RESTORATION LITERATURE

CRITICAL APPROACHES

Restoration Literature
Critical Approaches

Edited by
HAROLD LOVE

Methuen & Co Ltd
LONDON

First published 1972
by Methuen & Co Ltd
11 New Fetter Lane London EC4
© 1972 Methuen & Co Ltd
Printed in Great Britain by
T. & A. Constable Limited, Edinburgh

SBN 416 66240 4

Distributed in the U.S.A. by
HARPER & ROW PUBLISHERS INC
BARNES & NOBLE IMPORT DIVISION

Contents

Introduction

The Restoration marks the strongest assertion in post-mediaeval times of what we might call the Mediterranean component in British culture. The most obvious alien influences, mediated through the returned Cavaliers and their King, were French, but they came from a France whose first minister, premier musician, and favourite company of *farceurs* were all Italian-born and whose culture was vigorously reaffirming its own Mediterranean heritage against the Nordic infections of schism, democracy, and counterpoint. Among the courtiers of Charles II, the Roman Mass and the Roman carnival were celebrated with equal devotion. The King's gardeners laboured to supply him with oranges and even a pineapple or two; his tailors to clothe him in waistcoats in the style of the Persian Sophy. His poets had wandered as far as Italy (Rochester and Marvell), Spain (Killigrew), Tangier (Mulgrave), and even Constantinople (Etherege). For thirty years between 1660 and the early 1690's, the nation was exposed as scarcely before or since to the fermenting force of what Louis Macneice has called the Englishman's 'borrowed South'. In the end it was to need not one revolution but two – political under Dutch William and moral under the Society for the Reformation of Manners – to return the subjects of Charles and James to the paths of hyperborean seemliness.

One reason for assembling the present collection of studies of the period by writers who, with the exception of Professor Brooks, are natives or residents of Australia and New Zealand, has been that they too are participants in or observers of a culture which, for rather different reasons, has witnessed a clash of warm- and cold-latitude values. To claim that this has permitted them any insights denied to their British and American counterparts would be rash, but it has, I hope, qualified them to lay emphasis on a number of aspects of the period which have not been widely dealt with in recent writing and to circumvent some of the obstacles which the line of criticism descending from Collier, Johnson, and Macaulay has placed between the Restoration and ourselves.

Clayton,   H. L.
Victoria,
Australia.

Acknowledgements

The editor would like to express his gratitude to Sadie Stephens and Reuben Havin for their help in the preparation of this volume, and to Maureen Mann for compiling the index.

'The last Night's Ramble' is reproduced with the permission of the Bodleian Library.

A grant towards publication costs has kindly been made available by the Monash University Publications Committee.

Editions Used

Page references given with quotations from the principal Restoration authors are to the following editions. In the case of the older editions, an independent check for substantiative variants has been made against more recent editions of particular works or the originals.

References to contemporary printings are in the form '1673, p. 21' – the date being that of the first or most authoritative early edition.

Behn: *The Works of Aphra Behn*, ed. Montague Summers. 6 vols. London/Stratford-on-Avon, 1915.

Butler: *Hudibras*, ed. John Wilders. Oxford, 1967.

Congreve: *Complete Plays*, ed. Herbert Davis. Chicago, 1967.

Dryden (Verse and *The Dedication of the Aeneis*): *The Poems of John Dryden*, ed. James Kinsley. 4 vols. Oxford, 1958.

Dryden (Other prose): *Of Dramatic Poesy and Other Critical Essays*, ed. George Watson. 2 vols. London, 1962.

Dryden (Plays): *The Dramatic Works*, ed. Montague Summers. 6 vols. London, 1931-32.

Etherege: *The Dramatic Works of Sir George Etherege*, ed. H. F. B. Brett-Smith. 2 vols. Oxford, 1927.

Farquhar: *The Complete Works of George Farquhar*, ed. C. Stonehill. 2 vols. London, 1930.

Lee: *The Works of Nathaniel Lee*, ed. Thomas B. Stroup and Arthur L. Cooke. 2 vols. New Brunswick, 1954.

Milton: *Milton's Poems*, ed. B. A. Wright. London, 1956.

Rochester: *The Complete Poems of John Wilmot, Earl of Rochester*, ed. David M. Vieth. New Haven, 1968.

Shadwell: *The Complete Works of Thomas Shadwell*, ed. Montague Summers. 5 vols. London, 1927.

Traherne: *Poems, Centuries and Three Thanksgivings*, ed. Anne Ridler. London, 1966.

Wycherley: *The Complete Works of William Wycherley*, ed. Montague Summers. 4 vols. London, 1924.

Restoration Comedy
and the Provok'd Critic

ANDREW BEAR

Never in the whole field of literary endeavour have so few been
abused so often, for so long, by so many. Restoration comedy
was burned at the critical stake more than two hundred and
fifty years ago, and it is not done yet. Augustan, Romantic,
Victorian, and modern critics, major and minor, one after the
other. And still they come:

> Indeed if I may speak my Opinion of great part of the Writings
> which once prevailed among us under the Notion of Humour,
> they are such as wou'd tempt one to think there had been an
> Association among the Wits of those Times to rally Legitimacy
> out of our Island.   *[The Spectator, 525, 1712]*

> A blight fell upon England in the reign of Charles II. The King
> who stained his hands with the touch of French gold, and bar-
> gained away his country's greatness, corrupted its literature too
> with a debased French taste – and licentiousness and epigram
> took the place of love, earnestness, and passion.
>   *[Fraser's Magazine, December 1863]*

> I am disgusted that . . . you allowed your reviewer . . . to re-
> commend Wycherley's *The Country Wife* as a play that will
> 'delight anyone who cares to take the trip to Kensington'. . . .
> The aim of the Restoration dramatists was undoubtedly to
> corrupt and deprave the morals of the country, and, I would say,
> those who produce and commend such works are doing the same
> deadly work.   *[Letter to The Australian, June 10, 1965]*

Those are only collector's pieces, of course, but they are not
as unrepresentative as might appear.

1

Here is a curious tract of cultural and literary-critical history
which, perhaps perversely, I find both interesting and instructive. The purpose of the present essay is to illustrate and
explore some aspects of the controversies which broke out
over Restoration comedy during the eighteenth and nineteenth
centuries, and to show how these are linked with L. C. Knights's
'Restoration Comedy: The Reality and the Myth' the famous
essay which, although thirty years old, still seems to be the
most influential critique of the plays to have appeared this
century.[1] Like Collier and Macaulay before him, Professor
Knights was concerned to condemn Restoration comedy as
strongly as possible, and I want to examine the pressures in
modern moralistic criticism which made his condemnation so
much less forceful than theirs. In particular, I am interested in
the apparently timeless connection between moralistic criticism
and the belief that literature may produce an *effect* upon its
readers – that 'bad' books, on the one hand, can 'deprave and
corrupt', while 'good' books, on the other, can 'civilize'.
Restoration comedy, as all its enemies have agreed, is 'bad',
but how has this literary judgement been associated with the
further proposition that it is also bad 'for' its readers? And if it
is not bad 'for' its readers, what possible justification can there
be for attacking it?

Phase I: Eighteenth-Century Monism

All criticism of Restoration comedy begins, although it does
not end, in the Jeremy Collier Stage Controversy. The furious
exchange of pamphlets, of which only Collier's *Short View of the
Immorality and Profaneness of the English Stage* (1698) is
remembered, went on for nearly thirty years, and the resultant
tangling of critical questions with socio-moral ones is a heritage
which discussion of the plays has carried ever since. For
unlike the Milton controversy in our own day, this was not
merely an academic engagement bearing no relation to anything
outside itself. The Collier controversy was an integral part of
the 'Moral Revolution of 1688',[2] and more was involved than
the dislodgement of Etherege. It was a 'moral' controversy
because neoclassical critical theory defined the function of
literature in moral terms, and it was a social controversy

because the Restoration dramatists became counters in a confrontation of conflicting ideologies. The revolutionary settlement had to be saved, and the drama seemed to symbolize those
values in Restoration culture which a new age saw as threats
to the well-ordered state – metaphorically speaking, it was
associated with those 'hideous Phantoms' described in Addison's
apocalyptic dream in which he saw 'a young Man of about
twenty-two Years of Age' (James Stuart) lurking in wait
behind the dancing figures of Tyranny, Anarchy, Bigotry, and
Atheism.[3] The realm was in danger. The stage encouraged
immorality; therefore it was leading to social disruption; therefore it had to be put down: '. . . all endeavours for a national
reformation', wrote Nahum Tate in 1698, 'would prove in-
effectual without a regulation of the stage'.[4] Christopher Hill
has even claimed that Collier's interests were 'social rather
than moral'.[5]

The Collier controversy is noted for the violence of its
language, yet for all the scurrilous personal abuse to which both
sides resorted, the modern reader is likely to be struck more
by the extent of the common ground between the participants
than by their differences. A wide variety of people was involved,
ranging from some of the leading writers and critics of the day
to a fantastic band of clerics, self-appointed moral re-armers,
and representatives of the recently-formed Society for the
Reformation of Manners who took up the attack on the stage.
Despite many complicating factors, however, when it came to
specifically literary questions, they all shared the same basic
assumptions about what literature was, what it was for, and how
it might be judged. Even someone as sophisticated by the
standards of the time as John Dennis was actually speaking the
same critical language as the most fanatical of the moral
reformers: a single standard was available and the literary
intellectual was at one with the common reader in applying it.
To put it another way, if there had been a 'trial' of *The Country
Wife* in 1709, as there was a 'trial' of *Lady Chatterley's Lover*
two hundred and fifty years later, the prosecution would at
least have known what the defence was talking about. The
split in critical opinion and the division into 'levels' of taste,
which is so characteristic of our own day, had not yet taken
place.

Those who attacked the stage in the eighteenth century had no difficulty in justifying their action. As even the title of one of the pamphlets shows – Arthur Bedford's *The Evil and Danger of Stage Plays: Shewing their Natural Tendency to Destroy RELIGION, and introduce a General Corruption of Manners* (1706) – the stage was to be condemned because it was socially and morally *dangerous*. For men like Bedford, Restoration comedy was contemporary, or nearly so, and the charge that it was causing 'corruption' therefore had peculiar force. The Collier controversy, when compared with others like it, falls into place in a general pattern. Nearly all new forms of art and entertainment have been attacked by contemporaries: the first professional theatres in Elizabethan London, the realistic novel in the nineteenth century, the cinema in the 1930s, crime comics in the 'fifties, and, currently, television. In all cases (and there are many more that could be mentioned) the contemporaneity of the material has been claimed as a factor in its alleged power to corrupt. Restoration comedy is unusual in this only because it has continued to arouse opposition beyond its own time, and later critics have therefore faced problems of justification which did not exist in the eighteenth century. The stated motives of Bedford, Collier, and the rest, were clear and unambiguous. Restoration comedy was 'bad' and therefore, by definition, was producing harmful effects. The step from this position to the claim that it was actually *causing* 'a General Corruption of Manners' was then an easy one.

At this level, those who attacked the stage were able to draw on the established principles of the best criticism of the day. The doctrine of 'instruction' in neoclassical theory implied that the value of literature was actually to be defined by its effects – this, in fact, was the commonplace of Augustan criticism. Shadwell stated it briefly in his Preface to *The Humorists* (1671), and few would have disagreed with him:

> I confess, a Poet ought to do all that he can, decently to please, that so he may instruct. To adorn his Images of *Vertue* so delightfully to affect people with a secret veneration of it in others, and an emulation to practice it in themselves: And to render their Figures of *Vice* and *Folly* so ugly and detestable, to make People hate and despise them, not only in others, but (if it be possible) in their dear selves.   [*Works*, I, 184]

This meant that the identification of 'good' and 'bad' literature, in theory at least, was relatively easy. The one produced beneficial effects as described by Shadwell, while the other simply reversed the process to produce harmful ones. Charles Gildon's *A Complete Art of Poetry* (1718) shows how logical it all seemed:

> *Poetry* is an *Art* invented for the Instruction of Mankind, and consequently it must be *profitable*. 'Tis a general Truth, that every *Art* is a good Thing, because there is none whose End is not *good*. But as it is not less true, that Men often abuse the best Things, that which was design'd for a wholesome Remedy, may in Time become a very dangerous Poison.[6]

The striking feature of the Augustan controversy was that this repressive critical orthodoxy was universally accepted. Attackers and defenders of the stage, literary sophisticates and philistines: all argued from the same basic premises. For all the other issues that came up from time to time (including the charge that the dramatists were part of a deliberate conspiracy to corrupt the morals of the nation), the whole affair turned finally, from a critical point of view, on the interpretation of the moral 'examples' in plays and hence on their social effects. Not until the following century did an alternative theory of the nature of literature emerge, from which time those who would defend Restoration comedy could do so with more freedom than was possible or even conceivable for the Augustans.

The general tenor of the eighteenth-century attack on the stage may be sufficiently illustrated from two of the early pamphlets: the later ones tended to be mere repetitions of what had already been established. Indeed, the essentials of the case were laid down even before Collier by the epic poet Sir Richard Blackmore whose Preface to *Prince Arthur* started the controversy on its way in 1695:

> Our Poets seem engag'd in a general *Confederacy* to ruin the End of their own Art, to expose *Religion* and *Virtue*, and bring *Vice* and *Corruption of Manners* into Esteem and Reputation. . . . The *Man of Sense*, and the *Fine* Gentleman in the *Comedy*, who, as the chiefest Person propos'd to the Esteem and Imitation of the Audience . . . will appear a *Finish'd Libertine* . . . these Characters are set up on purpose to ruin all Opinion and Esteem of Virtue

B

. . . whence the Youth of the Nation have apparently receiv'd very bad Impressions. The *universal* Corruption of Manners and irreligious Disposition of Mind that infects the Kingdom seems to have been in great Measure deriv'd from the Stage, or has at least been highly promoted by it. . . . Sure some Effectual Care should be taken that these Men might not be suffer'd, by Debauching our Youth, to help on the *Destruction* of a brave Nation.[7]

Collier, however, was the central figure and, although he added little to what Blackmore had said, his *Short View* was by far the most influential of the anti-stage writings:

Being convinc'd that nothing has gone farther in Debauching the Age than the *Stage Poets*, and *Play-House*, I thought I could not employ my time better than in writing against them. . . . And what can be the Meaning of such a Representation, unless it be to Tincture the Audience, to extinguish Shame, and make Lewdness a Diversion? This is the natural Consequence, and therefore one would think 'twas the Intention too. Such Licentious Discourse tends to no point but to stain the Imagination, to awaken Folly, and weaken the Defences of Virtue.[8]

There are two points of particular interest here. The first is that this way of writing will still be familiar to many present-day readers, particularly those who have followed the modern debates about censorship and television. Blackmore's comment about the debauching of youth, for instance, has a distinctly contemporary ring about it, although these days, as far as I can imagine, no one would attempt to answer him in his own terms. The second is that the typical emphasis on the effects of the drama gains force from a universal agreement that the human process by which these effects are brought about has to do with the direct imitation of examples of behaviour presented in the plays. There was no *other* theory of how literature might function upon its readers or of how readers might respond to imaginative experience. This unanimous acceptance of what I like to call the 'example theory' is central in all the anti-stage writing. Blackmore ('the chiefest Person propos'd to the . . . Imitation of the Audience') is quite explicit about it, as is Steele in several of his periodical essays:

It is not every Youth that can behold the fine Gentleman of the Comedy represented with a good Grace, leading a loose and profligate Life, and condemning Virtuous Affection as insipid, and not be secretly Emulous of what appears so amiable to a whole Audience.[9]

Or again, even more explicitly:

It is, with me, a Matter of the highest Consideration what Parts are well or ill performed, what Passions or Sentiments are indulged or cultivated, and consequently what Manners and Customs are transfused from the Stage to the World, which reciprocally imitate each other.[10]

Nor is the idea restricted to the literary men – Collier reverts to it again and again:

To what purpose is *Vice* thus prefer'd, thus ornamented, and caress'd, unless for Imitation?

And at last that the Example may work the better, they generally make them rich, and happy, and reward them with their own Desires.[11]

*   *   *

Treating loose Characters with Sense and Respect, provokes to Imitation, and makes the Infection catching.[12]

More unliterary still, even the Upper House of Convocation shared exactly the same view. The profaneness and corruption of the age, they said (1711):

hath been much increased by the licentiousness of the stage, where the worst examples have been placed in the best lights and recommended to imitation.[13]

There is no mistaking the confidence with which this is put forward at all levels in the controversy: a rudimentary theory of the 'psychology' of reading had gained universal acceptance.

This condemnation of Restoration comedy did not go undisputed and the defenders of the stage included some of the leading writers and critics of the day. The characteristic feature of this controversy, however, and that which distinguishes it from the later ones, is that the defence attempted

to meet the attack on its own grounds. The universal acceptance
of the critical principles outlined above meant that the defenders
found themselves in a position from which they could only
argue that Restoration comedy was 'moral' after all and so
capable of fulfilling the instructive function described by
Shadwell. Insofar as the Augustan controversy touched on
specifically critical issues at all, disagreement could occur only
over the interpretation of the moral 'meaning' of particular
plays.

Steele's attack on *The Man of Mode* (in *Spectator 65*) offers
an absolutely typical illustration of the way the argument went.
His analysis of the play led him to conclude that the two most
attractive characters (Sir Fopling Flutter and Dorimant) were
in fact wicked knaves, while Harriet was everything Steele
thought she ought not to be. He therefore condemned the play
out of hand as likely to corrupt what he called the 'sense of
Innocence and Virtue':

> This whole celebrated Piece is a perfect Contradiction to good
> Manners, good Sense, and common Honesty; . . . there is nothing
> in it but what is built upon the Ruin of Virtue and Innocence. . . .
>   [I, 280]

The special feature of Augustan criticism is that all of Steele's
contemporaries would have accepted his conclusion so long as
they accepted his interpretation – i.e., agreed that the play was
immoral. The defenders of the stage could disagree at this point
only, and so, of course, they did. But the critical principle itself
was not at issue.

The whole controversy, therefore, reduces itself to disagree-
ments at points such as this. Dennis replied to Steele (*A
Defence of Sir Fopling Flutter*, 1722) by simply reversing the
interpretation in order to show that the vices of the characters
were 'exposed' rather than 'recommended', so that the play
functions to 'shew us what ought never to be done upon the
Stage of the World'.[14] It was as simple as that, and exactly
the same arguments were endlessly repeated in the replies to
Collier's *Short View*. Those of Dennis and Congreve may be
regarded as perfect paradigms of the discussion of Restoration
comedy as it was conducted by Augustan critics. One of Collier's
main complaints was that the indiscretions of the heroines were

regularly made attractive and hence morally dangerous – 'To what Purpose is *Vice* thus prefer'd . . . unless for Imitation?' Thus, he attacked the presentation of Olivia in *The Plain Dealer*, to which Dennis replied (*The Usefulness of the Stage*, 1698):

> I thought Mr. *Wycherley* had more than made Amends for it, [an 'indefensible' jest] by exposing Adultery, and making it the immediate Cause of *Olivia's* Misfortune, in that excellent Play, which is a most instructive, and a most noble Satire upon the Hypocrisy and Villainy of Mankind.[15]

Similarly, Collier found fault with the portraits of Belinda in *The Old Bachelor* and Miss Prue in *Love for Love*. This time Congreve himself replied:

> I only refer those two Characters to the Judgement of any impartial Reader, to determine whether they are represented so as to engage any Spectator to imitate the Impudence of one, or the Affectation of the other; and whether they are not both ridiculed rather than recommended.[16]

Perhaps the 'impartial Reader' of Restoration comedy does not exist, but even so this defence is hardly convincing. Nevertheless, within the monolithic orthodoxy of Augustan criticism it was the only one available. If further indication of the completely unanimous and totally crippling dependence on this doctrine throughout the century is required, however, it may be furnished by a brief glance at Johnson's *Life of Congreve*. Johnson, as we know from Boswell and even from the *Life* itself, was strongly attracted by Congreve's 'quick and sparkling' wit. Yet the weight of critical orthodoxy was too much for him. When he came to pass judgement it was utterly (and disappointingly) conventional:

> The cause of Congreve was not tenable: whatever glosses he might use for the defence or palliation of single passages, the general tenor and tendency of his plays must always be condemned. It is acknowledged, with universal conviction, that the perusal of his works will make no man better; and that their ultimate effect is to represent pleasure in alliance with vice, and to relax those obligations by which life ought to be regulated.[17]

Phase II: Nineteenth-Century Dualism

Restoration comedy continued to attract attention in the following century, but the pattern of discussion is more complex.

The critical revolution wrought by the Romantics' exaltation
of the Creative Imagination marks the decline of neoclassical
moralism in sophisticated criticism. Never again would a critic
of Johnson's eminence be hamstrung as he had been, although
the new emphasis on the imagination was not in itself a rejection
of the tendency to judge literature by its effects. English
literary theory remained essentially utilitarian, but the definition
of the *kind* of beneficial effect which 'great' literature could
produce underwent radical change. Shelley's *Defence of Poetry*
(1821) shows Romantic theory as at once a rejection and a
continuation of neoclassicism:

> Having determined what is poetry . . . let us proceed to estimate
> its effects upon society. . . .
>   The whole objection, however, of the immorality of poetry
> rests upon a misconception of the manner in which poetry acts
> to produce the moral improvement of man. Ethical science . . .
> proposes examples of civil and domestic life: nor is it for want of
> admirable doctrines that men hate, and despise. . . . But Poetry
> acts in another and diviner manner. It awakens and enlarges the
> mind itself by rendering it the receptacle of a thousand unappre-
> hended combinations of thought. . . . The great instrument of
> moral good is the imagination; and poetry administers to the effect
> by acting upon the cause. . . . Poetry strengthens the faculty which
> is the organ of the moral nature of man, in the same manner
> as exercise strengthens a limb.[18]

What I have called the 'example theory' was replaced as an
explanation of the function of literature by the doctrine of
'training the imagination' – a doctrine which has remained
influential in literary apologetics ever since.

As might be expected, the impact of this new understanding
of the function of literature was felt when people came to
discuss Restoration comedy, and there is now a conflict not only
of opinion but of critical method as well. In the previous age
leading writers and critics had 'concurred with the common
reader' in their basic agreement that the end of comedy was to

instruct by example. From the early years of the new century, however, it is clear that at least two sharply distinguished critical 'levels' had come into existence. The literary élite, recognizable as the main group of Romantic writers, diverged from the opinions and assumptions of the majority which tended still to uphold neoclassical orthodoxy. The old tradition went underground, intellectually speaking, and even on the comparatively minor topic of Restoration comedy, élite and majority opinion may be seen to diverge and to re-form in two recognizable schools of thought which Meredith was later to characterize as the 'Bacchanalian' (élite) and 'Puritan' (majority). The former shows the new trend, the latter the old. The result was that the 'defence' of Restoration comedy moved away from neoclassicism altogether, while the 'attack' continued in the old manner, though now at a level below that of the best criticism of the day. The two groups were no longer speaking the same critical language.

A curious situation emerged in which may be discerned further parallels to the modern debate about censorship. The literary intellectuals, superior in their emancipation from moralistic fallacy, took up the defence of Restoration comedy against the strictures of the majority, just as their counterparts today have taken up the cause of erotic literature against the censor. Furthermore, they were beginning to assert themselves as a social as well as a critical élite: the nineteenth-century defence of Restoration comedy contains strong elements of *avant-garde*ism. Thus, in the social atmosphere of an age which, according to Charles Lamb, could not 'bear' Restoration comedy,[19] we find some of the main Romantic writers and critics combining an enthusiasm for the plays with a rejection of bourgeois values. Lamb, Hazlitt, and Hunt all expressed themselves in this manner, while Byron, with characteristic exuberance, wrote: '*What Plays!* What wit! – *hélas!* Congreve and Vanbrugh are your only comedy. Our society is too insipid now for the like copy'.[20]

Byron's slighting reference to the insipidity of the age, echoed by the others, indicates the extent to which literary opinion no longer even wanted to concur with the common reader. Lamb, in his well-known essay 'On the Artificial Comedy of the Last Century' (1822), was just as slighting about the age and just as enthusiastic about Restoration comedy:

> The artificial Comedy, or Comedy of manners, is quite extinct on our stage. Congreve and Farquhar show their heads once in seven years only, to be exploded and put down instantly. The times cannot bear them. . . . In our great anxiety that our morality should not take cold, we wrap it up in a great blanket surtout of precaution against the breeze and sunshine. . . . We have not the courage to imagine a state of things for which there is neither reward nor punishment. We cling to the painful necessities of shame and blame. We would indict our very dreams.[21]

Lamb's defence is deliberately and forcefully controversial – that aspect of the discussion of Restoration comedy remains a constant factor. But from a critical point of view his argument is quite different from that which Dennis and Congreve had offered in the previous century. He defends Restoration comedy by insisting that the immorality of the plays is irrelevant to their literary quality and he explicitly denies that they will produce any harmful effects in society. This is partly because the dramas are no longer contemporary, but Lamb's most important revision of the eighteenth-century defence is his claim that there is an autonomous realm of *theatrical* experience – the 'neutral ground of character' – which is not reducible to real life. It is almost as if he had those words of Steele's directly in his mind. The stage and the world do *not* 'reciprocally imitate each other':

> We are spectators to a plot or intrigue, (not reducible in life to the point of strict morality,). . . . I could never connect those sports of a witty fancy in any shape with any result to be drawn from them to imitation in real life. They are a world of themselves almost as much as fairy-land. . . . [The characters] do not offend my moral sense; in fact they do not appeal to it at all. . . . They have got out of Christendom into the land – what shall I call it? – of cuckoldry – the Utopia of gallantry, where pleasure is duty, and the manners perfect freedom. It is altogether a speculative scene of things, which has no reference whatever to the world that is.[22]

But if that was the battle-cry of critical revolution it was not to be won easily. Old ways of thinking die hard and there are indications of a conflict between the old ideas and the new. Lamb was consistent in his rejection of the doctrine of the moral example but even in Hazlitt it could still reassert itself. In the lecture 'On Wycherley, Congreve, Vanbrugh, and Farquhar' (1819), Hazlitt defended Restoration comedy in terms similar to Lamb's. The main point is that the plays transport the theatregoer to an autonomous world of the imagination – 'from this dull age to one that was all life, and whim, and mirth, and humour' – and he too shows his scorn for the common man (and common reader) by remarking that 'the gross and palpable absurdities of modern manners . . . are too shallow . . . to make them worth the detection of the Comic Muse'.[23] That was the 'new' defence of Restoration comedy, the assertion of the élite's emancipation from neo-classicism. Yet Hazlitt did not achieve a consistent position. When he came to discuss *The Plain Dealer* all this was moment-arily forgotten and we find him echoing not Lamb but Dennis' reply to Collier. Far from transporting the reader to an imagin-ary 'Utopia of gallantry', the play is praised as a 'severe and poignant moral satire'. Like Dennis (who had called it 'a most noble Satire') Hazlitt selects the portrayal of the 'artful hypocrisy in Olivia' for special praise:

> The indignation excited against this odious and pernicious quality by the masterly exposure to which it is here subjected, is 'a discipline of humanity'. No one can read this play attentively without being the better for it as long as he lives . . . it shows the immorality and hateful effects of duplicity. . . . It is worth ten volumes of sermons.[24]

No wonder then that Lamb complained so bitterly about the pervasive influence of old-fashioned moralism: the doctrine of the imitation of example was still very much in the air. Indeed, where Restoration comedy was concerned, to have escaped from it was regarded by the minority who did as a mark of superiority. The attack on the plays went on exactly as before and Lamb could only complain:

> We carry our fire-side concerns to the theatre with us. . . . We dare not dally with images, or names, of wrong. We bark like foolish dogs at shadows. We dread infection from the scenic representation of disorder, and fear a painted pustule.[25]

Among those who attacked the comedies Thackeray is another who, like Hazlitt, seems to have felt the division of views within himself. In 1851 ('Congreve and Addison'), he was on the side of the literary men, Bacchanalian, Lamb-like in his admiration of Congreve:

> What a conquering air there is about these! What an irresistible Mr. Congreve it is! Sinner! of course he will be a sinner, the delightful rascal![26]

Only two years later, however, he was one of Lamb's barking-dogs, celebrating the victory of 'Dick Steele' over the dragon of Restoration comedy:

> He [Steele] took away comedy from behind the fine lady's alcove, or the screen where the libertine was watching her. He ended all that wretched business of wives jeering at their husbands, of rakes laughing wives, and husbands too, to scorn. That miserable, rouged, tawdry, sparkling, hollow-hearted comedy of the Restoration fled before him, and, like the wicked spirit in the Fairy-books, shrank, as Steele let the daylight in, and shrieked, and shuddered, and vanished.[27]

Perhaps the contradiction is due to the great performer knowing only too well how to please his audience – the second lecture ('Charity and Humour') was delivered at the Church of the Messiah in New York to the Ladies' Society for the Employment and Relief of the Poor. But if there seems something of the schizophrenic in Thackeray, the same could never be said of Macaulay. Completely unmoved by the critical revolution that had been going on around him, and by the moral defection of men like Lamb, the greatest common reader of them all, through the pages of the *Edinburgh Review*[28] asserted bedrock opinion. His view of Restoration comedy would stand no questioning: ' . . . in truth, this part of our literature is a disgrace to our language and our national character'. [LXXII, 493]. He would have none of it, and the issue that moved him most was the suggestion that the relationship between literature and morality was not the traditionally accepted one. Macaulay was reviewing Leigh Hunt's edition of the Restoration dramatists but his real target was Lamb. Hunt, it was true, had dared to suggest, in his critic's paraphrase, that 'there is little or no ground for the charge of immorality so often brought against the literature of the Restoration' [492], but he was let off relatively lightly as Macaulay turned to the main offender. Let us cease this nonsense, he said, with characteristic authority:

> Mr Charles Lamb, indeed, attempted to set up a defence for this way of writing. The dramatists of the latter part of the seventeenth century are not, according to him, to be tried by the standard of morality which exists, and ought to exist in real life. . . . We are sure that we do not wish to represent him unfairly. For we admire his genius . . . and we cherish his memory as much as if we had known him personally. But we must plainly say that his argument, though ingenious, is altogether sophistical.
>
> [494-495]

With that much by way of preliminary softening-up the onslaught began. *The Country Wife* was 'one of the most profligate and heartless of human compositions'; *The Plain Dealer* (which Hazlitt had thought 'worth ten volumes of sermons') was 'equally immoral' [506]; Wycherley, 'at seventy, was still the representative of the monstrous profligacy of the Restoration' [510] – his work was 'too filthy to handle, and too noisome even to approach' [513]. This of course is the moral tone of Victorian rather than Augustan England but at this level the neoclassical orthodoxy had remained unchanged. Macaulay, in his attack on the very basis of what Lamb had tried to establish, offers what is, I think, the last really impressive critical statement based on the theory of the moral example in literature:

> . . . what is immoral shall not be presented to the imagination of the young and susceptible in constant connexion with what is attractive. For every person who has observed the operation of the law of association in his own mind, and in the minds of others, knows, that whatever is constantly presented to the imagination in connexion with what is attractive, will commonly itself become attractive. . . . [The plays demonstrate a] systematic attempt to associate vice with those things which men value most and desire most, and virtue with every thing ridiculous and degrading. . . . The hero is in all superficial accomplishments exactly the fine gentleman, whom every youth in the pit would gladly resemble. . . . In the name of art, as well as in the name of virtue, we protest against the principle that the world of pure comedy is one into

which no moral enters. . . . Morality constantly enters into that
world, a sound morality, and an unsound morality; the sound
morality to be insulted, derided, associated with every thing
mean and hateful; the unsound morality to be set off to every
advantage, and inculcated by all methods, direct and indirect.

[493; 496-497]

Even in 1841 there must have been some for whom Macaulay's
seemed a voice from the past. Nevertheless, he asked the
questions which have remained crucial in the discussion of
Restoration comedy from his own day to the present. No one
after him, however, has been able to regain quite the same note
of authority and confidence:

And the question is simply, whether a man of genius, who constantly and systematically endeavours to make this sort of character
attractive . . . does or does not make an ill use of his powers. We
own that we are unable to understand how this question can be
answered in any way but one.

[497]

The strength of Macaulay's position was precisely that. Others
have responded to Restoration comedy with the same lack of
sympathy but they have been troubled by the awareness that
the question can be answered in many ways but one.

Phase III: Twentieth-Century Complication

Restoration comedy has continued to arouse strong feelings in
the present century: people are still moved to write 'for' or
'against' it, although the critical situation, particularly where
the question of morality is involved, has become increasingly
complicated.

As in the nineteenth century, those who would defend the
plays have taken the initiative. With the further retreat from
neoclassicism in serious criticism, one of the inherited defence
positions – the claim that Restoration comedy is really 'moral',
as Dennis, Congreve, and even Hazlitt had maintained – became
untenable, and the modern defence has tended to fall between
two extremes. The first, now going out of fashion, is to follow
Lamb's solution to the moral problem by simply denying its
existence and praising the plays for their lighthearted frivolity.

In his *Restoration Comedy* (1924) Bonamy Dobrée wrote: 'We take the same delight in the vagaries of Sir Fopling Flutter as we do at the sight of an absurdly gambolling calf' [p. 14]. It is odd to reflect that *The Man of Mode* is the very play that so aroused *both* Steele and Dennis: one wonders what either of them might have made of that. Predictably enough, however, many modern critics have found this unsatisfactory and a second, more up-to-date defence has become fashionable. This is really a throwback to the Augustan position, although the claim that the plays are 'serious' has replaced the claim that they are 'moral'. Thus, in one of the more recent exchanges, John Wain (*Essays in Criticism*, 1956) excepted, of all things, the same *Man of Mode* from a general condemnation of Restoration comedy on the grounds that it, alone among all these plays, shows the 'consequences' of moral action and has a 'harsh ring of truth' [VI, 381-382]. F. W. Bateson, in a reply to Mr Wain (*Essays in Criticism*, 1957), took the same position considerably further when he analyzed the 'china scene' in *The Country Wife* in order to demonstrate the 'implicit seriousness' of even this, and went on to conclude that it approaches an 'allegory of sex' [VII, 65-66]. That certainly is an answer to his question that never occurred to Macaulay.

The nineteenth-century controversy produced a new 'defence' of Restoration comedy but not a new 'attack' – when it came to the point Macaulay anachronistically fell back on the Augustan doctrine of the moral example. The sophisticated modern critic, of course, cannot take this step and if he feels moved to condemn the plays he is therefore in an awkward situation. There are few precedents for publishing strongly-worded attacks on non-contemporary literature, largely, I believe, because the force and conviction of condemnatory criticism almost inevitably depends not on the mere assertion of distaste ('this is a bad book') but rather on the further claim that it will produce harmful effects upon its audience ('this is a dangerous book'). The problem is that it must seem absurd or melodramatic to argue that *The Country Wife*, for example, still has the power to 'deprave and corrupt': one can see why some people think that *Tropic of Cancer* or *Bonnie and Clyde* have such power but it is difficult to believe of a two-hundred-and-fifty-year-old comedy. How, then, can a modern critic who disapproves of that

play and others like it justify the time spent in writing against
them, given that he cannot claim, as Collier did, that they
represent an immediate danger to the social order; nor believe,
as Macaulay still did, that people respond to imaginative
experience by directly imitating 'examples' of behaviour?

These problems were faced by L. C. Knights, whose 'Restoration Comedy: The Reality and the Myth' has become the focal
point in discussion of the plays this century.[29] As John Loftis
has remarked: 'it was difficult in Addison and Steele's time
to write about Restoration comedy without taking Collier's
charges of immorality into account; it has been difficult in the
mid-twentieth century to write about it without taking sides
for or against Knights'.[30] That being so, the essay will be
worth discussing in some detail for Professor Knights attempted
to fill the critical gap left during the nineteenth century. With
him, the Collier controversy seems to come full circle in the
attempt to justify an unfavourable literary judgement of the
plays which depends neither on the charge of immorality nor
on the claim that they produce corrupting effects. It is as if he
was trying to do for the 'attack' case what Lamb had done for
the 'defence' and since the essay therefore represents a new
direction in the criticism of Restoration comedy we may
reasonably ask how far it succeeds. But there is a larger question
involved as well: given these limitations, is condemnatory
criticism possible or justifiable at all?

Professor Knights's conclusion is well known: 'The criticism
that defenders of Restoration comedy need to answer is not that
the comedies are "immoral", but that they are trivial, gross
and dull' [143]. There are then three separate charges which
relate fairly closely to the three main stages of Professor
Knights's argument, and it will be convenient to examine them
in order of presentation. It should be noticed, however, that
the conclusion is stated in that way for a specific reason.
Professor Knights begins the essay by indicating the pitfalls
which he wishes to avoid. He points out (rightly) that the
debate about Restoration comedy, and always the case against,
has previously been conducted 'almost entirely in moral terms'.
He then points out (again rightly) that just for this reason it
has never been satisfactory simply because it can so easily be
turned 'upside down', as of course it can, either by the Augustan

defence which claims that the plays are really satirical or by those modern critics he refers to who 'find freedom of manners where Macaulay found licentiousness'. For this reason Professor Knights sets out to state the case against Restoration comedy in explicitly *non-moral* terms and hence reaches the conclusion quoted above. He seeks to 'make possible a free and critical approach', although he leaves the odd proviso (perhaps to dissociate himself from anything like the Lamb position) that '"Morals" are, in the long run, decidedly relevant – but only in the long run' [122].

The first of Professor Knights's non-moral charges, which is brought forward in the first sentence and reiterated in the last, is that Restoration comedy is 'dull'. Now this, it seems to me, must be dismissed at once as critical subterfuge. If readers over the years had shared that view the need for the present essay, and for all its predecessors, would never have arisen. If literary criticism at the level of formal publication amounts to no more than the mere assertion of such subjective opinion then it has never been worth anyone's serious attention. The obvious and unanswerable reply to this proposition is simply that 'I find it engrossing', and at such a point criticism reaches an absurd and profitless impasse. This is the way to stop a literary conversation, not to start a critical essay.

The second major objection, which appears to be related to the use of the term 'gross', may be called a sociological one. Restoration comedy, Professor Knights argues, reflects the 'disintegration of the old cultural unity' of Elizabethan times. It is limited to the attitudes and ideals of the 'upper class' and anyway (or perhaps therefore) bears 'no significant relation with the best thought of the time . . . it is artificial in a completely damaging sense, *and by contemporary standards*' [125; italics original]. The latter judgement is supported by an analysis showing the nervelessness and unsubtlety of Congreve's prose against a passage from Halifax.

I find this one of the most interesting parts of the essay, but I am not at all sure what Professor Knights wants us to assume from it. In the first place I am not sure that I accept his implicit judgement that Halifax is a 'better' writer than Congreve: the discursive prose of the *Life of Charles II* does not seem to me qualitatively comparable with passages of dramatic dialogue. Furthermore, as John Wain remarks, a critic can always seem to prove a point by 'juggling with quotations'[31] (particularly when he does not attempt to justify the selections), and in this case it is not difficult to see that one could juggle a few more and thus prove Congreve a better prose writer than someone else – other passages in Halifax would do. There are larger problems than these, however. If Professor Knights had been content with the claim that none of the dramatists 'achieved a genuinely sensitive and individual mode of expression', one would know what he meant and know how to dispute his judgement if one happened not to agree with him; that would be a recognizably literary-critical procedure. But in fact the weight of the argument falls elsewhere. Professor Knights is careful to say that Restoration comedy does not stand condemned because it reflects the 'impoverishment' of Restoration culture in comparison with the racy vigour of Elizabethan life (though that broader suggestion, once it has been introduced, does seem to carry evaluative meanings). Nevertheless, he insists that literary and cultural judgements are inseparable:

> If the drama is inferior it is not because it represents – by Elizabethan standards – a limited culture, but because it represents contemporary culture so inadequately; it has no significant relation with the best thought of the time. . . . the comedy of manners exhibits [an] . . . attenuation and enfeeblement of what the age, taken as a whole, had to offer.
>
> [125-126]

Two very large assumptions are being made there. The first is that passages of imaginative literature may be taken to 'exhibit' or 'represent' certain qualities of a culture, and the second is that the culture of a period may be 'taken as a whole'. Both assumptions seem to me to be questionable – or at least in need of very careful justification and definition – but, more important at the moment, I cannot see how either of them relates to the judgement that the drama is 'inferior'. It is certainly true, and this seems to be what Professor Knights is talking about here, that we often read literature in order to gain insight into the cultural mode of a period: we may also, of course, read parish-registers and sermons for the same purpose. I entirely fail to see, however, that a *literary judgement*, which is what

Professor Knights purports to be making, can be derived from cultural or sociological investigations. If (granting the assumption) Congreve reveals something about upper-class culture in Restoration England then surely this is as valuable *if one is studying the culture* as anything Halifax might reveal (again granting the assumption) about 'the best thought of the time'. I do not see that 'good' literature necessarily represents the culture of its time 'adequately' – or at least I do not know what 'adequate' might mean in this context – but it is certain that in the study of a culture one wants to know about the 'worst' that is in it as well as the 'best'. In other words I think that literary *judgement* is out of place in the study of cultural meanings – out of place in the sense of being irrelevant. Some literature may be found to reveal more about a culture than most but it is not necessarily that which one values most as literature. I do not value Collier's *Short View* as a work of literature but I am sure it reveals a great deal about Augustan life.

If this distinction is granted it makes Professor Knights's essay rather difficult to follow. As far as I can see the only point in writing strongly-worded dismissive criticism would be to dissuade people from reading the literature in question, but if they were not interested in studying Restoration culture – as many devoted readers of the comedies obviously are not – then the knowledge that the best thought of the time is only 'inadequately' represented will hardly deter them. This argument, it seems to me, quite fails to justify the obvious animus of the essay as a whole – unless Professor Knights is implying that knowledge of a nerveless and decadent part of a society (granting the assumption yet again) will somehow affect us in the direction of nervelessness and decadence? If that is so I simply do not believe it.

Professor Knights turns from these issues and in the third section of the essay approaches – from his own explicitly non-moral point of view – the long-vexed question of the immorality of Restoration comedy: he calls it 'the matter of sexual relations'. He had already made the point in passing (while rebutting a critic of the 'serious' school) that the plays have nothing 'fresh and penetrating to say on sex and social relations' but the main charge, which is perhaps an elaboration of this,

c

is that the persistent implication of Restoration comedy is that 'constancy in love, especially in marriage, is a bore', while sex itself is always regarded as an unimportant or merely diverting pastime: 'Sex is a hook baited with tempting morsels; it is a thirst quencher; it is a cordial; it is a dish to feed on; it is a bunch of grapes; it is anything but sex' [135-136]. From this point on Professor Knights seems to me to be working under difficulties. There can be no doubt that he disapproves of these social and moral attitudes yet he has to insist that it is not their conventional immorality that bothers him. Thus, having presented his analysis, he resolutely refuses to pass the judgement of Collier and Macaulay, and states his condemnation of the plays on other grounds. The following is a list of some of the terms in which the value judgement is couched: 'narrow'; 'dull'; 'nothing but the titillation of appetite'; 'hovers on the outskirts of sexual relations'; 'monotonously' the 'same'; 'the easiest, the most superficial response'; 'trivial'; '*merely* of the public surface . . . relies on the conventional assumptions'; 'limited range of human potentialities'; 'meagre'; and 'vulgar'. It is from all this that he arrives at the final dismissive statement that has already been quoted.

That does not seem to me very satisfactory, primarily because, for all the protestations that he is not talking in moralistic terms, it soon becomes clear that that is exactly what he *is* doing. It is obvious that he disapproves of the sexual code that he finds in the plays and the preference for these apparently neutral terms only superficially disguises the familiar moral stance that is actually being taken. Norman N. Holland has written that 'Mr Knights's essay did Restoration comedy a great service by substituting the aesthetic question for the moral question',[32] yet the implications of these 'aesthetic' terms of disapprobation are rather more complex than the easy flow of the essay at first suggests. Their cumulative import seems inescapable: Professor Knights is placing a positive value on those human qualities which he takes to be the *opposite* of 'triviality', 'superficially', 'conventionality', and the rest. And the trouble with this is that, although it is not the language of moralistic discourse, it is open to exactly the same objection that Professor Knights himself so neatly turned against Macaulay. This too can be turned 'upside down' by anyone who would maintain, for example, that the plays present a desirable, or at least a realistic, attitude towards sex and marriage; that conventional solemnities about sex ought to be deflated; that such cynicism is the only possible approach to life; and that triviality and superficiality have a positive value as sources of relief or detachment from the pressures of an increasingly absurd civilization.

These attitudes seem to me just as tenable as Professor Knights's, and it is plain that a large number of highly intelligent people hold them at the moment. While that is so I can see no valid reason for taking 'Restoration Comedy: The Reality and the Myth' any more seriously *as criticism* than Professor Knights himself says we should take the *Short View*.

One crucial point remains, however. As I remarked earlier I am of the impression that strongly condemnatory criticism can have little force or conviction – indeed, is probably not possible – without the assumption that the condemned literature will somehow do harm to its audience. I have discussed Professor Knights's essay at length because it is the only serious and sustained attempt at such criticism I know of which sets out to be neither 'moralistic' nor 'effects'. Yet if my analysis holds it fails in the former attempt – it is, finally, an ordinary piece of moralistic criticism conducted in only superficially non-moral terms. I would go further, however, and claim that it fails in the latter attempt as well. It seems to me that in order to justify his animus and his decision to publish the essay in the first place, Professor Knights simply *must* be assuming that Restoration comedy is not only 'bad' but 'dangerous': I do not know if this is conscious or unconscious, deliberate or accidental, but I think it is there.

The difficulties in Professor Knights's position arise only because of his sophistication. Collier and Macaulay before him were aware of no such problems. For them the availability of the doctrine of the moral example meant that they could write condemnatory criticism which was immediately and obviously justifiable. But Professor Knights, in deliberately eschewing the traditional support of their argument, can hardly answer the objection that might run: 'All right, you don't like Restoration comedy, but why make such a fuss about it? Why publish a long essay about something you think has no literary value at all?'

The third major charge brought against the plays, after all, is not that they are 'immoral', not that they will 'rally Legitimacy out of our Island', but that they are 'trivial' – 'it is the triviality that one comes back to' [137] – and it seems to me that the only possible explanation for the force of this emphasis is that Professor Knights is assuming that triviality is harmful.

In other words, the circle of the Collier controversy is now complete: the attack position retains the essentials of its traditional form although the kind of harmful effect which Restoration comedy is supposed to produce is now very different from that alleged by Collier. People do not imitate the indiscretions of Horner or Lady Fidget but they are affected in other ways. One possible explanation is I. A. Richards's theory of the stock response,[33] which provided an apparently scientific justification for the view that superficial and conventional responses *are* harmful to the personality, and an examination of the context and phraseology of Professor Knights's essay will suggest that he was probably drawing to some extent on this aspect of Richards' work. But apart from this, I think it can be shown that for him the concept of 'triviality' already has inherent overtones of evil and danger. The idea cuts right to the heart of English puritanism, and Restoration comedy, whatever else it is, is a challenge to all that puritanism stands for in English life. The traditional fear of 'idleness' re-emerges in the modern hatred of triviality. 'Ydleness is the Mother of Vice', as the Elizabethan preacher put it; 'Insignificance, to speak softly, is the Natural Consequence of Lewdness', wrote Collier in the *Second Defence*, putting it the other way about; 'Triviality', as the Pilkington Committee was reminded in 1960, is 'more dangerous to the soul than wickedness'[34]; and, in Professor Knights's own circle, there is the example of F. R. Leavis' defence of George Eliot against the charge of over-seriousness. The alternative to maintaining serious values, he argues, is to maintain trivial ones, and 'I will add (exposing myself completely) that the enlightenment or aestheticism or sophistication that feels an amused superiority to them leads, in my view, to triviality and boredom, and that out of triviality comes evil'.[35]

Restoration comedy, in failing to be serious, is therefore trivial and therefore not only 'bad' but 'dangerous': that, in the end, is what Professor Knights reacted against, and perhaps he remains closer to Collier and Macaulay than has been suggested. It is, as I remarked at the outset, a curious and many-faceted tract of cultural and critical history, yet this interminable debate has a disturbing tendency to throw us back to first principles. And the challenge of the plays themselves is still there.

NOTES

1. L. C. Knights, 'Restoration Comedy: The Reality and the Myth', *Scrutiny*, VI (1937), 122-143. Repr. in *Explorations* (London, 1946), pp. 131-149, and elsewhere. All subsequent references are to *Scrutiny*.

2. See Dudley W. R. Bahlman, *The Moral Revolution of 1688* (New Haven and London, 1957).

3. Joseph Addison, Richard Steele, *et al.*, *The Spectator*, ed. Donald F. Bond (Oxford, 1965), I, 16. All subsequent references to *The Spectator* are to this edition.

4. Quoted Bahlman, p. 6.

5. Christopher Hill, *Society and Puritanism in Pre-Revolutionary England* (London, 1964), p. 509.

6. *Critical Essays of the Eighteenth Century 1700-1725*, ed. W. H. Durham (New Haven and London, 1915), p. 71.

7. *Critical Essays of the Seventeenth Century*, ed. J. E. Spingarn (Oxford, 1908), III, 229-232.

8. Jeremy Collier, *A Short View of the Immorality and Profaneness of the English Stage* (London, 1698), Preface and p. 5.

9. *The Lover*, No. 5, in *Richard Steele's Periodical Journalism 1714-1716*, ed. Rae Blanchard (Oxford, 1959), p. 22.

10. *Spectator*, III, 393.

11. *Short View*, pp. 141 and 148.

12. *A Second Defence of the Short View of the Profaneness and Immorality of the English Stage* (London, 1700), p. 98.

13. Quoted Bahlman, p. 6.

14. *The Critical Works of John Dennis*, ed. E. N. Hooker (Baltimore, 1939-43), II, 245.

15. *Critical Works*, I, 157.

16. *Amendments to Mr. Collier's False and Imperfect Citations*, 1698, in *The Mourning Bride, Poems, and Miscellanies*, ed. Bonamy Dobrée (London, 1928), p. 411.

17. *Lives of the English Poets*, ed. G. Birkbeck Hill (Oxford, 1905), II, 222.

18. 'A Defence of Poetry', in *The Complete Works of Percy Bysshe Shelley*, ed. Roger Ingpen and Walter E. Peck (London, 1926-7), VII, 116, 117, 118.

19. 'On the Artificial Comedy of the Last Century', in *The Life Letters and Writings of Charles Lamb*, ed. Percy Fitzgerald (London, 1875), III, 361.

20. *Journal*, March 10, 1814. *Works of Lord Byron*, ed. Rowland E. Prothero (London, 1903), *Letters and Journals*, II, 398.

21. Lamb, III, 361, 363, 366.

22. Lamb, III, 362-364.

23. *Complete Works of William Hazlitt*, ed. P. P. Howe (London and Toronto, 1931), VI, 70 and 151.

24. Hazlitt, VI, 78.

25. Lamb, III, 362, 363.

26. W. M. Thackeray, *The English Humourists of the Eighteenth Century* (London, 1853), in *The Oxford Thackeray*, ed. G. Saintsbury (Oxford, 1908), XIII, 521.

27. *The Oxford Thackeray*, X, 621.

28. *The Edinburgh Review*, LXXII (1841), 490-528.

29. See Note 1.

30. *Restoration Drama: Modern Essays in Criticism*, ed. John Loftis (New York, 1966), p. ix.

31. John Wain, 'Restoration Comedy and Its Modern Critics', *Essays in Criticism*, VI (1956), 374.

32. Norman N. Holland, 'The Critical Forum: Restoration Comedy Again', *Essays in Criticism*, VII (1957), 321-322.

33. I. A. Richards, *Principles of Literary Criticism* (London, 1924), 199-206.

34. HMSO, *Report of the Committee on Broadcasting, 1960* (London, 1962), p. 35.

35. F. R. Leavis, *The Great Tradition* (London, 1948), pp. 13-14. The approved serious values under discussion are chastity, industry, and self-restraint.

Restoration Tragedy
as Total Theatre

PHILIP PARSONS

I

Studies of Restoration tragedy almost always begin with Dryden, the most literary playwright of the period. A great non-dramatic poet, a major critic, and the finest rhetorician of the Restoration theatre, he holds strong interest for the literary critic. To a theatrical sensibility, however, the picture is rather different. In this most intensely theatrical of all periods in English drama, Dryden's verbal brilliance remains a unique strength, but his command of the theatrical medium is less certain. Here Lee and Otway are often his superiors. And since the serious drama of the Restoration is the most full-blooded attempt until the Expressionist theatre of our own century to create significant drama out of the resources of the theatre itself, Dryden's preoccupation with literary issues can sometimes be a source of weakness rather than strength.

This was the first great age of the proscenium-arch theatre, invented to house the scenic spectacles of such courtly entertainments as the *intermedio* in Italy, the masque in England, and above all the opera that developed with these. Audiences accustomed to allegorical painting, to emblem books, to emblematic pageantries and masques, were acutely sensitive to the wonder of perspective painting – often described as a kind of magic – and to the new, sensuous, and colourful world of the stage. To such a medium the externalized passions and patterns of heroic drama were highly sympathetic. Dance, spectacle – including even aerial display – and, of course, music, assumed a new prominence in the public theatre in

27

response to a new interest in their expressive potential. Dramatists have always conceived their plays for the stage but the radically expanded resources of the public theatre meant that now more than ever they must conceive their work in theatrical space and in more than verbal terms. In his command of the full resources of the baroque Restoration stage, Lee is the outstanding creative figure, while Crowne, Congreve, even Settle, can claim attention as imaginative artists of some consequence. Since this view of the period's dramatists is less flagrantly at odds with contemporary audience response than today's preoccupation with Dryden to the exclusion of all the rest, it has perhaps something to commend it.

Restoration tragedy is a misnomer. If tragedy means an exploration of human life, a following of the obscure currents of consciousness wherever they may lead, no Restoration play may claim the status of tragedy. Instead we find a formulation of problems, a demonstration of dilemmas, rather in the manner of the problem play, or, better still, of the mediaeval morality. In the strictest sense, these are plays of ideas. The derivation is partly through the Jacobean and Caroline court masque, where character is nothing and sensuous demonstration everything. The figures embodying Union or Love or Wisdom that once circled about James or Charles as God's vice-gerent, and the embodiment of Kingship, are replaced now by tokens of Will, Magnanimity, Ambition and, of course, Love, though they no longer move in hieratic order about an assured centre. They clash in constantly moving patterns as the dramatists attack from every conceivable position the obsessive problem of reconciling reason with the dangerous stuff of passion.

Drama of this kind must stand or fall by its handling of situation, for it is by manipulating his characters through a series of revealing situations that the dramatist expresses his meaning. This is the technique of melodrama, and indeed the term Restoration melodrama is to be preferred to the traditional and misleading label, Restoration tragedy. Unfortunately melodrama today has become a term of abuse, conjuring up the simple-minded confrontations of Vice and Virtue of certain Victorian melodramas. These were, in fact, the last degenerate flicker of a tradition dating back two hundred years to Lee, Dryden, Otway, Congreve – anything but simple-minded men.

Developing the situational techniques of Fletcher to their own ends, they gave the English theatre poetic melodrama of real complexity and distinction.

Like all melodrama, the serious drama of the Restoration is given to violent overstatement and finds its power in the theatre rather than on the printed page. It is in this context that the literary qualities of the genre are to be assessed. Words are designed as a vigorous rhetoric to match the stage conception rather than embody it; they are conceived as an appropriate and expressive drapery to clothe the dramatic ideas – as Dryden's own critical writings abundantly testify. The aim is finally illustrative and pictorial – to 'paint the passions'. Thus characters live in their surfaces, visual and verbal, to be read like a complex charade. Concepts of depth, of a compelling inner life, are irrelevant to character conceived not as individual personality but as illustrated moral trait. Instead a series of sensuously apprehended ideas is propelled by a violent and dazzling theatricality.

Just as illustration implies a pre-existing entity to be illustrated, so the dramatic idea is conceived prior to the language that illustrates it and can exist independently of it in purely mimetic or stage terms. The emblematic stage tableau is, of course, the extreme case, but the point may also be illustrated by reference to a striking, because atypical – in the light of the author's generally lesser regard for visual effects – passage from Dryden's *All For Love*. For clothing dramatic ideas in language Dryden, of course, had no peer, yet here he deliberately lays aside language to present ideas in as purely theatrical terms as may be found in any court masque. At the crisis of Act III, Octavia, supported by Antony's old general, Ventidius, and his friend Dolabella, confronts Antony with their children. She motions them towards their father to beg him to return to his duty and forsake his unlawful passion for Cleopatra:

Ventidius.   Was ever sight so moving! Emperor!
Dolabella.   Friend!
Octavia.   Husband!
Both Children.   Father!
Antony.   I am vanquish'd: take me,
    Octavia; take me Children; share me all.

[IV, 226]

This is theatrical gesture, powerful in its context – any competent director can make it work by timing and grouping – but the words themselves are obviously not intended to realize personalities. Rather they are the blueprint for a formal sculptural composition which will crystallize with mathematical lucidity the meaning of the whole act. This begins with Cleopatra triumphing with Antony and ends with Cleopatra's despair at having lost him. Between this celebration of passion and its reversal come the rational claims of duty, presented to Antony in stern gradation: first, Ventidius enters, representing soldierly duty, forsaken for Cleopatra's sake; he then brings in Dolabella, representing the more personal claims of friendship, wronged for Cleopatra's sake; he in turn introduces Octavia, bringing the claims of a wife abandoned for Cleopatra's sake; and with her the children, fatherless for Cleopatra's sake. The order of entry is vital, moving with inexorable logic from the public to the most personal areas of responsibility. The lines just quoted climax the sequence and recapitulate it precisely. They gather up the issues of the whole act in a violently theatrical, violently disciplined statement, its melodramatic pressure expressing exactly the force of Dryden's logic. The movement of the whole act has a mathematical lucidity like that of music. Indeed if it has a fault it is perhaps a little too elegant, too controlled. Dryden is always comfortable in his reasonable poise – an Augustan temper to which the violent stresses of the Restoration were never so personally destructive as to the tortured sensibility of Lee or Otway.

Today we are peculiarly well placed to reappraise sympathetically the serious theatre of the Restoration. We have our own total theatre of music, light, and form. After the constrictions of the realist theatre with its box sets and its psychological inwardness, we are again externalizing, rediscovering the amplitude of the theatre's expressive resources. There is a new, sharper awareness of visual communication (back-projected illustrative slides are a commonplace of the post-Brechtian theatre) and of the actor as an expressive body. In the following pages I shall point out some of the more obvious examples of kindred techniques in the Restoration. But it is not only the technique that invites attention, for there is also a striking congruence of tone and theme with contemporary issues. In our time of shifting moral values, of spiritual violence and political atrocity, Antonin Artaud's Theatre of Cruelty has taught our stage an amoral ruthlessness. We may well look with new eyes on the treacherous, shifting world in which the Restoration hero confronts anarchy with his existential gesture and the libertine coolly pursues his ruthless Hobbist principles.

When Dryden wrote that 'an heroic play ought to be an imitation, in little, of an heroic poem' [I, 158] he was announcing a more radical break with dramatic tradition than appeared at first glance. Drama had already absorbed much of the heroic spirit, and the close resemblance between tragedy and the epic or heroic poem was a commonplace of the age: Milton was in long debate before deciding that his major work should be an epic rather than a tragedy,[1] and Hobbes, approving D'avenant's decision to model *Gondibert* on the five-act play, wrote: 'The Heroique Poem narrative (such as is yours) is called an *Epique Poem*. The Heroique Poem Dramatique, is *Tragedy*'.[2] Dryden merely reversed D'avenant's procedure: 'I have modelled my heroic plays by the rules of an heroic poem' [I, 162]; and that, in his view, was D'avenant's own intention, imperfectly realized, in *The Siege of Rhodes*. We may doubt, however, whether such a seasoned dramatist as D'avenant would have modelled a heroic play by anything but the rules of drama. Indeed it was his enthusiasm for drama which decided the form of *Gondibert*[3] – an enthusiasm which Dryden found misplaced: 'But this, I think, is rather a play in narration, as I may call it, than an heroic poem' [I, 159]. Oddly enough, it did not occur to him that the argument cuts the other way, and that *The Indian Emperor*, *The Conquest of Granada*, and even *Aureng-Zebe* are heroic poems in dialogue rather than plays.

A minor but instructive mark of epic as opposed to dramatic conception in Dryden's heroic plays is his fondness for extended simile and metaphor. Such devices are not in themselves undramatic – they sit quite well at the end of a scene, for instance, when the time has come for reflective commentary. But Dryden confesses that on occasion he used them to disastrous effect. He cites a scene from *The Indian Emperor*:

Montezuma, pursued by his enemies, and seeking sanctuary,

stands parleying without the fort, and describing his danger
to Cydaria, in a simile of six lines:

> As on the sands the frighted traveller
> Sees the high seas come rolling from afar, etc.

. . . The image had not been amiss from another man, at another
time: *sed nunc non erat hisce locus*: he destroyed the concernment
which the audience might otherwise have had for him; for they
could not think the danger near when he had the leisure to invent
a simile.

[I, 256-257]

So elementary a blunder in dramatic pace will seem incompre-
hensible until we remember the epic, where it is standard
practice to intensify and enlarge a moment of crisis by precisely
such means. Dryden was not thinking dramatically. He was
too busy imitating in little the heroic poem to see and feel
the movement of the scene in the theatre. In *The Rehearsal*
Mr Bayes lays down as 'a general Rule' that 'you must ever
make a *simile*, when you are surpris'd; 'tis the new way of
writing'.[4] It was a very old way of writing, but not a dramatic
one.

Dryden's preoccupation with the heroic poem often takes him
dangerously far from drama's most basic principle – that it
must enact. It encourages him to confuse dramatic with narrative interest, as in the opening scene of *Aureng-Zebe*, which
runs to one hundred and thirty-six lines of static exposition
before the action begins. Audiences will absorb expository information only for the sake of the action taking place before
their eyes. Thus Lee in a classic example of dramatic exposition
opens *The Rival Queens* with a duel which is at once frustrated
by the intervention of a third character. The angry exchanges
which follow reveal the situation in both subplot and main
plot. Dryden opens *Aureng-Zebe* with a complex political discussion about a battle to be fought that day – or, rather, with
three court officials reciting information already known to each.
This takes up the first forty-seven lines. Then a fourth court
official enters with two lines of news – the battle has begun –
and Dryden, plainly assuming that quite enough excitement has
been generated for the moment, devotes the next seventeen
lines to generalized comment before moving on to a further

recital of information. He proceeds in this fashion for a further seventy lines before the Emperor enters in argument with an ambassador – and at last drama has begun. For Dryden, of course, it began with the opening line. Even in the leisurely heroic theatre of the Restoration, and even if the five actors were as many Bettertons, it is difficult to believe that the scene held the audience. It must surely have been cut drastically. Yet the verse is distinguished by Dryden's most supple mastery of the couplet. It reads beautifully – as the opening of a heroic poem in dialogue form.

Again, the epic as Dryden conceived it (that is, with Tasso very much in mind) is responsible for the extreme proliferation of subplot and incident about his central heroic action. (Here Dryden's practice differs in degree rather than in kind from that of his fellow-dramatists – luxuriant incident is essential to the romantic heroic spirit. But it must be carefully disciplined and dramatized if the multiple action is to register clearly in the theatre.) Lee interweaves several plots successfully in *Sophonisba*, but each is relatively simple and presented as a sequence of dramatic event. While it would be grossly unjust to single Dryden out for exclusive censure on this score, it is certainly true that he tends to crowd his interwoven plots with part-enacted, part-reported incident and reversals of fortune, so that the complex actions of his heroic plays defy memory more successfully than some, if not most. This intricacy is carefully designed to reflect thematic comment back and forth through the play in a series of parallels; but its effectiveness in the theatre is to be doubted. The most acute member of the audience would be unlikely to appreciate to the full the texture of *Aureng-Zebe* or *The Conquest of Granada*, especially since this abundance of imperfectly dramatized incident tends to obscure the play's central development. Even on the printed page these works need close and reflective examination before the kaleidoscopic action settles into the ample, lucid statement of Dryden's design.[5] The stage action is the index of his intention rather than its embodiment. He demands that we look beyond it, as he himself does, in scene after scene. If the opening of *Aureng-Zebe* shows this demand at its most pernicious, it also appears in many more lively scenes where the dramatic conflict is that of debate, Dryden's most typical formal unit: 'The favourite

exercise of his mind was ratiocination . . . When once he had
engaged himself in disputation, thoughts flowed in on either
side: . . . he had always objections and solutions at command;
"verbaque provisam rem" – give him matter for his verse, and
he finds without difficulty verse for his matter'.[6] Despite Dr
Johnson's rather sour tone, in this kind of poetic dialectic
Dryden can, of course, be brilliant; when the debate is grounded
in a strong clash of wills or personalities he gives us some of his
best scenes, such as the first act of *All For Love* or the quarrel
between the Emperor and Nourmahal in *Aureng-Zebe*. But there
is an ever-present danger that Dryden will lose sight of the
debaters in the debate. In the second act of *All For Love*, where
Antony presents the case against Cleopatra and she rebuts the
charges, the dramatic tug-of-war is so closely identified with
the severe investigation of events long past that the scene
tends to evoke the tedious argumentation of a court of law
rather than the urgent concerns of the theatre. The admired
reconciliation between Sebastian and Dorax in *Don Sebastian* is
open to the same criticism, though here the danger is mitigated
by the play's whole backward-looking theme; the past is raked
over in quest of the truth behind today's unhappiness and
conflict, and Dryden digs towards the heart of his drama.
Similarly crucial is Indamora's conversion of Morat in *Aureng-
Zebe* but here, where extremes are made to meet, it is dis-
concerting to find the debate conducted with an air of academic
calm; if it succeeded in the theatre it is to be hoped Dryden
congratulated the actors quite as much as himself. Examples of
Dryden's fondness for debate could be multiplied from *The
Conquest of Granada*, *Tyrannic Love*, and *The Indian Emperor*;
one thinks in particular of Almanzor and Boabdelin disputing
sovereign right, of Saint Catharine arguing the merits of
Christianity with Apollonius – a scene staged quite frankly as a
debate. However, since the habit, at once Dryden's strength
and weakness, extends beyond his avowed heroic period, it can
hardly be traced directly to his epic interpretation of drama.
Rather, both that and this suggest an imagination of no
particular dramatic bent. As he confesses in the dedication of
Aureng-Zebe and again eighteen years later,[7] his heart was in
the epic, not in drama; and the enormous contemporary prestige
of the epic was responsible for his theory of the heroic play:

'I have modelled my heroic plays by the rules of an heroic poem. And if that be the most noble, the most pleasant, and the most instructive way of writing in verse, and withal the highest pattern of human life, as all poets have agreed, I shall need no other argument to justify my choice in this imitation' [I, 162]. The reasoning is understandable but it has nothing to do with drama. Dryden's heroic plays are his substitute for the great epic he was never to write. Thanks partly to the extreme heroic taste of the day, partly to the brilliant acting talents at his disposal,[8] most of all to his native literary and acquired dramatic skills, he enjoyed a string of triumphs in the theatre. For, despite the weakness pointed out here, Dryden was, of course, abundantly endowed with critical acumen to profit by experience and learn the craft of the theatre as he went along; and he learned, too, to cover his dramatic weakness by exploiting his genius for poetic rhetoric to its full theatrical value.[9] But the theory enunciated in the essay *Of Heroic Plays* remains misconceived. It is a spirited charge up a blind alley.

It is proper to emphasize the distinction made above between the theatrical value of Dryden's heroic rhetoric and his limited dramatic sense. Probably at no other period in the history of our theatre was it possible for sheer rhetorical impact to carry a play so far towards success. Cibber often reminds us how dearly the Restoration audience loved to have its eardrums soundly rattled[10] and deplores this standing temptation to the greenhorn actor; but by the same token the excellence of a Betterton or a Barry appeared in the subtlety of their rhythms and modulations – in the 'enchanting harmony' with which they poured out the rhetoric of the passions: ' . . . The least Syllable too long, or too slightly dwelt upon in a Period, depreciates it to nothing; which very Syllable if rightly touch'd, shall, like the heightening Stroke of Light from a Master's Pencil, give Life and Spirit to the whole. I never heard a Line in Tragedy come from *Betterton*, wherein my Judgment, my Ear, and my Imagination, were not fully satisfy'd'.[11] Over the years Dryden provided the Restoration actors with vocal scores of increasing subtlety and consistently high finish. The kind of excitement that *stilo recitativo* had brought to *The Siege of Rhodes* is supplied now by Dryden's feeling for tonal change and colour in the heroic couplet and later in blank verse. Here lies his signal contribution to the development of the heroic play.

II

The development of the heroic play is usually discussed in terms of English, French, Italian, Spanish, or other influence – which is not, of course, our present interest. We are concerned here with observable changes in dramatic form and function, and in this light we must consider a second vitally important formal influence, that of the masque, and in particular the crucial marriage of masque to tragedy solemnized by Sir William D'avenant in the first true heroic play, *The Siege of Rhodes* (1656). *The Siege of Rhodes* was mounted as a masque with scenery, music, actresses, and no curtain-fall between acts (here called masque 'entries'), a convention continued in the Restoration theatre; it was printed in masque format in the Restoration as well as the Commonwealth editions, and it was entered in the Stationers' Register as a masque; and yet it is also a play, a pure development of D'avenant's Caroline heroic strain. He is rarely given full credit for his originality and doggedness. *The Siege of Rhodes* is still too often dismissed as a makeshift freak, devised purely to avoid the Commonwealth ban on outright stage-plays. It is, in fact, the culmination of his plans for a lyric theatre, developed before the Civil War.

Modern readers of *The Siege of Rhodes* may well be puzzled to find the reason for its enormous popular success and greet with frank ridicule Pepys's judgement that it was 'the best poem that ever was wrote'.[12] Yet Pepys's enthusiasm cannot be dismissed as an echo of modish acclaim for a new sensation. It is based on long and close familiarity. He went not only to the opening season of 1661 but to revival after revival during the following years. On 26 February 1661/2 he spent a pleasant morning with John Berkenshaw, his music master, setting 'This Cursed Jealousie, what is't' – a chorus from Part 1 – to their own accompaniment, and as late as January 1666/7, long after D'avenant's first brave venture in Restoration heroics had lost the gloss of novelty, Pepys's fiddling teacher is promising to get him the whole score. No doubt his keen enjoyment of the score, now lost, colours Pepys's high regard for D'avenant's text;

but D'avenant intended the play to stand on its own feet, and on some of his visits to *The Siege of Rhodes* Pepys would have seen the piece stripped of its music and 'acted as a just drama', for so, Dryden tells us, it was later revived [I, 158]. The text, especially Part 1, has the extreme simplicity and bareness of words designed for music, but D'avenant sees the music as secondary to the dramatic language it carries:

> In Tragedy, the language of the Stage
> Is rais'd above the common dialect;
> And Vocal Musick adds new wings to all
> The flights of Poetry.[13]

Pepys and his wife would read the text to each other, and his high opinion, already quoted, is dated 1 October 1665, more than four years after D'avenant's initial triumph at Lincoln's Inn Fields. Yet the poetic pressure of the text in the literary sense is minimal, and even Dryden, with his deep affection and admiration for D'avenant, suggests mildly that 'something might have been added to the beauty of the style' [I, 158] – a monumental understatement. In fact Pepys is probably using the word 'poem' in the catholic sense of his century. He is carried away by the total poetry of D'avenant's opera, to which the text is the guide.

D'avenant states clearly the poetic nature of his new kind of drama – a useful corrective to the view that he was an irresponsible showman, fathering upon the theatre an unworthy tradition of bread and circuses: 'Vertue, in those Images of the *Heroes*, adorn'd with that Musick, and these Scenes, is to be enliven'd with Poetry. Poetry is the subtle Engine by which the wonderful Body of the *Opera* must move'.[14] It is a striking analysis. D'avenant's operatic conception of drama posits an art of the *ensemble*, a total 'Poetry (whose several beauties make up the shape of the *Opera*)'.[15] Action, scenery, words, and music are the poet's language in the theatre; it is the voice of Edward Gordon Craig two and a half centuries before his time and the battle-cry of today's *avant-garde*: 'The Art of the Theatre is neither acting nor the play, it is neither scene nor dance, but it consists of all the elements of which these things are composed: action, which is the very spirit of acting; words, which are the body of the play; line and colour, which are the very heart of the

D

scene; rhythm, which is the very essence of dance. Action,
words, line, colour, rhythm!'[16] And poetry, the poetic spirit of
Craig's 'artist of the theatre' and of D'avenant's theatrical
poet, is the informing life by which the wonderful body of the
ensemble must move. This means, of course, that a literary
approach to drama (never entirely satisfactory) becomes quite
inadequate. Indeed Craig kicks up his heels and argues that any
play which is completely satisfying when read is no true theatre-
piece, and on this ground dismisses Shakespeare from his
theatre of the future – an intriguing comment on D'avenant's
operatic *Macbeth*. In the Elizabethan age, says Craig, the true
art of the theatre flourished outside the playhouse: 'I will tell
you, on the other hand, what at that period was made for the
theatre – the Masques – the Pageants – these were light and
beautiful examples of the Art of the Theatre'.[17] And, of course,
The Siege of Rhodes stems directly from D'avenant's court
masques.

At its best the court masque was just such a poetic unity of
movement, colour, and sound as D'avenant and Craig describe.
The published text was a very incomplete record, as Ben
Jonson laments in his description of his *Hymenaei*: 'Onely the
enuie was, that it lasted not still, or (now it is past) cannot by
imagination, much lesse description, be recouered to a part of
that *spirit* it had in the gliding by'.[18] The text will indicate
the theme but can realize only its verbal manifestation. In fact
the masque's primary appeal is to the eye (a fundamental law
of the theatre, says Craig), for a masque is distinct from a play
in that it does not deal with people but with visual ideas –
Mercy, Justice, Peace, and so forth. In this it is more closely
related to the morality play than to contemporary drama. Thus
we find D'avenant setting out in *The Siege of Rhodes* 'to advance
the Characters of vertue in the shapes of Valor and conjugal
Love'; 'nor have I wanted care' he adds, 'to render the *Ideas* of
Greatness and Vertue pleasing and familiar'.[19] But where in a
true masque such characters would actually be called Valour
and Love, here they bear such names as Alphonso and Ianthe.
For D'avenant has applied the principles of the masque to
traditional dramatic form. His characters are presented as
people, but in behaviour each runs through a series of masque
absolutes, chiefly Love, Jealousy, and Magnanimity. So that,

despite the surface appearance of individual character, *The Siege of Rhodes* presents, as Dryden points out, 'the examples of moral virtue writ in verse, and performed in recitative music'[20] – the business of the court masque. And that is the level at which the text must be approached.

This infusion of the masque has influenced the dramatic form in other ways. It has simplified the story to the barest outline of a plot. All that is required of it is the instructive juxtaposition of D'avenant's small selected range of masque values. For instance, Magnanimity (Solyman) is played against Love (Ianthe) and then against Jealousy (Alphonso). Or Honour (Alphonso) is played against Power (Solyman). The idea is to throw light on each from a number of angles, and this D'avenant has achieved with great economy. In brief, the function of the plot is to provide a series of revealing situations; situation is the mainspring of the court masque, of *The Siege of Rhodes*, and of succeeding heroic melodrama.

It must be added, however, that situation is also central to Fletcher's dramatic method and to D'avenant's after him. Indeed, that is what made the fusion of masque and drama possible. Fletcher has often been reproached with skin-deep, inconsistent characterization, and sensational plotting. Of late we are coming to see, however, that another view is possible – that through his situations Fletcher makes his limited but serious comment on the world in which he lived: 'Almost every one of the Beaumont and Fletcher plays, and of the plays of later date that belong to the same mode, is an attempt to record the case-history not of a man but of a situation. Analogies can be found in the pages of Burton, where we learn little concerning individuals but much concerning the pattern of human responses to abnormal situations'.[21] D'avenant's Caroline tragedies take Fletcher's method to its logical conclusion. Personality becomes nothing, situation everything. The movement is as fascinating as it is clear. His first play, *Albovine* (1626?), is a post-Jacobean blood tragedy, a failure but full of promise. Albovine himself is conceived and fitfully realized as a Tamburlaine-like figure of titanic energy, pride and irresponsibility, but also of disarming innocence. There are real flashes of life here – never to be repeated in D'avenant's later work. For he never again essayed the old grand manner. The influence of Fletcher, already strong in *Albovine,* dominates the following plays. Individual actions may be caught well enough but they are disembodied – there is no attempt to realize sustained character. Instead D'avenant begins to investigate ideas through situation, and here he soon goes beyond Fletcher. Given that a play is not to be like life but like a discussion of it, there is no point in picturing even such limited personality as Fletcher's characters present. Ideas are best worked out with moral and emotional counters; the presence of more than one or two qualities in a character merely confuses the pattern. Thus in *Love and Honour* (1634) D'avenant flouts psychological probability in showing three young men so altruistically united in love of two young women (all three love both) that they devoutly accept a quite arbitrary allocation at the end. But of course these men and women are primarily figures in an allegory – personified ideas of Beauty and Love manipulated into a situation to show (among other things) that Beauty cannot be possessed and that Love is unpossessive. Here we are only a step away from the masque, and in *The Siege of Rhodes* D'avenant took that final step.

What D'avenant handed on to the Restoration was not his concern that men should measure themselves against the ideal but – as Dryden tells us – a new dramatic form. In many respects, of course, it was not new, as D'avenant's own Caroline heroic plays witness. But what made the old material new was the discipline of the masque. One need only set *The Siege of Rhodes* beside *Love and Honour* to see that the masque has simplified, heightened, and hardened the heroic material. The very brevity of D'avenant's story in *The Siege of Rhodes,* itself a legacy of the masque,[22] throws attention on the new feeling for heroic character. The postures are sharply defined and absolute like those of the masque; in *Love and Honour* there remains something of the relaxed atmosphere of Fletcherian romance – a certain soft, fairy-tale quality. *The Siege of Rhodes* is dry, artificial, and hard. The last lingering traces of something personal in the old heroic figures have been shorn away and the new gestures are impersonal as those of a puppet. They are also more exaggerated, so that the new heroic form stands forth as at once more flamboyant and more austere than its precursor. It is the paradoxical combination of wildness and discipline which gives the new form its baroque excitement; theatrical turbulence is rigidly confined within a narrow, simple range of gestures.[23]

As Dryden saw, the idea was capable of development. D'avenant had provided the discipline; what was needed now was even greater flamboyance.

Future dramatists were to modify the formula still further. When Dryden's high heroic melodrama had run its course, Restoration taste returned to blank verse and a lower-toned, more supple melodrama which looks back to the Jacobeans. But set Otway beside a Jacobean dramatist and it is at once apparent that the Jacobean sense of realized personality is lacking in the characters. Otway's figures are assembled from a range of isolated, sharply defined, impersonal gestures no less than Dryden's or D'avenant's before him. He is still working within the legacy of the masque.

III

The most obvious and familiar evidence of the influence of the masque upon legitimate drama is, of course, the physical theatre building of the Restoration. D'avenant's little improvised stage for the Commonwealth première of *The Siege of Rhodes* was designed by John Webb, assistant to Inigo Jones, and is identical in layout with the final masque stage. With the Restoration, D'avenant at once constructed a more permanent theatre along the same lines, with such popular success that the rival company, the King's Men, was forced to follow suit. The old Elizabethan stage was finished; the masque's painted wings, shutters, backcloths, and machines had taken over the public theatre. The huge Elizabethan open stage remained in front of this framed three-dimensional picture, still filling half the house; the musicians' gallery remained above and the entrance doors on either side, giving directly on to the open stage. But the character of the theatre was transformed. An essentially verbal theatre had been modified to create the conditions for what we should call today a total theatre.

Such revolutionary changes do not occur in that most conservative of artistic media, the theatre, without good artistic cause. Drama is made for theatres and theatres for drama; the one cannot change independently of the other. D'avenant's drastic overhaul of dramatic form and the theatre itself in *The Siege of Rhodes* represents a solution to a difficulty created by the dramatization of heroic material – a difficulty made plain already in *Love and Honour* by the uneasy status of the serious characters. Are these creatures, with their impossible psychology, to be approached as dramatic characters in the traditional sense or as masque-like embodiments of moral qualities? Clearly, the play will make sense only on the latter assumption; we read the emergence of these buried lovers into a blustering world as an allegory of the spring, and in this context we can accept the three men's undemanding worship of springlike beauty in the two women. Yet the allegorical status of these characters is by no means underlined. While they are clearly idealized, D'avenant seems to offer them as idealized men and women – models of impossible aristocratic refinement. They are neither quite fairy-tale creatures, nor credible human beings. Nor is their language convincing. D'avenant's blank verse is fairly regular but it is rarely functional. He can rise on occasion to a pleasing rhetorical prettiness in which the iambic beat regains something of its old vitality, but, in general, language is far more lively in the comically realistic subplot; and, of course, the proximity of this subplot world, itself part of the allegory, obscures the status of the main-plot characters still further by encouraging a realistic view of the whole play. In brief, while the serious characters seem calculated to give delight by a brilliant fairy-tale quality, we still seem invited to approach them as human beings with an implied inner life – which they very obviously lack.

Ideal postures of love and valour clearly demand a world of their own, a theatre devoid of real life, yet which establishes contact with the audience at some new level. In *The Siege of Rhodes* D'avenant takes a decisive step towards its creation. He boldly heightens and emphasizes the artificiality of his material to make it all-of-a-piece as a theatrical object, a thing made, inviting no direct reference to a world of ordinary life. At the same time he gives it a new, violent life by a transformation of the dramatic medium itself. Elizabethan, Jacobean, and even Caroline drama had addressed the mind directly, chiefly by verbal means. *The Siege of Rhodes* does not address the mind directly; it assaults it by way of the senses in coordinated appeal

– sculptural, painterly, musical, balletic, rhetorical. The logic is excellent. The realistic dramatic development of earlier seventeenth-century drama had invited the audience into the life of the characters to explore and experience; with that relationship no longer possible the play will now project itself and its meaning at the audience to compel attention and wonder – admiration. Had this technique of theatrical assault proved less than highly sympathetic to the rising tide of heroic taste in the theatre, it is difficult to believe that it would have left much mark on heroic drama. It was very expensive, demanding the rebuilding of theatres and a continuing outlay on scenery and machines. Reasonable unity of heroic impact might have been obtained, after all, merely by excising realism and continuing with the old stage, while *The Siege of Rhodes* might have been left as a tentative model for opera. But, in fact, when Dryden comes to write his lengthy essay on opera he makes no reference at all to *The Siege of Rhodes* – a striking omission in view of his generous acknowledgements elsewhere to D'avenant, 'whose memory I love and honour', and to whose originality, 'quick and piercing imagination', and personal kindness, he pays touching tribute in the *Preface to the Tempest* [I, 134]. For the significance of *The Siege of Rhodes* was, of course, dramatic, even to the *stilo recitativo* which Buckingham parodies so delightfully as one of the techniques of the heroic theatre in *The Rehearsal*.[24] D'avenant's expensive experiment made dramatic history because it set off splendidly heroic material. His heightening and stylization of character underlined the idealized quality of heroic romance, brought it into sharper focus; and the principle of total theatrical assault was entirely attuned to the heroic play's sensational development of Fletcherian dramatic techniques – the strong situations, surprising developments, exciting incidents, amazing villainies, and superb acts of virtue. The exalted heroic spirit, as Dryden insists again and again, was directed to admiration – or, as Buckingham has it, 'given altogether to elevate and surprise'.[25] D'avenant's infusion of the masque in *The Siege of Rhodes* was adapted to the theatrical expression of precisely these qualities.

Seen in this context, Dryden's advocacy (and practice) of rhyme makes very good sense. It stressed still further the artificial nature of the heroic spirit but also provided a

much-needed external discipline. The verse of *Love and Honour*
sprawls so badly that the inversion of an iambic foot means
nothing; there are no rules by which to play the game and so it
is impossible to score. What Dryden calls 'the Pindaric way
practiced in *The Siege of Rhodes*' is a step in the right direction,
but, again, the capricious freedom of the form (designed,
says D'avenant in the preface to the 1656 edition, for musical
setting) limits its expressive potential. The severe discipline of
the rhymed couplet was to prove at last too limiting, but for
the narrow, clear-cut emotional range of extreme heroism it was
ideal. The regular rhymed heroic play (first conceived by the
Earl of Orrery in imitation of the French, first essayed by Dryden
with Howard in *The Indian Queen*) seems the natural vehicle for
heroic speech. In terms of drama the heroic couplet means
extreme stylization ('Serious plays', Dryden warns us, 'ought
not to imitate conversation too nearly' [I, 157]), and the
portrayal of big, uninflected emotions, sustained perhaps to the
length of a *tirade*; it means remote, incantatory drama with
something of the dignity of ritual. The play's argument and
characters must be great and noble to support rhyme, and 'the
scenes which . . . most commend it, are those, . . . on the result
of which the doing or not doing some considerable action should
depend' [I, 9]. Significantly, rhyme was often reserved at
first for a play's grand moments, or to strike an attitude at the
end of a scene. Such foretastes led audiences to want the ritual
of the grand moment and the heroic attitudes sustained from
beginning to end – and, indeed, to miss this singing, hieratic
quality in *Tyrannic Love* or *The Conquest of Granada* is to miss
something of the play's spirit. 'By the harmony of words we
elevate the mind to a sense of devotion, as our solemn music,
which is inarticulate poesy, does in churches', writes Dryden, a
piece of special pleading to justify his religious subject in
Tyrannic Love [I, 139]. But it also leads indirectly back to the
heroic play's grand object – admiration. Formally, rhyme
helped to give the heroic play its all-of-a-piece unity but it also
hit the taste of the day because it gave heroic dialogue the
right 'feel', an almost physical quality; sharpening the play's
impact on the stage, it was welcomed into the armoury of
theatrical assault.

While literary usage of the term 'baroque' is highly contentious, there can be no reasonable doubt that D'avenant's theatrical technique in *The Siege of Rhodes* – his simultaneous address to several senses – is strongly marked by the baroque spirit in the art-historian's sense:

> [The emblematists] associated the arts, brought together both the sensuous and the intellectual, and fulfilled an ancient dream that somehow the sister arts of painting and poetry would profit by formal union. . . . Similar reflections arose in attempting to define the masque spectacular in the days of its glory under James I. But one element that is new, or at least that received greater emphasis in the century of the baroque than in the Renaissance, is the notion that in the union of body and soul, picture and word, sense and intellect, there was some kind of interpenetration.[26]

Miss Hagstrum, whose extreme caution makes her study of this difficult field the more valuable, is stating here only the most general principles. It might, of course, be argued that the relationship between visual and verbal elements in Jonson's masques is very different from that in D'avenant's, or in *The Siege of Rhodes*, while the emblematic thought of some of the metaphysicals bears no comparison with either. But whatever the temper of the practitioner, the practice itself was, as Miss Hagstrum says, widely diffused throughout the period, and cannot be ignored in the theatre. Mr Bayes appeals to its prestige directly in his melodious two-man war fought in *recitativo*: 'you have at once your ear entertained . . . with Music and good language; and your eye satisfied with the garb, and accoutrements of war'.[27] But the union of the arts in the Restoration heroic theatre expresses a further aspect of baroque in the heroic violence, the theatrical assault of its sensuous appeal. This aspect of the baroque spirit does not argue, but proclaims. One cannot argue with a physical, sensuous experience – one can only react to it; and so 'baroque is able to win assent from the spirit through its power over the sensorium alone'.[28] That assent, of course, must be confirmed by the mind; the sensuous vision must proclaim acceptable values. Yet the power of sheer violence over the audience – violence of rhetoric and spectacle – is witnessed by the contemporary success of Dryden's most baroque play, *Tyrannic Love*, where he 'loos'd the Reins, and bid his Muse run mad' in Maximin's rants,[29] and where the core of Dryden's conception of warring powers, heavenly and terrestrial, is expressed in a baroque visual image as St Catharine's guardian angel swoops down to smash the wheel on which she is to be tortured. Equally baroque in the visual sense are the singing aerial spirits who hover over the sleeping saint, their ambiguous spirituality a vital strand in the theme. This full-blooded baroque manner in the theatre was not really to Dryden's taste and he was never to essay it again.[30] But, while *Tyrannic Love* is not among his better work for the theatre, it is usually criticized for the wrong reason. Maximin's impossible rants and the supernatural apparatus are all part of an effort to transcend reality, to enter the baroque world of contemporary heroic painting (in England Verrio's Heaven Room at Burghley may be cited as an example); in short, to win assent from the spirit through power over the sensorium alone. Today we withhold that assent. We find more smoke than fire in Dryden's passions, while his figures are not all to scale; so the play remains disastrously earthbound. But the example is interesting as an extreme development of the baroque theatre inaugurated with *The Siege of Rhodes*, where, for the first time on the public stage, we find deployed the baroque tactic of 'overstatement in the flesh, energy, mass, space, height, colour, and light'.[31] These qualities, both in the tangible, physical sense and in the literary sense, were to constitute the medium of Restoration melodrama. The dramatist constantly presents a visual and verbal picture, or a physical experience; spiritual or emotional experience is typically imaged in the flesh – pain as the bloodiest physical torture – love as a paradisial physical bliss. Verbal and literary elements must always dominate drama this side of ballet or opera, or mime, but we can hardly overstress the large extent to which serious drama had to be conceived physically and composed in the theatre after D'avenant had revolutionized it.

Like its forerunner, the court masque, this new, sensational dramatic medium was open to abuse. There was every temptation to assemble eye-catching spectacle, dancing, and music about a trivial text crammed with surprising twists and turns and larded with rant. These were the weapons of theatrical assault, the means of holding attention: 'The grand design upon the Stage is to keep the Auditors in suspence; for to guess presently at the plot, and the sence, tires 'em before the end of the first Act: now, here, every line surprises you, and brings in new matter. And, then, for Scenes, Cloaths and Dances we put 'em quite down, all that ever went before us: and these are the things, you know, that are essential to a Play'.[32] This view from *The Rehearsal* is, of course, hardly objective. It was no part of Buckingham's intention to suggest that the age had produced poets of the theatre, in D'avenant's and Gordon Craig's sense, who were creating dramatic *ensembles* of great distinction. Nor need such men have quarrelled with Buckingham's strictures here, which amount in substance to a complaint that preoccupation with the theatrical medium for its own sake obscures the plot and sense instead of forwarding them. But Buckingham's further assumption, that respect for plot and sense demands a retreat to 'the old plain way', does not follow. On the contrary, given the multiple appeal of this new dramatic medium, the best plays will be those which exploit it most sensitively. For instance, the big visual set-piece, with its immediate impact, should be used only to drive home an idea central to the dramatic conception. Its nature is climactic rather than diversionary. For its simplest effective use, we may look back to Ford, who time and again fills his stage at the play's close with a powerful emblematic statement of his theme. By contrast, Dryden's free use of spectacle and music in *The Indian Emperor* tends to be decorative (on the whole, tastefully so) rather than functional. That he did understand their expressive potential is witnessed by *Tyrannic Love* – though Buckingham's parody of the aerial spirits here is not entirely undeserved; the opening song is almost as silly as Buckingham would have it, and the whole scene goes on rather longer than dramatic necessity requires. *The Conquest of Granada* is the stronger for Dryden's sparing use of spectacle and reliance upon the one weapon of theatrical assault of which he is undisputed master – rhetoric. We may pause to praise the spectacular trial by arms of Almahide; in a play rooted in the idea of power, it is apt that the accusation of unchastity should be tried, not by rational process of law, but by a chivalric clash of brute force. But Dryden's heroic rhetoric in this play is at times almost beyond praise. Nobody but he could have brought off such a *tour de force* as the opening, where there is no vestige of dramatic action or conflict. Instead we have the magnificent narration of Almanzor's prowess at the bullfight (delivered originally by Mohun, one of the finest actors of the day) which enthrals the audience at the outset and establishes brilliantly the play's world of power and valour. For the rest, though it was not his *forte*, Dryden could sculpt space in the theatre, as appears in the reconciliation of Antony and Octavia in *All For Love* (quoted earlier), where the successive appeals 'Emperor!' – 'Friend!' – 'Husband!' – 'Father!' declare themselves as a sculptural group. But scenes such as this, which so clearly demand visual and theatrical realization, are comparatively unusual with Dryden. His imagination – including his image-making – and his great theatrical strength were overwhelmingly verbal.

Dryden's uncertain visual sense in the theatre contrasts strongly with the expressive feeling for stage imagery shown by some other Restoration dramatists. Settle, for instance, is Dryden's complete antithesis. Endowed with limited verbal poetic gifts (though his language often has vivid theatrical quality[33]), he shows remarkable visual imagination. His talent was operatic and spectacular, and after his appointment, probably in 1691, as City Poet, he designed a long succession of city pageants.[34] It is not surprising that when he published *The Empress of Morocco* he broke with tradition by incorporating 'sculptures' of the scenery; for the scenery is as much the text of his play as the words. The tradition of the masque continues with Settle more obviously than with any other of the more important dramatists of the period. A story from his last unhappy and impoverished years – that in Mrs Mynn's booth at Bartholomew Fair he 'acted a dragon, enclosed in a case of green leather of his own invention' in a droll called *St George for England*[35] – sticks in the mind with the tenacity of symbol; for *The Empress of Morocco* reminds one of nothing so much as a horrific and haunting puppet-play or fairground entertainment – a quality still present in his more impressive but erratic work *The Female Prelate*. He had in him the vulgar, popular stuff of the theatre.

Yet Settle is more than a purveyor of sensation to a popular audience. If *The Empress of Morocco* was a signal popular success, it also enjoyed prestige at court. His crude, simple, and violent theatricality expresses an imaginative vision to which it is wholly appropriate. In the Morocco presided over by the monstrous figure of the dowager Empress, the final realities are self-seeking, rage, and lust. They seem, as it were, the very ground from which all else derives. In such a world, altruism, tenderness, fidelity, become logically absurd. One is irresistibly reminded of Hobbes's 'state of nature' that precedes all law and all moral value. Seen from this point of view, it is Settle's achievement to have dramatized the terrifying insecurity of an order where hell may claim an older authority than heaven, where the powers of good are derived from a brutish vision of man's primal nature. The stink of the shambles that pervades *The Empress of Morocco* is the necessary violence of an imagination obsessed with crisis. The Jacobean tragic dramatists could still bear to realize what happens to men. For Settle there is only convulsive protest.

Settle's unprecedented 'sculptures' for *The Empress of Morocco* testify not only to great theatrical success but also to the nature of his dramaturgy. For, as Professor Wilson Knight writes of another play, Settle's dialogue is as much gesture as language; the whole melodrama strives to realize itself as a *tableau vivant*. Appropriately, the poetic core of his conception is stated in a masque – not a true court masque as James I and Charles I had known it, but more properly a masquerade. Its theme is the great redemptive myth of Orpheus and Eurydice. In the dowager Empress's realm, this is the crucial challenge to heaven: can love still descend and redeem life from death? It is rather a female hell into which Orpheus descends, full of 'Women-Spirits . . . attended by Furies'. With his music Orpheus calms the tortured spirits, 'And Hell in spite of Vengeance is at Peace'. Challenged by Pluto to state his business Orpheus replies boldly that Pluto is a ravisher:

> *No Tears nor Prayer*
> *Your unresisted Will Controules,*
> *Who Commit force on Vertue, Rapes on Soules.*
> [1673, p. 46]

Pluto promptly condemns him to damnation and commands the Furies to fling their snakes into Orpheus' bosom. But Proserpine intervenes on behalf of 'a Lover and a Stranger' and Orpheus goes on to ask for Eurydice, with whom, if need be, he is willing to endure hell – 'Oh take me down to Her or send Her back to me'. Pluto is unmoved but Proserpine pleads that he may take Eurydice with him, 'Releast by Love from that Eternal Chain, / Which destin'd Kings and Conquerours cannot break' [p. 48]. After further refusals Pluto is at last persuaded to relax the laws of hell, and Orpheus proclaims the power of redemptive love in a triumphant song:

> For this signal Grace to the World I'le declare,
>   In Heaven Earth and Hell Loves Pow'r is the Same.
> No Law there nor here, no God so Severe,
>   But Love can Repeale, and Beauty can Tame.
>
> [p. 48]

The chorus take up the refrain and love is celebrated in the harmony of a dance. But, as Orpheus reaches his hand to Eurydice, she turns on him and stabs him to death.

This perversion of a noble myth gathers up Settle's theme of deceit and corruption. The Jacobeans had, of course, known that a man may 'smile and smile and be a villain'. Fair appearance may hide an appalling reality. But Settle's masked company in hell carry the theme of disguise to a still more disturbing conclusion, making virtue play the part of vice. For this murderous Eurydice is the loyal and loving wife of the man she kills, the young Emperor of Morocco. The intended escape from hell extends beyond the masque to the court of the treacherous Crimalhaz, who arranges this entertainment for his sovereign. The Emperor is told privately that he is to be murdered that night and that he must take his wife's hand at the end of the masque and with her slip out of the camp and back to his capital. But the young Empress has been told that the Orpheus of the masque is in fact Crimalhaz, who will try to snatch her away from the revels and rape her. And so when the masked Emperor takes her hand, she cries out, 'Take that Ravisher', and stabs him. The powers of hell, 'Who Commit force on Vertue, Rapes on Soules', have turned an obscene trick. They have caused love to violate itself in the very moment of its symbolic triumph over death. They would show the world corrupted to the heart.

We in the audience may protest that love is still love, that Eurydice was abused, that the sea-marks of good and evil have suffered no alteration. But the Empress has killed her husband

and seems a murderess none the less. The truth is known only to the instigators of the plot, for whom good and evil are anyway meaningless. To all others, belief in goodness must become an act of faith. Good acts the part of evil, evil masquerades as good. 'On what Ill subjects I my Favours cast?' says the bewildered young Emperor:

> Kings Bounties act like the Suns Courteous smiles,
> Whose rayes produce kind Flowers on fruitful Soyles:
> But cast on barren Sands, and baser Earth,
> Only breed Poysons, and give Monsters Birth.
>
> [p. 34]

How is even the most astute ruler to delegate his power wisely or to avoid breeding poisonous monsters in a world where good and evil so interpenetrate and bear each other's shapes? Not only may good breed evil, but evil may breed good, with cynical inconsequence. At the play's opening it is the Dowager Empress who brings release to her imprisoned son and his mistress, merely as preliminary to his murder. Later she pleads passionately and successfully for her son's loyal general, Muly Hamet, whom she has brought to prison with her slanders and whose assassination she has well in hand – a situation she finds full of humour. The terms of the argument may be the crudest blacks and whites but the point is the ease with which one may replace the other. In these deceptive shifts Settle draws to a focus the whole world of the play. Is goodness merely a freak development in a world of evil? Are the heavens finally benign, hostile, or indifferent?

Settle reserves his major statement on the ambiguous heavens for another of his big visual set-pieces:

> *The Scene open'd, is presented a Prospect of a Clouded Sky, with a Rain bow. After a shower of Hail, enter from within the Scenes* Muly Hamet, *and* Abdelcador.
>
> [p. 36]

Upon this desert scene of mingled threat and promise arrives persecuted loyalty, in the persons of Muly Hamet and his faithful friend on their way to exile. There is more than a hint

here of Macbeth's blasted heath and of Lear's storm: 'Stormes
to my Miseries like attendants look . . .' says Muly Hamet,
while Abdelcador fears the shower of hail – 'an Object strange
and new' in Morocco – as some dire portent. Courts and cities
have been left behind; beggared virtue encounters here the
powers of heaven in a naked pictorial statement of man's
predicament. Within the puppet-like convention of the play,
the scene becomes strange and haunting. First Mariamne
appears from nowhere, having fled the city to join Muly
Hamet, her lover. 'Devotion is the rise of Pilgrimage', she
says; 'led by Love', she now:

> Leaves Palaces, and does to Desarts Rove.
> Wing'd by that zeal united Souls do beare.
>
> [p. 37]

Both here and throughout the play, the imagery of religion and
that of physical love interpenetrate to express the good. The
language of religion retains its traditional dramatic function to
imply a world-view, but it also endows with supreme value the
beloved mistress and other personal relationships. As Abdelcador
says, his master's poverty and persecution shall not make 'my
Esteem grow faint, or my Zeal less. . . . The Saint's not less,
although the Shrine's defac'd'. But immediately there appears a
priest with a band of his fellows to announce:

> Sir, our great Prophet has pronounc't your Fate,
> Your Love is doom'd to be Unfortunate.
>
> [p. 38]

And he goes on to interpret 'the language of the Sky':

> A mourning Garb of thick black Clouds it wore.
> But on the Sudden –
> Some aery Demon chang'd its form, and now
> That which look't black Above look'd white below.
> The Clouds dishevel'd from their crusted Locks,
> Something like Gems coin'd out of Chrystal Rocks.
> The Ground was with this strange bright Issue spread,
> As if Heav'n in affront to Nature had
> Design'd some new-found Tillage of its own;
> And on the Earth these unknown Seeds had sown.

Of these I reacht a Grain, which to my sence
Appear'd as cool as Virgin-innocence:
And like that too (which chiefly I admir'd)
Its ravisht Whiteness with a touch expir'd.
At the approach of Heat, this candid Rain
Dissolv'd to its first Element again.

[p. 39]

Muly Hamet robustly rejects the portent, identifying this strange stuff as a freak shower of hail, whereupon the priests set upon him (they are 'Hametalhaz, *disguis'd in the Habit of a Priest, with Villains in the same Dress'*) and in a trice have carried off Mariamne. Like the hail, she has disappeared as suddenly as she came, after as brief a stay. Abruptly Muly Hamet's divine imagery changes its character:

Condemn'd never to see *Morocco* more!
Thus am I doom'd to quit all I Adore:
As prophane Sinners are from Altars driven,
Banish'd the Temple to be banisht Heaven.
Horrour and Tortures now my Jaylours be,
Who paints Damnation needs but Copy me;
For if Mankind the pains of Hell e're knew,
T'is when they lose a Mistress as I do.

[p. 41]

The imaginative function of the scenic clouds, rainbow, and hailstorm has now been defined. Black clouds deliver white portents, interpreted – perhaps truly – by false priests. In a world rooted in evil, virgin innocence disappears at a touch. Or perhaps the portents mean nothing at all. Perhaps behind the threatening clouds and the fragile promise of the rainbow the heavens are empty.

The complete and unselfconscious acceptance by Restoration dramatists of visual communication as integral to their craft is witnessed by John Crowne's epilogue to the first part of *The Destruction of Jerusalem*. Though the curtain rose on 'the Brazen Gates of the Temple', though in the third act 'the Vale flies open, and shews the *Sanctum Sanctorum*', and though shortly afterwards 'an Angel descends over the Altar' [1677, p. 25] to

E

prophesy destruction, Crowne boasts his avoidance of mere spectacle:

> *But he at shew and great Machines might aim,*
> *Fine Chairs to carry Poetry when lame,*
> *On Ropes instead of Raptures to relye,*
> *When the sense creeps, to make the Actors flye.*
> *These Tricks upon our Stage will never hit,*
> *Our Company is for the old way of Wit.*
>
> [Part I, p. 56]

He is quite right. This weird and disturbing play has remarkable unity of impact. The golden, spirit-haunted Temple of Herod dominates the drama poetically from the moment of its revelation till the awesome scene of its burning ten acts later in 'Rivers of Fire, of Bloud, and liquid Gold'. There is spectacle in plenty, but none for its own sake. According to a supposed letter[36] from St Evremond to the Duchess of Mazarin, *The Destruction of Jerusalem* 'met with as wild and unaccountable success as Mr Dryden's *Conquest of Granada*'. Unaccountable it may have seemed to French taste, but by the canons of English heroic drama Crowne's is a work of outstanding interest. Nothing in his prentice piece, *Juliana*, or his rhymed, competently carpentered *The History of Charles VIII of France* prepares one for the violent baroque conviction of *The Destruction of Jerusalem* – precisely the quality lacking in Dryden's *Tyrannic Love*, a more proper parallel than *The Conquest of Granada*. Crowne's verse is sometimes clumsy, his action wordy; he never achieves Dryden's verbal refinement and definition. But neither can Dryden's evocation of 'things above' in the calm, if not prim, confidence of his Saint Catharine, and the pretty eloquence of her guardian angel, challenge comparison with Crowne's flaming messenger and the vision of his High Priest:

> And this once blessed House, where Angels came
> To bathe their aiery wings in holy flame,
> Like a swift Vision or a flash of light,
> All rapt in Fire, shall vanish in thy sight;
> And thrown aside amongst the common store,
> Sink down in Times Abyss, and rise no more.
>
> [Part I, p. 26]

So ends the angelic pronouncement of doom. The ardent imagery and spatial sweep make Dryden's angel seem more glittering than golden as he descends to St Catharine's aid:

> To guard thee from the Daemons of the Air;
> My flaming Sword, above 'em to display,
> (All Keen and Ground upon the edge of Day;)
> The Flat to sweep the Visions from thy Mind,
> The Edge to cut 'em through that stay behind.
>
> [II, *363*]

The energy here is intellectual, acrobatic, rather than passional – one of those 'wild and daring sallies of sentiment' which were so repugnant to Dr Johnson's neoclassic temper. We may demur at Dr Johnson's severity yet grant – with some qualifications – his main contention: 'The mind can be captivated only by recollection or by curiosity; by reviving natural sentiments or impressing new appearances of things: sentences were readier at his call than images; he could more easily fill the ear with some splendid novelty than awaken those ideas that slumber in the heart'.[37] To assault the ear with splendid novelty was a perfectly proper technique of the heroic theatre; but it should also awaken those ideas that slumber in the heart. Dryden's angelic rhetoric does not, while Crowne's spirits of air and fire appeal convincingly to old elemental tradition. So does the faithful High Priest's inability to believe that Jerusalem's holy of holies must be destroyed:

> Yes, on these Columns the whole Arch is bent,
> This Golden Roof supports the Firmament.
> The Sun with Altar-Flames adorns his head,
> And from this Oyl the heav'nly Lamps are fed;
> And all the Order which in Nature dwells
> But dances to the sound of *Aaron's* Bells.
> That to say Heav'n will ruine on us send,
> Is to declare the world is at an end;
> And Nature is disbanding all her Powers –
> Then falls the Temple of the world, and ours.
>
> [Part I, 1677, p. *27*]

It is true. The shaken temple of the world, in which God's vice-gerent had officiated, did finally fall in the catastrophe of the

mid-century. That terrible vision of supernatural destruction
authorizes every aspect of Crowne's theatrical violence – the
reported vision of a stormy army of the air 'so bright, / As if
their prancing Steeds were shod with Light' [p. 22]; the earth-
quake groans of the dying Temple; the small voice from beneath
the altar; the great voice that cries 'Let us depart'; the torn
veil 'as if the starry Heaven were rent, / And Angels shone
through the torn Firmament'; the descending messenger 'all
clad in Robes of fire' [p. 25]; the assembled Sanhedrin struck
with sleep while 'the Ghost of *Herod* the great *Edomite*: /
Greatest of all abandon'd *Esau*'s Line' rises to curse Jerusalem
and inspire with destructive rage his nation [I, pp. 37-39] and
the canting Pharisees, those puritan fanatics who will assault
the Temple from within. Deserted by heaven, the High Priest
can only affirm heroic will to defend the sacred things in his
charge:

> Heav'ns Will be done! But better I were slain,
> Than I my self my Diadem prophane; . . .
> If Heav'n's pleas'd t'abandon their defence,
> I'le guard them in the room of Providence.
>
> [Part I, 39-40]

It was a bold stroke on Crowne's part to send to Jerusalem's
aid his rationalist, sensual hero, King Phraartes of Parthia – a
cheerful Restoration atheist who would refer all the supernatural phenomena to the Royal Society for investigation but
who has his own holy of holies in the fleshly temple of love. He
too is swept up into the unearthly fire of the blazing Temple at
the spectacular climax of the play's second part, as Jerusalem
goes down before the assault of Titus Vespasian. Titus, himself
in love with the Jewish Queen Berenice, is obsessed by the
Temple's beauty and desperately anxious to keep it from harm.
His triumph among the ruins is empty, even though it has
made him Emperor; for it must also rob him of Berenice, whom
Rome would never accept as Empress. As Emperor and Queen
take their separate ways in the final scene, Crowne strikes the
note of saddened realism which echoes in Solyman's clear-eyed
perception of his position at the end of *The Siege of Rhodes*: the
will to power over the unruly world must come first, love must
remain unfulfilled; something vital has been destroyed.

Crowne projects upon the flat, masque-like stereotype of the heroic play a poetic statement of great vitality and richness. His characters are no more alive than Dryden's or Settle's. It is the brilliance of pigment, shape, and movement which communicates the play's abundant life. If Settle's *Empress of Morocco* is a vigorously drawn cartoon, Crowne's *Jerusalems* (as he conveniently calls them) are an opulent history piece, where form melts into form and colour into colour; his pairs of lovers are aspects of each other, his love and religion opposed yet alike. In the same way music melts into spectacle, spectacle into rhetoric, and each poetic image into the next. At curtain rise, 'the Brazen Gates of the Temple appear; Musick is heard within. Above, without the Temple as in the Womens Court, behind guilded Lettices, appear Queen *Berenice* and *Clarona* at their devotion'; Levites are heard singing this evening hymn:

> Day is dismounted on the watry Plain,
>   And Evening does begin to fold
>   Up Light's rich Cloth of Gold,
> And Nature's Face the Night begins to stain.
>   Holy Angels round us keep,
>   While our sense dissolves in sleep.
>   While the half of us is dead
> Let the living half be lead
> To your Gardens, to your Bowers,
> Where you pass your pleasing hours.
> Treat within your heav'nly Tents
>   Your Brethren Spirits thus in state
>   While they wait
> The leisure of their slumb'ring sense.
>   [Part I, a4ᵛ]

The 'sense dissolves' in the languorous richness of the whole. Each image is no sooner perceived than it disappears. The horseman melts as he dismounts into the watery plain, folds of shadow in cloth-of-gold become a dark, spreading stain upon a face, while the singers themselves dissolve into death and life, bodies and souls, and the souls become angels. The sense of an intangible, beautiful presence richly hidden is echoed in the image of the great brazen doors closed on the sacred ritual within, in the gilt lattices enclosing the praying women, in the invisible singers.

Such full-blooded interpenetration of the visual, verbal, and musical is not uncommon. Settle uses it – though to simpler purpose – in *The Empress of Morocco*, where a dance about an artificial palm-tree is performed before the Emperor and Empress, while a song with the refrain 'Long live and reign' is sung by a priest and chorus [p. 13]. The palm, traditional emblem of eternal life, bulked very large, as the contemporary illustration of the scene shows. As late as 1697, when such effects in serious drama are becoming rarer, Congreve makes a striking musical and visual point in *The Mourning Bride*. At the play's opening, he directs: 'The Curtain rising slowly to soft Musick, discovers *Almeria* in Mourning, *Leonora* waiting in Mourning'; then Almeria comes forward to speak the famous opening lines:

> Musick has Charms to sooth a savage Breast,
> To soften Rocks, or bend a knotted Oak.

The soft music and mourning are soon associated with Almeria's separation from the world: she is married to the dead and dreams of union with her husband's spirit; she is bitterly opposed to the world ruled by her predatory warrior father, King Manuel. Then her father's triumphant return from the wars is announced:

> *Almeria.*   My Women. I would meet him.
>   *Attendants to* Almeria *enter in Mourning.*
> *Symphony of Warlike Musick. Enter the King, attended by* Garcia
> *and several Officers. Files of Prisoners in Chains, and Guards, who
> are ranged in Order, round the Stage.* Almeria *meets the King and
> kneels: afterwards* Gonsalez *kneels and kisses the King's Hand,
> while* Garcia *does the same to the Princess.*
>
>   [I.i.263-270]

The clash is perfectly explicit without the use of words. This is not Almeria's music or her world; the black-clad figures advance upon the gaudy military brilliance ranged round the stage. In the end they will conquer the conqueror. The arrival of Almeria's husband-in-death, the despaired-of Alphonso, is among the most telling visual moments in Restoration melodrama. It follows shortly upon the passage so much admired by Dr Johnson, when Almeria has gone to mourn at the tomb of Alphonso's father, a 'Monument fronting the View, greater than the rest'. In her grief she calls Alphonso's name, whereupon he rises from his father's tomb – an event as eloquent as it is spectacular. 'We both have backward trod the paths of Fate', says Alphonso [II.ii.92], and as the play moves forward this unearthly pair continue to move backward, reversing fate, until the world of predatory passion has disappeared and lost happiness is recovered.

IV

Lee's visual effects are among the most assured and various of the period. The opening of *Theodosius, or the Force of Love* recalls the full manner of the masque:

> A stately Temple, which represents the Christian Religion, as in its first Magnificence: Being but lately establisht at Rome and Constantinople. The side Scenes shew the horrid Tortures with which the Roman Tyrants persecuted the Church; and the flat Scene, which is the limit of the prospect, discovers an Altar richly adorn'd, before it Constantine, suppos'd kneels, with Commanders about him, gazing at a bloody Cross in the Aire, which being incompass'd with many Angels, offers it self to view; with these words distinctly written, (In hoc signo vinces!) Instruments are heard, and many Attendants; The Ministers at Divine Service, walk busily up and down. Till Atticus the chief of all the Priests, and successor of St Chrysostom, in rich Robes, comes forward with the Philosopher Leontine. The Waiters in ranks bowing all the way before him. A Chorus heard at distance.

Those distinctly written words 'In hoc signo vinces!' bear enigmatic meaning in the context of the meek, inefficient sway of a Christian emperor, or of the destructive tortures inflicted by love. Of a more obvious emblematic kind is the fantastic scene from Act two scene two of *Sophonisba* presaging Hannibal's overthrow by Scipio in the clash of two world-orders:

> The SCENE drawn, discovers a Heaven of blood, two Suns, Spirits in Battel, Arrows shot to and fro in the Air Cryes of yielding Persons: Cries of Carthage is fallen, Carthage, &c.

Yet Lee is by no means confined to emblematic visual statement; in *The Rival Queens*, for instance (where he also has a similar portentous set-piece) he uses the spectacle of Alexander's

feast quite differently as ironic backdrop for Alexander's
petulance and vanity; or in *Mithridates* he can deliberately show
a piece of stage machinery breaking, a fake portent to throw
in doubt the existence of metaphysical and moral reality as
anything but priestly hocus-pocus:

> . . . my Brother Tryphon is
> High-Priest o'th'Sun, whom all the rest obey:
> Him have I wrought, that when the Nuptial Rites
> Begin, some strange presages shall fall out,
> Disorders unexpected, to forshow
> The Gods are much offended at the Marriage.
>
> [I.i.71-6]

And so, of course, it happens. Mithridates will learn from painful experience the existence and autonomy of his moral nature.

But the play in which Lee's mastery of theatrical effect is
most movingly and effectively put to the service of a poetic
vision is *Lucius Junius Brutus*. Much has been written about the
political element in this play, in particular its daring and un-
disguised equation of the Stuarts and the Tarquins,[38] less about
the dramatically more significant fact that it is a play about
revolution and even more profoundly about sacrifice. Indeed,
overtones of Christian blood sacrifice haunt the whole play.
However, it is not so much the dialogue as the play's three
visual climaxes, each centred upon a sacrificial image, which
gather up the main action and clarify the main themes, very
much as Settle's visual images gather up and clarify those of
The Empress of Morocco.

The first act brings news of Lucrece's rape and ends with the
sacramental kissing of her bloody poignard as her husband and
her kinsmen, Brutus and his two sons, swear over her body to
drive the Tarquins from Rome. Brutus' son Tiberius, however,
is a royalist at heart and sponsors a conspiracy to restore
Tarquin. In the play's most spectacular scene, Tarquin's
Fecialian priests adminster to the conspirators an obscene
travesty of the Mass to bind them to the plot:

> The Scene draws, showing the Sacrifice; One Burning, and
> another Crucify'd: the Priests coming forward with Goblets in
> their hands, fill'd with human blood.
>
> [IV.i.102+]

The plot is discovered and the conspirators arrested, including Brutus' loyal son, Titus, who is morally innocent despite his involvement with the traitors. Yet Brutus determines that both his sons must die. First, it is necessary in strict law, and the whole revolution has been inspired by the sovereignty of law. Rome under the Tarquins had imaged a society founded upon the tyranny of man's chaotic passions – bloody, lecherous, unjust:

> Invading Fundamental Right and Justice,
> Breaking the ancient Customs, Statutes, Laws,
> With positive pow'r, and Arbitrary Lust.
>
> [II.i.182-184]

But now 'no man shall offend because he's great' [V.ii.45]. To pardon Titus, let alone Tiberius, would compromise the revolution. But, further, Lee had 'read Machivel's Notes upon the place' [*Ep. ded.* ll. 36-37] pointing the principle that a new régime must confirm its authority by some signal stroke of punishment or strict piece of justice, after which it is safe to proceed more gently. This is the argument which Brutus puts to Titus – or, rather, which he need not put, for the young man is there before him:

> Yes, Sir; I call the Powers of Heav'n to witness,
> Titus dares dye, if so you have Decreed;
> Nay, he shall dye with joy, to honor Brutus,
> To make your Justice famous through the World
> And fix the Liberty of Rome for ever.
>
> [IV.i.478-482]

And so, in this understanding, father and son proceed to the blood sacrifice of the last scene. Each has accepted his role, Titus that of the willing victim, Brutus that of the implacable avenger of the Republic:

> Yes, Titus, since the Gods have so Decreed,
> That I must lose thee; I will take th'advantage
> Of thy important Fate, Cement Rome's flaws,
> And heal her wounded Freedom with thy blood:
> I will ascend my self the sad Tribunal,
> And sit upon my Sons; on thee, my Titus;
> Behold thee suffer all the shame of death,
> The Lictor's lashes, bleed before the People;

> Then, with thy hopes and all thy youth upon thee,
> See thy head taken by the Common Ax,
> Without a groan, without one pittying tear,
> If that the Gods can hold me to my purpose,
> To make my Justice quite transcend example.
>
> [IV.i.521-533]

His purpose holds. In the final act, the scene draws first on a horrible picture[39]:

> See here the Bodies of the Roman youth
> All headless by your Doom, and there Tiberius.
>
> [V.ii.116-117]

On all sides Brutus is besieged with pleas to spare Titus. His heartbroken wife declares him mad, curses 'Tyrannic Brutus' and his purposed 'murder'. But he is not to be moved. Titus, however, escapes the shameful axe by the pre-arranged sword-thrust of a friend; nor is Brutus able to preserve the severe face of the judge to the end. His son dies in his arms. There is an appalling pathos in the bereaved father's last request as he sits in the havoc he has himself willed, holding the bloody, scarcely-breathing body of his son:

> . . . ere thou goest, I beg thee to report me
> To the great Shades of Romulus and Numa,
> Just with that Majesty and rugged Virtue
> Which they inspir'd, and which the World has seen.
>
> [ll. 175-178]

But suddenly, with Titus' death, the atmosphere of the play is transformed; the feverish brazen clamour is succeeded by a majestic calm as Brutus rebukes the bitterness of Valerius:

> Peace, Consul, peace; let us not soil the pomp
> Of this Majestick Fate with Womans brawls.
> Kneel Fathers, Friends, kneel all you Roman People,
> Hush'd as dead Calms, while I conceive a pray'r
> That shall be worthy Rome, and worthy Jove.
>
> [ll. 191-195]

The prayer, which ends the play, is no petition; it is a universal benediction upon the stars, upon heaven and earth, upon man. The sacrifice is fulfilled.

These three big scenes of blood sacrifice keep the theme visually before the audience – and the visual image, especially when it is placed at a dramatic peak, as these are, has, of course, tremendous impact. The kissing of the bloody dagger to confirm the oath of righteous vengeance clearly finds its diabolic parallel in the blood drunk by the conspirators to seal their plot; and the overtly religious nature of the latter scene, given the prominence of the play's big showpiece, elicits powerfully the religious echoes in the story of the godlike father who sacrifices his son and the son who freely gives his life for the people. Nor is there any doubting the nature of the final majestic benediction.

Further citation of examples to show the total theatrical conception of Restoration melodrama would be burdensome. The range extends from the elaborate masquing spectacle (of which Orrery should also be noticed as a prime exponent) to the chastened visual and overwhelming situational appeal of Otway's later work; but common to all is the tangible object in theatrical space – and this it is which underlines Dryden's exceptional attitude:

> What credit it [i.e., *The Spanish Friar*] has gained upon the stage, I value no farther than in reference to my profit, and the satisfaction I had in seeing it represented with all the justness and gracefulness of action. But as 'tis my interest to please my audience, so 'tis my ambition to be read: that I am sure is the more lasting and the nobler design: for the propriety of thoughts and words, which are the hidden beauties of a play, are but confusedly judged in the vehemence of action. All things are there beheld as in a hasty motion, where the objects only glide before the eye and disappear.
>
> [I, 278]

This contempt for the stage, or, at least, this refusal to grant that a play is unrealized outside the theatre, contrasts sharply with poor Lee's distress for his banned *Lucius Junius Brutus*. He tells Dorset: 'I show'd no passion outward, but whether through an Over-Conceit of the Work, or because perhaps there was indeed some Merit, the Fire burnt inward, and I was troubled for my dumb Play, like a Father for his dead Child. 'Tis enough that I have eas'd my heart by this Dedication to your Lordship' [*Ep. ded.* ll. 56-61]. In fairness to Dryden it must be added that he is feeling rather sour about some unperceptive comments made on *The Spanish Friar* in performance. But there is no reason to doubt the sincerity of his complaint that the theatre obscures the qualities of his work which he valued most highly:

> In a playhouse, everything contributes to impose upon the judgment: the lights, the scenes, the habits, and, above all, the grace of action, which is commonly the best where there is the most need of it, surprise the audience, and cast a mist upon their understandings; not unlike the cunning of a juggler, who is always staring us in the face, and overwhelming us with gibberish, only that he may gain the opportunity of making the cleaner conveyance of his trick.
>
> [I, 275]

The theatre, pretty clearly, is no place for a good play.

NOTES

1. See *The Reason of Church Government*, in *Complete Prose Works of John Milton* ed. Don M. Wolfe *et al.* (New Haven, 1953), I, 812-816.

2. *The Answer to the Preface*, in D'avenant's *Works* (London, 1673), p. 23. [First pagination block.]

3. *The Preface to Gondibert*, in *Works*, 1673, p. 9. [First pagination block.]

4. George Villiers, Duke of Buckingham, *et al.*, *The Rehearsal*, ed. Montague Summers (Stratford-upon-Avon, 1914), p. 22.

5. See Eugene M. Waith's account of these two plays in *The Herculean Hero* (New York, 1962), Chapter VI.

6. Samuel Johnson, *Lives of the English Poets*, ed. G. Birkbeck Hill (Oxford, 1905), I, 459.

7. In *A Discourse Concerning the Original and Progress of Satire*, in Watson, II, 91-92.

8. Even when an elderly man's nostalgia is discounted, Cibber's account of the Restoration theatre supports persuasively Montague Summers' view: 'When Hart and Mohun, Mrs Marshall and Nell Gwynn, Betterton and Smith, Mrs Barry and Mrs Bracegirdle acted what Dryden, Wycherley, Otway and Congreve wrote, the theatre

with all its drawbacks had reached a zenith of brilliance which was certainly not sustained. . . .' (*The Restoration Theatre* [London, 1934], p. 289). Of Hart in *A King and No King*, Rymer writes: 'Mr *Hart pleases*; most of the business falls to his share, and what he *delivers*, every one takes upon *content*; their *eyes* are prepossest and charm'd by his *action*, before ought of the *Poets* can approach their *ears*; and to the most wretched of *Characters*, he gives a lustre and *brillant* which dazles the *sight*, that the *deformities* in the Poetry cannot be perceiv'd'. (*The Tragedies of the Last Age Consider'd etc.*, in *The Critical Works of Thomas Rymer*, ed. Curt A. Zimansky [New Haven, 1956], p. 19.)

9. Bonamy Dobrée draws attention to Dryden's constant tonal change throughout the individual scene and speech (*Restoration Tragedy* [London, 1929], pp. 98-107). Experience in the theatre with a production of *All For Love* brought home to me both Dryden's skill in this respect and the degree to which he depends upon it to sustain audience interest during his lengthy debates. He taxes very heavily his players' technical ability to exploit every fluctuation of mood, especially in this highly statuesque neoclassic play.

10. *An Apology for the Life of Mr Colley Cibber*, 2nd edn. (London, 1740), pp. 85-86.

11. Colley Cibber, p. 93.

12. *The Diary of Samuel Pepys*, ed. H. B. Wheatley (London, 1920), V, 99.

13. *The Play-House to be Lett*, Act I, in *Works*, 1673.

14. *The First Dayes Entertainment at Rutland-House* in *Works*, 1673, p. 345. [First pagination block.]

15. *First Dayes Entertainment*, p. 349.

16. *The Art of the Theatre* (London, 1962), p. 138.

17. Craig, p. 143.

18. *Ben Jonson*, ed. C. H. Herford, Percy and Evelyn Simpson, 11 vols. (Oxford, 1925-52), VII, 229.

19. 'To the Reader' in *The Siege of Rhodes* (London, 1656), A3^v, and 'Epistle Dedicatory' to *The Siege of Rhodes: The Second Part* (London, 1663), II, A3^r.

20. *Op. cit.*, pp. 157-58. The fact that this masque-like approach to character was refined rather than obliterated in the Restoration emerges very clearly in a passage from *The Tragedies of the Last Age Consider'd etc.* (*The Critical Works of Thomas Rymer*, ed. Curt A. Zimansky [New Haven, 1956], p. 20): 'It may be remember'd that there are but five vowels; or be consider'd, from *seven* Planets, and

their several positions, how *many fates* and fortunes the *Astrologer* distributes to the people. And has not a Poet more *vertues* and *vices* within his *circle*, cannot he observe them and their influences in their several *situations*, in their *oppositions* and *conjunctions*, in their *altitudes* and *depressions*: and he shall sooner find his *ink*, than the *stores* of Nature exhausted'. Rymer looks beyond the interplay of characters (in the modern sense) to the interplay of moral qualities.

21. Clifford Leech, *The John Fletcher Plays* (London, 1962), p. 38.

22. D'avenant deplores the simplicity of his story in his address 'To the Reader' (1656), and when a larger cast and a larger stage gave him the opportunity, he amplified it with the Roxolana entries and the other additions. But the piece remains shorter than an orthodox play, as does the rather longer second part; for D'avenant had also 'to prevent the length of *Recitative* Music', a necessity which applied with equal force to the singing in the court masque. Singing is, of course, slower than speech.

23. It is not fanciful to extend this view to the larger conflict between formal severity and flamboyant material which Bonamy Dobrée notices: '. . . the dramatists of that day were trying to express romantic ideas in a form specially evolved for the classical' (*Restoration Tragedy* [London, 1929], p. 26).

24. Ed. Summers, pp. 64–65.

25. *Ibid.*, p. 2. Failure to interpret 'admiration', a key term in Restoration dramatic theory, in the vigorous baroque sense current at the time has given rise to much modern misunderstanding. During the Restoration and even later, the word still retained its Elizabethan meaning of wonder, awe, surprise; in Bailey's *Dictionary* of 1721 this is still the sole usage given: 'To ADMIRE: to look upon with Wonder, to be surprized at'. The word was also beginning to acquire its modern sense, but the Restoration heroic dramatists, like the masque writers before them, regularly invoke the older meaning.

26. Jean H. Hagstrum, *The Sister Arts* (Chicago, 1958), p. 97.

27. *The Rehearsal*, p. 64.

28. Wylie Sypher, *Four Stages of Renaissance Style* (New York, 1956), p. 185.

29. 'Prologue to *Tyrannic Love*', l. 19.

30. In his odes, however, Dryden's imagery is often highly baroque in the pictorial sense. See J. H. Hagstrum, *Sister Arts*, pp. 197–209. Miss Hagstrum's examination of 'the sister arts' commands more confidence than that in Wylie Sypher's brilliant but erratic book because she sticks strictly to literary techniques, while Sypher

attempts to parallel literary with painterly techniques. When Miss Hagstrum points out that, in the ode to Mrs Anne Killigrew, 'the deceased young lady, addressed as the "youngest virgin-daughter of the skies", is imagined as bearing a palm in paradise, "rich with immortal green"; or rolling above in "procession fix'd and regular", like a star; or as treading "with seraphims the vast abyss",' there seems obvious justice in her contention that this imagery expresses 'celestial themes in the baroque plastic manner'. This is only one detail chosen at random from Miss Hagstrum's fascinating comparison of Dryden's imagery with that of painting popular in England at the time, and with which she often establishes a striking correspondence. In the same way, considered purely as an image, Crowne's angel in *The Destruction of Jerusalem* (discussed below) is unmistakably and splendidly baroque.

31. Wylie Sypher, *Four Stages*, p. 181.

32. *The Rehearsal*, p. 6.

33. Settle's verbal quality is rarely poetic in the sense of memorable language; but he sometimes generates intense rhetorical excitement. The *Empress of Morocco* is never less than declaimable, and occasional passages which practically act themselves hint at the abilities which take fire in *The Female Prelate* and provide some fine moments in *Distress'd Innocence*. There has even been a suggestion that Settle must have cribbed from a much earlier play for *The Female Prelate* (see J. Crossley in *Notes and Queries*, Series I, V, 52, discussed by F. C. Brown, *Elkanah Settle: His Life and Works* [Chicago, 1910] pp. 90-91, n.). G. Wilson Knight (*The Golden Labyrinth* [London, 1962], pp. 155-6) notes of certain scenes in this play that 'the language lives and stings', as indeed it does; but not in the old Elizabethan way. It lives purely in its movement, not in its conceptual quality. The nearest parallel, oddly enough, is Milton's feeling for the sway and power of language – though, of course, he uses it to very different purpose.

34. See F. C. Brown, *op. cit.*, Chapter V. To his duties as City Poet Settle brought 'his reputation as "a contriver of machinery" and his experience in devising and managing the most elaborate Pope-burning pageants on record' [p. 28]. In *The Fairy Queen* (music by Purcell) and *The World in the Moon* he gave the theatre two of the most spectacular operatic pieces of the period.

35. F. C. Brown, *op. cit.*, pp. 35-36. Brown is quoting from *Biographica Dramatica* (London, 1812), I, Part II, 640.

36. Quoted from James Maidment and W. H. Logan, eds., *The*

Dramatic Works of John Crowne, 4 vols. (Edinburgh, 1873-74), II, 218.

37. 'Life of Dryden', in Birkbeck Hill, I, 458-459.

38. See, in particular, the discussion by John Loftis in his *The Politics of Drama in Augustan England* (Oxford, 1963), pp. 15-17, and in the introduction to his edition of the play in the Regents Restoration Drama Series (1967).

39. The sense demands that the scene be drawn here, though there is no stage direction to this effect in any edition.

The Extravagant Rake
in Restoration Comedy

ROBERT JORDAN

I

Critics of Restoration comedies still find themselves much disturbed over the moral significance of the rake-hero, or at least
over the preoccupation of other critics with this matter. It is my
intention in this essay to consider a clearly-defined type of rake
to whom such considerations are in fact irrelevant – one, indeed,
to whom some of Lamb's much-despised comments are applicable. This particular character type has not attracted much
attention from the critics, since he is not significant in the major
works of Etherege, Wycherley, or Congreve, the only authors
with whom many of these critics concern themselves, but he is a
significant figure in some of the most charming of the minor
Restoration comedies, the second rank of quality. I have chosen
to call this figure the 'extravagant rake'.

The extravagant rake is the first type of libertine gentleman
to emerge with any clarity in Restoration Comedy. Between
1663 and 1668 he can be seen as Wellbred in James Howard's
The English Mounsieur, Alberto in Rhodes's *Flora's Vagaries*,
Felices in Porter's *The Carnival*, Philidor in James Howard's *All
Mistaken*, Bellamy and Wildblood in Dryden's *An Evening's
Love* and, quintessentially, as Celadon in *Secret Love*, also by
Dryden. He is visible in a more subdued form in the only other
gentleman-rakes to have been created up to 1668, Loveby in
Dryden's *The Wild Gallant*, Sir Frederick in Etherege's *The
Comical Revenge*, and Don John and Don Frederick in Bucking-
ham's adaptation of Beaumont and Fletcher's *The Chances*, an
adaptation that gives a clue to at least one source for the type,

though *Monsieur Thomas* better exemplifies the Fletcherian achievement in the style. After 1668, although no longer monopolizing the market, the extravagant rake continues in full vigour. There is, it is true, something of a slump in the mid-sixteen-nineties, but the last two years of the century can provide such excellent specimens as Wildish in John Cory's *A Cure for Jealousie*, Beaumine in Mrs Trotter's *Love at a Loss*, and, most notably, Sir Harry Wildair in Farquhar's *The Constant Couple*, as well as rather incompetent renderings such as Bernardo in Manning's *The Generous Choice*, and Claremont in Burnaby's *The Reform'd Wife*. Between these two dates he has been the staple diet in the plays of Dryden and Mrs Behn and the centrepiece of works by a multitude of other writers.

One of the main characteristics of this rake is the wildness of his actions. The frantic intensity with which he applies himself to the life of the moment is caught in many a wondering description. Wildish in John Cory's *A Cure for Jealousie*, for example, 'Whores, Games and Drinks, at that abominable rate, he would run out the *Kings Revenue* in less time then 'tis gathered' [1701, p. 6],[1] while an exhausted serving-man in Francis Manning's *The Generous Choice* complains, 'Was there ever such a Cormorant at Whoring as this Don Bernardo? no Place, no Time, nor no Woman almost can be free from his Persecutions. A Pox of these Night-doings' [1700, p. 25]. Occasionally the information becomes statistical. Ramble, in Crowne's *The Country Wit*, 'has not been come from *France* above three months, and here he has debauch'd four Women, and fought five Duels; not a keeper in the town can preserve his doe from him' [1675, pp. 6-7], while Trivultio in Sir Francis Fane's *Love in the Dark* is forced to lament: 'Was ever Man so disappointed? I have no less than Fifteen Marriages on foot; four of 'em are already consummated, by the help of some slight Vows, without the solemn Perjury in a Church; five or six more are finely warm'd and soften'd, and ready for the Seal; and all are at a stand, for want of these same little scraps of Paper, call'd *Bills of Credit*' [1675, p. 1]. In some cases at least, the numbers mount up in this way because of the rake's complete inability to withstand temptation, no matter what the circumstances. Alonzo, in Aphra Behn's *The Dutch Lover*, talking quietly to a friend, is suddenly galvanized by the appearance of a masked woman, and, mindless of everything including the dangers of an ambush, sets off in pursuit [I, 230]. Roebuck, in *Love and a Bottle*, suddenly noticing the splendid wenches in the street outside, has to be physically restrained from rushing out to them: 'Prithee let me go; 'tis a deed of charity; I'm quite starved. I'll just take a snap, and be with you in the twinkling' [I, 29-30].

Weathercock figures such as this, of course, are prone to particularly spectacular falls from grace when, having vowed fidelity to one woman, they are suddenly confronted with a new face. But this is not the only disaster to which they are subject. Because of their promiscuity and impulsiveness, they are continually finding themselves in trouble and their predicaments often match in extravagance the deed that begets them. Here, for example, is James Howard's *All Mistaken*:

> *Phili.* . . . I have been haunted by a Pack of Hounds this three Hours, and damn'd deep-Mouth'd Hounds too. No less then three Couple of Nurses. Three Couple of Plaguy hunting Bitches. And with them three Couple of Whelpes *alias* Children Sir, they have Rung me such a Ring this Morning through every by turning that leads to a Bawdy house, I wisht my self Eartht a thousand times, as a Fox does when he is hard Run, but that they wou'd have presently dig'd me out with their Tongues.
>
> *Duke.* Faith Philidor t'is no news to me, for I have known thee from sixteen at this course of Life, what and these Children were all your Bastards, and their Nurses coming to dun you for money?
>
> *Phili.* Something of that's in't I think Sir.
>
> [1672, pp. 7-8]

So it continues to the climax of the scene when, trapped by three clamorous nurses demanding their arrears in pay, he makes a final effort to escape:

> *Phili.* . . . Boy was the Woolf fed to day.
> *Boy.* No Sir.
> *Phili.* Go fetch him quickly to dine with these Ladies.
> *Exeunt Nurses.*
> So, I thought I shou'd set them going. Ha! the Devil they have left the Children behind them, this was a very cunning device

of mine, now am I in a pretty condition. Troth a very noble
Anabaptist Progeny, for the Devil a one of these were ever
Christned; For I have run so much upon tick to the Parsons
for Christning of Children, that now they all refuse to make
any Bastards of mine a Christian without ready money, . . .
what shall I doe when these Infants begin to be hungry and
youle for the Teat. O that a milk Woman wou'd come by now,
well I must remove my flock from hence. Small Cole, small
Cole, will you buy any small Cole, Pox on't I cou'd never
light of any but fruitful whores, small cole small cole.

Exit.

[pp. 11-12]

This instance is crazier than most but the tendency in this
direction is evident in all the extravagant rakes.

I have quoted this example at length because, as well as
illustrating the wild adventures of the rake, it also illustrates
his manner, and it is this manner that is the surest guide to the
type rather than voracity of appetite or ridiculousness of situation, since most rakes make some claim to the former and any
farce can provide the latter. Thus Philidor's remarks are no
sober assessment of his position. They are shot through with
extravagance of language, with witty (or would-be witty) turns
of phrase, and with wry jests. It is a quality of this kind of rake
that he cannot take himself, or anybody else, at all seriously.
This is one of the most heavily exploited features in Sir Harry
Wildair, the extravagant rake in Farquhar's *The Constant
Couple*, who cannot treat even a personal insult with any
earnestness [I, 189-190]. Few of them, it is true, are as frivolous
as that but most are well on the way to it and none can even
begin to be solemn when the subject is love. Alberto, in
Richard Rhodes's play *Flora's Vagaries*, who 'loves all Women
in Jest' [1670, p. 8], is in this quite characteristic. It is this
turning of everything to jest which so bewilders Catherine
Trotter's Lesbia in her efforts to pin down Beaumine to a
promise of marriage. As she complains in *Love at a Loss*: 'I can
never be satisfy'd, or angry with this Man; Is it impossible for
you ever to answer seriously and directly, Beaumine? . . . Thus
may this gay Humour fool me on for ever. . . . Well, thou art
the madest Fellow' [1701, pp. 11-12]. Even danger is unable
to shake this habit of jesting and frivolity. Mrs Behn's Willmore,

with an irate mistress suddenly clapping a pistol to his chest
and threatening to kill him for his infidelity, can cheerily reply:
'Why, then there's an end of a proper handsome Fellow, that
might have liv'd to have done good Service yet' [I, 94].
Nathaniel Lee's *The Princess of Cleve* probably provides the best
generalized statement of the spirit in which this intense life was
pursued. As Nemours scuttles off with a boast and a flourish
to recover a mistress who threatens to desert him, his lady-
procuress and occasional bedfellow declares: 'Go thy ways Petronius, nay, if he were dying too, with his Veins cut, he wou'd call
for Wine, Fiddles and Whores, and laugh himself into the other
World' [II, 218]. Most of them manage to sustain this tone
even into matrimony, a state that they profess to fear much more
than death.

Closely related to this reckless frivolity of the extravagant
rake is another characteristic, his cheekiness. 'Impudence, was
ever a successful Quality', says Cleremont in William Burnaby's
The Reform'd Wife, 'and 'twou'd be very unlucky if I shou'd be
the first that did not thrive by it' [1700, p. 13]. Thrive he does.
The heroine of Thomas Scott's *The Mock-Marriage* [1696, p. 13]
remarks on the same quality in Willmot, who on the very first
day he met her announced that he loved her, and Loveby in
John Smythe's *Win Her and Take Her* reveals it when, confronted with a beautiful woman he has never seen before and
whose name he does not know, he immediately persuades her
that he is an old acquaintance [1691, pp. 12-13]. Apart from
this readiness with the grand lie, their impudence is apparent
in the breezy vanity, the taste for boasting, and the enormous
self-assurance of these characters. 'In the meantime will I go
see what divertisement the Church affords, where I shall meet
all the good company', Sir Francis Fane's Trivultio remarks in
Love in the Dark, 'I love to shoot at a whole Covey at once; ten
to one but some will drop' [1675, pp. 17-18]. The most perfect
of all these rakes, Dryden's Celadon in *Secret Love*, indulges in
complete orgies of self-glorification in his encounters with
women:

Fla. . . . could you not be constant to one?
Cel. Constant to one! I have been a Courtier, a Souldier, and a
Traveller, to good purpose, if I must be constant to one; give

me some Twenty, some Forty, some a Hundred Mistresses:
I have more Love than any one woman can turn her to . . . Yet
for my part, I can live with as few Mistresses as any man. I
desire no superfluities, onely for necessary change, or so, as I
shift my Linnen.

[II, 14-15]

Comparable fantasies can be found in the mouths of other
extravagants.

This same cheekiness, the 'natural itch of talking and lying',
as Alonzo in Mrs Behn's *The Dutch Lover* calls it [I, 259], helps
to explain what might otherwise appear a rather dangerous tendency in some of these rakes. Several of them are the spokes-
men for quite outrageous libertine sentiments on love, Nature,
marriage, and the like. Sometimes this is a matter of passing
comments but occasionally it takes the form of an harangue
such as the following from Sir Francis Fane's *Love in the Dark*:

And shall I then attempt his wife again? Ingrateful God of Love;
Pox on't, in matter of Women, the deceit is Trivial. Civiliz'd
Mankind that live in Towns, lye with one anothers Wives, as
Gentlemen cheat in Horses, by a *Tacit compact*, and rule among
themselves. Let *Cornant* pursue his inclinations, I'll follow mine.
Man's Gratitude may sometimes rise from Pride; Friendship
to others from the first writ Law of pleasing of himself; why may
not I endure the burden of a wilful obligation; and not be tossing
it still back again to one who throws it upon me to ease himself?

For why should Mankind live by Rule and Measure
Since all his Virtue rises from his Pleasure?

[1675, p. 77]

Libertine sentiments are not limited to the extravagant rake, of
course. They are part of the whole tissue of a play such as
Otway's *The Atheist* and one can find examples even in such a
late play as Farquhar's *The Beaux' Strategem* (especially in I, i).
But I think it would be true to say that most of the really
explicit cases come from extravagants. On the other hand, the
effect of these utterances may be qualified in the case of the
extravagant rake by a characteristic that is sometimes made explicit and in most other cases could be inferred from the general
frivolity – that is, that on matters intellectual these rakes are

hardly to be taken as serious or profound commentators. Thus Mrs Trotter's Beaumine in *Love at a Loss* can trumpet on human and divine laws as 'chains to our Wills, our Inclinations? Destroyers of Liberty, the dear Prerogative of Nature', and so on [1707, p. 6], but the heroine is quite untroubled by his philosophy: 'I believe there's more Humour and Affectation than any serious Reflection in it . . .' [p. 4]. Similarly Crowne's Ramble in *The Country Wit* may have one of the most outrageous expressions of libertine philosophy in Restoration comedy[2] but another character can see his wildness as springing from heedlessness rather than heterodoxy:

> *Chris.* . . . has he not deny'd 'em still with Oaths, such Oaths that if he thinks he has a Soul, he must believe it damn'd if he be false. . . .
> *Isab.* . . . he think he has a Soul! alas good man, he seldom sets his thoughts on those affairs: he loves his Soul, but as he loves his Bawd, only to Pimp for pleasures for the Body, and then, Bawd-like it may be damn'd, he cares not.
>
> [1676, p. 8]

In Fane's *Love in the Dark* [1675, p. 20] we find Trivultio's respectable friends deliberately egging him on into a tirade against marriage as a trick of the priests: 'Oh, pray let's humour him a little'. This hardly suggests that they are taking his ideas seriously. On the whole, libertine philosophy in the mouth of such a rake seems designed more to reinforce the sense of hyperbolic extravagance and impertinence than to constitute a serious case seriously advanced.

This, then, is the extravagant rake. Faced with such a character his bewildered companions fall back on a whole range of adjectives which quickly become more-or-less standard. He is 'mad',[3] 'airy',[4] 'extravagant',[5] 'gay',[6] 'wild',[7] and so on. In addition he tends to be regarded as unique, not a typical young man or a common type but a phenomenon. When Lucy goes into breeches as an extravagant rake in Southerne's *Sir Antony Love*, those who mistake her for the real thing speak of this rake, Sir Antony, as 'above Example, or Imitation' [1691, p. 3]. In this phrase one seems to have the aspirations of the whole tribe of the extravagants.

From what I have said the basic fact about the extravagant

rake should be fairly clear – he is a comic figure. One not only laughs with him in his verbal sallies, one also laughs at him in his extravagances. But though he may be comic he is not a comic fool. He is not like the lecherous old men, the hypocritical puritans, and the grosser fops, figures at once to be laughed at and to be despised for their weakness and their folly. He is to be laughed at, certainly, but there is no contempt involved, and very little that can seriously be called satire. For in the first place he has self-awareness. He knows what he is, whereas the fools proper are nearly all characterized by their failure to realize the picture they present to other people. The fops all believe they are the mirrors of refinement, the lecherous old women that they are outwardly models of chastity, the country blockheads that they are worthy gentlemen. But there is no suggestion that the extravagant rake sees himself as anything but an extravagant rake. Indeed, one of the openings for the lunatic romance that blossoms between the extravagant rake and the extravagant heroine in so many of these plays is the sudden realization that here at long last is a woman who is 'mad' in exactly the same way he is.[8] Moreover it is a characteristic of this rake that he is what he wants to be. The fools are nearly all aspiring to qualities they do not possess, whereas the extravagant rake is delighting in those with which he is endowed. He is also, of course, exploiting them, working on the principle that his follies are not only amusing but also engagingly amusing, that they are attractive follies. Thus Vizard, in Farquhar's *The Constant Couple*, can declare of Sir Harry Wildair: 'He's a gentleman of most happy circumstances, born to a plentiful estate; has had a genteel and easy education, free from the rigidness of teachers and pedantry of schools. His florid constitution being never ruffled by misfortune, nor stinted in its pleasures, has rendered him entertaining to others, and easy to himself: – turning all passion into gaiety of humour, by which he chooses rather to rejoice his friends than be hated by any; as you shall see' [I, 134]. All of this leaves him rather much in the category of the entertaining puppy. But if he is a puppy, he is a pure breed and ultimately has to be treated with a kind of respect.

There are, it is true, one or two cases in which the comicality of the extravagant rake is stressed in a way that does reduce his stature as a human being and as a member of the social élite. In Edward Howard's *The Man of Newmarket*, for example, there is, as a minor figure, an extravagant gentleman called Breakbond, 'a Wilde Gentleman, obliging the Sex of Women, and of generous character, except in payment of Bonds' [1678, A4^r]. But the central characters in the play are so sedate, and Breakbond's singularity is so frequently remarked upon, that he begins to appear odd rather than extravagant. This sense is fortified by his role in the play, for he is not there as a figure pursuing an independent course through a subplot of his own but is rather one of a whole crowd of types and eccentric personalities who are there to display their eccentricities rather than to act out a story. Furthermore, much stress is laid on his indebtedness and the poverty his wild courses have brought upon him. He becomes, in fact, a mildly pathetic eccentric putting on a show of cheerfulness in spite of his predicament, and one of the sober heroes can declare, 'I pity him' [p. 8], a reaction which could not conceivably be elicited by a Celadon. But at the same time, it should be noticed that Howard is at great pains to prevent Breakbond from being taken for a buffoon or a basically inferior person such as are some of the other eccentrics in the gallery of portraits in which he appears. On practically every occasion on which a character exclaims at his eccentricity, there is an immediate qualification to the effect that, even so, he is a worthy gentleman or a pleasant companion (see, for example, pp. 8, 19, 38, 60). This may be something of a distortion of the extravagant gentleman but the very distortion is such as to emphasize the dual nature of the type, at once true gentleman and eccentric.

Something of the same sort is true of Trivultio in Fane's *Love in the Dark*. The play is an extraordinary medley of reminiscences from earlier dramatic forms, and Trivultio has in his composition much of the Elizabethan ingenious trickster and author of merry pranks. These elements do give him a slightly primitive and unsophisticated air which is not found in most extravagant rakes but which makes all the more marked the extent to which such an impeccable gentleman as Sforza accepts him as a friend – as he does [1675, p. 64]. It is, in fact, a characteristic of practically every extravagant rake, and the clearest evidence of his status, that when he shares a play with a more conventional hero (rakish or otherwise) this character is quite ready to accept him as a friend no matter how psychologically implausible that may seem.

II

So far I have described the surface characteristics of the extravagant rake. What I would now like to investigate is the inner nature of the type as his creators and first appreciators conceived it, the bases, whether psychological-physiological or literary-aesthetic, on which he is constructed.

The immediate possibility is that this rake is a humours figure in the tradition of Ben Jonson. The extravagant rakes of Restoration comedy are regarded in the plays themselves not only as 'mad', 'wild', 'extravagant', 'brisk', and the like; they are also spoken of with some frequency as possessed of a humour. Thus there is a reference in Thomas Scott's *The Mock-Marriage* to 'that thirst after variety, that wandering inconstant humour' that the extravagant rake has 'been hitherto so famous for' [1696, p. 6]. Sir Frederick in *The Comical Revenge* has a 'freeness of . . . humour' [I, 8], Careless in Edward Ravenscroft's *Careless Lovers* a 'lewd wild humour' [1673, p. 10], and the rake in Catherine Trotter's *Love at a Loss* a 'gay Humour' [1701, p. 11], something that he apparently shares with the eponymous hero of Thomas Southerne's *Sir Antony Love* [1691, p. 10], while the aim of much of the widow's plotting in James Howard's *The English Mounsieur* is to break her wild young wooer of his humour [1674, p. 27]. Similarly, the mutual attraction of wild hero and wild heroine is often expressed in terms of a compatibility of humours. The most notable example of this is James Howard's *All Mistaken*, where we get exchanges such as the following:

> *Phili.* Was there ever so witty a wench, 'tis the Woman of women for my turn, I'le to her, thou most Renowned Female I cannot hold . . . why, you are just of my Humour, when I heard thee say how many men you had fool'd, I was very glad to hear you come one short of me, for I have fool'd six women, and you but five men. . . . Nay hear me, we two will Love how we please, when we please, and as long as we please, doe not these Propositions tickle your heart a little.

Mir.   I don't mislike them. Now cou'd I take him about the
Neck and Kiss him for this humour of his, and do you say you
will Love me.

[1672, pp. 20-21]

Other examples can be found in James Carlile's *The Fortune-
Hunters* [1689, p. 13], Mrs Behn's *The Rover I* [I, 48], and in
Dryden's *Secret Love* [II, 14].

It must be granted, of course, that the word, 'humour' is often
used very loosely in the Restoration to signify a momentary
whim or the wildest of inclinations, but the older meaning did
persist and the extravagant rake with his excessiveness and
lunatic intensity of commitment could well warrant the term.
Indeed, it has already been argued by F. H. Moore that some
of Dryden's heroes and heroines are to be seen as humours,
though his effort to apply the term to the married couple of
Marriage-à-la-Mode[9] seems to me to be rather misguided, as
does his argument that the humours rake is Dryden's personal
application of Jonsonian techniques of characterization to a
Fletcherian milieu.[10] The objection to this is that Fletcher
himself seems to have developed the extravagant rake to a
considerable degree. Mirabel, for instance, in *The Wild Goose
Chase* is a clear example of the extravagant rake and one moreover whose extravagance is seen as a product of the humours.
His father, on hearing that he has returned from his Grand
Tour, can ask:

And how (for I dare say, you will not flatter him)
Has *Italy* wrought on him? has he mew'd yet
His wild fantistic Toyes? they say that Climate
Is a great purger of those humorous Fluxes.[11]

Even some of Shakespeare's young men have a little of the
extravagant rake's quality – Berowne, for example, in *Love's
Labour's Lost*, who is described at one stage as a 'merry mad-
cap lord' [II.i.215]. Nor has Jonson himself overlooked the
type. In *Bartholomew Fair* Quarlous is distinguished from
Winwife on the grounds that he is the 'madder' of the two,[12]
and Truewit in *The Silent Woman* seems to be an essay in the
style, although these Jonsonian examples differ from those of
Fletcher and the Restoration in that, while they have the
effervescence and the verbosity, they lack the obsession with

love. Dryden himself seems to be thinking primarily of this type of character in the 'Defence of the Epilogue', when he compares Fletcher's Don John, Jonson's Truewit, and Shakespeare's Mercutio with the [unspecified] Restoration efforts to depict the gentleman in comedy. The claim here is simply that the Restoration does this sort of thing better, not that it or Dryden breaks entirely new ground [I, 180-181].

There are then grounds for regarding the extravagant rake as a 'humours' figure. A certain amount of caution is, however, necessary, for the age itself does not seem to be entirely clear on the matter. The most striking evidence of this comes from Thomas Shadwell, self-appointed champion of the humours tradition in literature. A pair of quotations should make the point. The first is from the Preface to *The Sullen Lovers*:

> Though I have known some of late so Insolent to say, that *Ben Jonson* wrote his best *Playes* without Wit; imagining, that all the Wit in *Playes* consisted in bringing two persons upon the Stage to break Jests, and to bob one another, which they call Repartie, not considering that there is more wit and invention requir'd in the finding out good Humour, and the Matter proper for it, then in all their smart reparties. For, in the Writing of a Humour, a Man is confin'd not to swerve from the Character, and oblig'd to say nothing but what is proper to it: but in the *Playes* which have been wrote of late, there is no such thing as a perfect Character, but the two persons are most commonly a Swearing, Drinking, Whoring, Ruffian for a Lover, and an impudent ill-bred *tomrig* for a Mistress, and these are the fine People of the *Play*; and there is that Latitude in this, that almost any thing is proper for them to say; but their chief Subject is bawdy, and profaneness, which they call *brisk writing*.
>
> [I, 11]

The second is from the Preface to *The Royal Shepherdess*:

> I find, it pleases most to see Vice incouraged, by bringing the Characters of debauch'd People upon the Stage, and making them pass for fine Gentlemen, who openly profess Swearing, Drinking, Whoring, breaking Windows, beating Constables, *etc.* and that is esteem'd, among us, a Gentile gayety of Humour, which is contrary to the Customs and Laws of all civilized Nations.
>
> [I, 100]

It seems to me highly likely that Shadwell has the same target
in both these quotations and that this target is the extravagant
rake and his consort. At the time Shadwell wrote, Dryden was
the pre-eminent purveyor of extravagant rakes and the first
of the two passages appears to be a direct attack on sentiments
expressed by Dryden in the *Essay of Dramatic Poesy* [I, 69], an
attack answered by Dryden in the Preface to *An Evening's Love*
[I, 148]. From the first quotation, then, it is quite clear that
Shadwell does not even conceive of the type as a humour. From
the second quotation, the most that can be wrung is the possibility
that others defend him as one and Shadwell regards the claim
as weak, though another (likelier?) possibility is that 'gayety
of humour' is being used in the loose, non-technical sense, just
as Dryden uses it when he claims he lacks the 'gaiety of humour'
necessary to a comic writer [I, 116]. In any case, the extravagant rake's claims to consideration as a 'humour' could hardly
have been strikingly evident if Shadwell could sail so un-
knowingly past them.

Another example, from the first years of the eighteenth
century, is provided by John Dennis. In his 'Large Account of
Taste' we find Dennis claiming that comedy of humours almost
invariably has to deal with the 'lower sort of people', since well-
bred people are, by definition, free of humorous excess. Later it
appears that he can think of only one dramatic masterpiece in
which 'a great deal of Humour is shewn in high Characters',
Wycherley's *The Plain Dealer*.[13] Much obviously depends on
one's definition of a masterpiece but it still remains fairly significant that throughout the discussion no thought is given to one
of the most popular character types of the age, the extravagant
rake. A few minutes later in the discussion another tantalising
sentence appears. Dennis is developing a distinction between
comedy of Humour and comedy of Love (in view of the extravagant rake's love obsession, this in itself is striking). In the
process he attempts a definition of Humour and declares:' . . . to
every Passion there is a Humour which answers to it, which
Humour is nothing but a less degree of that Passion. As for
example, Anger is a Passion, Peevishness and Moroseness are
Humours, Joy when it is great is a Passion, Jollity and Gayety
perhaps may be said to be Humours' [*Critical Works*, I, 284].
It is the 'perhaps' that is significant, breaking across the certitude

of the previous utterances. When it comes to the point Dennis seems to have some difficulty conceiving of 'gayety' as a Humour.

As a final example one might quote Dryden himself. As Moore contends, the logical inference of the Prologue to *Secret Love* seems to be that Dryden regards Celadon as a humour.[14] But if this is the case, his attitude to the gentleman as humour can only be described as wavering for, in other texts, the trend seems quite the reverse. Thus Dryden's Preface to *An Evening's Love* contains his reply to Shadwell's attack and one might expect him to point out Shadwell's failure to recognize the Celadon type as a humour. Instead one finds him declaring that 'as I pretend not that I can write humour, so none of them [Dryden's contemporaries] can reasonably pretend to have written it as they ought' [I, 147], and later remarking, 'I declare that I want judgement to imitate [Jonson]; and should think it a great impudence in myself to attempt it' [I, 148]. These remarks are reinforced [I, 150] by a sharp distinction between Jonson's Truewit and his humours figures (Truewit being Jonson's closest approximation to the Celadon type), and the whole is capped by the statement that 'to entertain an audience perpetually with humour is to carry them from the conversation of gentlemen, and treat them with the follies and extravagances of Bedlam' [I, 151].

One does not have to look far to find a reason for this hesitancy in classifying the extravagant rake as a humour. The overwhelming tendency is for humours figures to be more-or-less contemptible – witness Neander's remark that they 'beget that malicious pleasure in the audience which is testified by laughter' [I, 73]. As I have suggested, however, the extravagant rake always remains socially acceptable. There is no suggestion of contempt for him. This factor alone may be enough to throw his status as humour into doubt.

The humours theory itself provides a further loophole. Rakish extravagance is best described in the theory's terms as an excess of the blood, a sanguine humour.[15] This is the characteristic humoral quality of the young man, leading him to venery, inconstancy, great gaiety, and the like,[16] and presumably the extravagant rake would be said to have this bias to an exceptional degree. But the sanguine humour is often placed in a special position. Theoretically the ideal personality is one in which the four humours are perfectly balanced, but at the same time there is a strong tendency to regard the sanguine disposition as very attractive or desirable so that it, rather than the perfect balance, sometimes appears the ideal.[17] The excess of the extravagant rake, in consequence, is a bias built on essentially sound qualities and so could fall into a different category from an excess of choler, phlegm, or bile.

The extravagant rake, then, can be considered in terms of the humours theory, but the age itself seems somewhat reluctant to accept the identification, presumably because the aesthetic connotations of humours comedy seem inappropriate to the extravagant rake. In view of this, a different approach to the character may be more useful, an approach that relates this character type to the obsessive Restoration interest in wit.

The starting-point for this is a distinction between the extravagant rake and the more normal rakish gentleman of Restoration comedy such as Dorimant in Etherege's *The Man of Mode*, Rodophil and Palamede in Dryden's *Marriage-à-la-Mode*, Horner in Wycherley's *The Country Wife*, Longvil and Bruce in Shadwell's *The Virtuoso*, and Truman and Valentine in Otway's *Friendship in Fashion*. The distinction here is largely one of manner or style. Dorimant in Etherege's *The Man of Mode* may be as sexually active as many of the extravagant rakes but his style of behaviour is much more controlled and a quite different set of qualities tends to be emphasized. Dorimant is not particularly renowned for scatterbrained lightheartedness. Rather he is noted for his command of the smooth social manner, the cultivated charm, and for his ability to 'fathom all the depths of Womankind' [II, 244]. Potency aside, Wycherley's Horner is probably most notable for his 'understanding', his perception of the nature of people and society – his ability also to fathom the depths. The triumphant success of his plot, which is a central issue of the play, is a tribute both to his ingenuity and to his understanding of human nature.

Somewhat more precise information is provided by Shadwell. In *Bury Fair* he presents us with the rake Wildish disavowing the title of wit in what, for my present concern, is a rather pointed fashion:

I had as leive be call'd a Pick-pocket, as a Wit. A Wit is always a Merry, Idle, Waggish Fellow, of no Understanding: Parts

indeed he has, but he had better be without 'em; Your solid Fop
is a better Man; he'll be Diligent and Fawning, always in the
way, and with his Blockhead do his business at last; but your Wit
will either neglect all Opportunities for Pleasure, or if he brings
his business into a hopeful way, he will laugh at, or draw his Wit
upon some great Man or other, and spoil all.

[IV, 299]

Even more pointed is the opening of *The Virtuoso*. Here we
have Bruce after a night's debauch reading Lucretius, a 'profound Oracle of Wit and Sence', in the Latin, and observing
that 'we should not live always hot-headed; we should give
our selves leave sometimes to think' [III, 105]. Out of this
comes an attack on the heedless youths of the age which
culminates in the observations: 'These are sure the only
Animals that live without thinking: a Sensible Plant has more
imagination than most of 'em. . . . The highest pitch our
Youth do generally arrive at, is, to have a form, a fashion of
Wit, a Rotine of speaking, which they get by imitation; and
generally they imitate the extravagancies of witty Men drunk,
which they very discreetly practise sober' [III, 106]. In view
of Shadwell's hostility to the extravagant rake, the target of
these attacks may well be that literary type, but, even if it is
not, the nature of the attack pretty clearly distinguishes Wildish
and Bruce from the extravagants. In them is made explicit what
is largely implicit in the case of the Dorimants and the Horners
– a concern with 'sense', with 'understanding', with intellectual
awareness, and a cool sophistication even in their pleasures.

It seems to me that these two types, the extravagant rake and
this more thoughtful, more judicious rake, can be seen as reflect-
ing different biases in the seventeenth-century definition of wit.
When, in the Prologue to *Madam Fickle*, Thomas D'Urfey
speaks of 'Fancy and Sence the glorious Twins of Wit' [1677,
A4ᵛ], he is expressing one of the standard ideas about wit,
fancy, and sense (or judgement, to use the more usual word),
true wit being a quality made up of a due proportion of fancy
and judgement. But there is some disagreement in the age about
the relative importance of these components to wit.[18] In this
context, then, a Bruce or a Dorimant is a wit in some sense of
the word that emphasizes the importance of judgement, a Celadon is a wit with the emphasis on the role of fancy. The relation

between the extravagant rake and fancy is adequately enough suggested by the sort of description of fancy that is commonly given. Here, for example, is Thomas Rymer in *The Tragedies of the Last Age*: '*Fancy* leaps, and frisks, and away she's gone; whilst *reason* rattles the chains, and follows after'.[19] And here is the author of the Postscript to *Notes and Observations on The Empress of Morocco*: 'Fanciful poetry and music, used with moderation, are good; but men who are wholly given over to either of them, are commonly as full of whimsies as diseased and splenetic men can be. Their heads are continually hot, and they have the same elevation of fancy sober, which men of sense have when they drink.'[20] It is also worth noting that an over-abundance of fancy is frequently seen as the excess to which the young are naturally prone. Joseph Glanvill is one who describes it as such[21] and William Wycherley seems of much the same opinion in the Preface to the *Miscellany Poems* [III, 7]. In both places there is the implication that this excess of fancy constitutes the wit of the young man.

In the terminological chaos of the Restoration, of course, wit, fancy, and judgement do not always stand in the relationship I have suggested. Shadwell would not be alone in limiting the word 'wit' to fancifulness and then slating the word, and the quality, as he does in *Bury Fair*. Nor would he be alone in taking wit as a word with favourable connotations, equating it with what others describe as judgement and then denying the extravagant manner the right to be called wit (which is substantially what he does in the Preface to *The Sullen Lovers*). Another example of the former tactic, which further points the role of the extravagant as a fanciful wit, comes from a conversation about an extravagant rake in Southerne's *Sir Antony Love*:

> *Val.* . . . he has a great deal of Wit.
> *Ilf.* Pretty good Natural Parts, I confess; But a Fool has the keeping 'em, no Judgment in the world; and what he says, comes as much by chance –
> *Val.* As *Epicurus*'s World did; Perfect, and Uniform, without a design.
> *Ilf.* He flies too much at Random to please any man of discretion.
> [1691, p. 9]

For the purpose of the example it matters little that the rake

G

discussed here is, unknown to the speakers, a woman in disguise.

III

I began this essay by suggesting that the extravagant rake was one concerning whom moral judgements were largely irrelevant. I would now like to return to this point and consider the means whereby this escape from moral difficulties is effected. Partly this is a matter of the excuses for the rake that are made in, or can be inferred from, the text. Beyond this, however, is the broad effect of the tone or atmosphere of many of these plays. I shall look at these features in that order.

At the simplest level I think it could be claimed that the essence of this rake lies more in his manner than in his deeds. One can then have a completely satisfying extravagant rake who in fact is seen to do very little that is seriously wicked. One can have lots of talk and very little else. Moreover, most of the talk is fairly unspecific, and as the rake is marked by a wild extravagance of speech, generalized claims to profligacy are just as likely to be fantasy as fact. Where the author has presented his extravagant in this way, then, the whole question of the morals of the character can be wished out of sight. At most there is evidence for a few venial sins of lying, lack of respect for elders, and so on. It seems to me that Celadon in Dryden's *Secret Love* is one who can be construed in this way.

In addition to this there is the possibility that if the extravagant's wildness can be attributed to a humour, and to a youthful humour at that, then this may provide a basis for a permissive attitude towards his profligacy. If his licentiousness is seen as an upsurge of the blood of a kind 'natural' in a young man, then it becomes a product of physical factors and as such is something for which the character cannot be blamed entirely (perhaps not at all). In addition it is something that is bound to pass as physical conditions inevitably change with age and so is all the more tolerable for being transient. Expressions of this sort of sentiment are a commonplace in the plays. To give a few random examples, Welbred in James Howard's *The English Monsieur* is justified on the ground that his behaviour 'is onely a fault and miscarriage of his Youth' [1674, K1ᵛ] and Careless in Edward

Ravenscroft's *The Careless Lovers* can defend himself against the heroine's charges of being wild in similar terms – 'I have my Froliques as most young men have' [1673, K3ʳ]. The extravagant rake in Southerne's *Sir Antony Love* is justified in similar terms, 'Youth will have its Sallies' [1691, p. 9], and in John Cory's *A Cure for Jealousie* a worthy old gentleman defends the extravagant against a narrow moralist with the words, 'we must make large allowances for Youth' [1701, p. 5]. Whether this sort of appeal is as persuasive now as it was then, of course, is another question.

In the event, however, the sheer comicality of these rakes is one of the strongest influences towards the throwing of a mellow glow over their misdemeanours. If the rakes themselves are risible in the fashion that I indicated earlier then it is difficult to treat their sins very seriously. 'Now, if I should be hang'd, I can't be angry with him, he dissembles so heartily' is how Helena excuses Willmore on one occasion in Mrs Behn's *The Rover I* [I, 47] and the adverb 'heartily' is one that could be applied to any action of the extravagant rake.

This particular idea, however, is capable of much further extension – extension in terms that are implicit in some of the plays. The opening lines of Sir Francis Fane's *Love in the Dark* have Trivultio, an outstandingly extravagant rake, pronouncing: 'The Carnival's begun; the Feast of free-born Souls, / Where Nature Reigns, and Custom is depos'd' [1675, p. 1]. Embedded in these lines is the whole concept of carnival as a time in which release of restraint is accepted. Such a release is generally held to be therapeutic – the tensions built up by the need for social conformity are relaxed by a licensed explosion. Several Restoration comedies, especially those containing extravagant rakes, are in fact set at a time of carnival or at least of public celebration. In addition to Fane's play, for example, there are Thomas Porter's *The Carnival*, Dryden's *The Mock Astrologer*, *The Assignation*, and *The Spanish Friar*, and Mrs Behn's *The Rover I*.

It can, I think, be argued that the extravagant rake in his own person is actually filling a carnival role.[22] To experience him in the safe confines of the play is to experience the spirit of carnival. He is a one-man *mardi gras* and provides the appropriate therapeutic release for the audience irrespective of whether or not he is put in a carnival setting. In him customary restraints are thrown off with a wild exuberance and an unashamed joy, and if he does finally dwindle into a husband this could be said to mark the passing of carnival and the acceptance of responsibility.

The carnival release provided by the extravagant rake, it seems to me, is not simply from the tensions created by sexual restraint. The Restoration aspired to be an age of great social refinement. It sought to cultivate the controlled and polished social manner. The possible gap between the graceful, easy surface and the real emotions is tellingly illustrated in Etherege's Dorimant and seems to be one of the preoccupations of Congreve, notably in *The Way of the World* where wit, elegance, and politeness are a mask not only for villainy, illicit passion, and hatred but also for quite honest emotions. A situation of this kind then is one of great tension and one release for such a tension is to rejoice in the antics of those who are free of the inhibitions of decorum. It seems to me, for example, that in Vanbrugh's *The Relapse* so much delight is taken in the unashamed swagger, freedom, and joy of self-display of the traditional fop figure that he pretty well ends up as comic hero. The extravagant rake, who is at times rather close to the fop, provides the same sort of release but in a much safer, more reassuring form. He also has spontaniety and uninhibited self-display but at the same time he manages to remain socially acceptable within the world of the play. The wages of freedom are not ostracism but an amused acceptance.

NOTES

1. Plays cited from the first London edition will be referred to simply by the year of publication and page number, enclosed in square brackets, in the body of the text.

2. '. . . the order of Nature is to follow my appetite: am I to eat at Noon, because it is Noon, or because I am a hungry? to eat because a Clock strikes, were to feed a Clock, or the Sun, and not my self: let dull grave Rogues observe distinction of seasons; eat because the Sun shines, and when he departs lye drown'd some nine hours in their

own Flegm; I will pay no such homage to the Sun, and time, which are things below me: I am a Superiour being to them, and will make 'em attend my pleasure. . . . The World is Nature's house of entertainment, where men of wit and pleasure are her free Guests, ty'd to no rules, and orders; Fools indeed are her Houshold-stuff, which she locks up and brings forth at seasons; handsome Fools are her Pictures; studious, plotting, engineering Fools, are her Mechanic Implements; strong laborious Fools, are her Common Utensils; valiant bold Fools, are her Armoury; and dull insignificant Fools, are her Lumber: which by Wars, Plagues, and other conveniences, she often throws and sweeps out of the World. [1675, pp. 22-23.]

3. For example, James Carlile's *The Fortune-Hunters* [1689, pp. 1, 7, and 13], Mrs Behn's *The Rover II* [I, 196], John Cory's *The Cure for Jealousie* [1701, p. 48], Catherine Trotter's *Love at a Loss* [1701, pp. 11 and 23], and Francis Manning's *The Generous Choice* [1700, p. 14].

4. For example, James Carlile's *The Fortune-Hunters* [1689, p. 4], John Crowne's *The Country Wit* [III, 25], and George Farquhar's *The Constant Couple* [I, 124].

5. For example, in John Crowne's *The Country Wit* [III, 40] and George Farquhar's *Love and a Bottle* [I, 115].

6. For example, in Mrs Behn's *The Dutch Lover* [I, 228] and Catherine Trotter's *Love at a Loss* [1701, p. 14].

7. For example, in John Dryden's *The Wild Gallant* [I, 109], Sir Francis Fane's *Love in the Dark* [1675, pp. 22 and 56], and John Smythe's *Win Her and Take Her* [1691, p. 12].

8. The most extended example of this comes from James Howard's *All Mistaken* [1672, pp. 20-21]. See also James Carlile's *The Fortune-Hunters* [1689, p. 13], Aphra Behn's *The Rover I* [I, 48], and John Dryden's *Secret Love* [II, 14].

9. Frank Harper Moore, *The Nobler Pleasure: Dryden's Comedy in Theory and Practice* (Chapel Hill, 1963), p. 108.

10. Moore, pp. 40, 45-6, and *passim*.

11. *The Works of Francis Beaumont and John Fletcher*, ed. A. R. Waller, 10 vols. (Cambridge, 1906), IV, 317.

12. *Ben Jonson*, ed. C. H. Herford and Percy and Evelyn Simpson, 11 vols. (Oxford, 1925-1952), VI, 21-22.

13. *The Critical Works of John Dennis*, ed. Edward Niles Hooker, 2 vols. (Baltimore, 1939), I, 283.

14. Moore, p. 45.

15. The element corresponding to the sanguine humour is air, possibly the source of one of the standard descriptive adjectives for the extravagant rake – airy.

16. See, for example, John W. Draper, *The Humours and Shakespeare's Characters* (Durham, North Carolina, 1945), pp. 23-24.

17. Draper, pp. 18, 81-82.

18. This necessarily compressed account of the general situation can be expanded by reference to Chapter Two of T. H. Fujimura's *The Restoration Comedy of Wit* (Princeton, 1965), and to Chapter Four of C. S. Lewis's *Studies in Words* (Cambridge, 1960).

19. *The Critical Works of Thomas Rymer*, ed. Curt A. Zimansky (New Haven, 1956), p. 20.

20. *The Works of John Dryden*, ed. Sir Walter Scott and George Saintsbury, 18 vols. (Edinburgh, 1882-1893), XV, 406. The authors were Dryden, Shadwell and Crowne.

21. Joseph Glanvill, *A Whip for the Droll, Fidler to the Atheist* (London, 1700), p. 5.

22. I am using the idea of the carnival here chiefly as an analogue. For a more seriously intended investigation of carnival elements in Restoration drama, see Harold Love's unpublished Cambridge University Ph.D. thesis, *Satire in the Drama of the Restoration*, pp. 48-61. Love's concern is with traditional plot motifs rather than character types and the comic release seems to be primarily from puritan/political pressures rather than from neoclassic social restraints. What results is a list of plays in many of its titles different from my list of extravagant-rake comedies but with enough plays in common to make the comparison interesting.

The Last of the Epics:
The Rejection of the Heroic in
Paradise Lost and *Hudibras*

MICHAEL WILDING

With the English Civil War, the forward youth who would write an epic poem was presented with first-hand material for his muse. The images of martial valour, the scenes of military glory, were played out before his eyes, providing ready themes for the epic poem England's literature awaited.

But the realities of civil war were less glorious than the literary images of heroic grandeur. Although past civil wars had later found epic treatment, the contemporary slaughter of fellow-countrymen could have little appeal. The two most famous heroic poems of the Restoration concerned themselves with questioning the very idea of military glory; these two epics questioned the basic assumptions of traditional epic. That they should ask such questions at such a time suggests that their authors had been reconsidering the heroic epics and romances of the past in the light of the tragic experience of civil war. The epic found itself transformed in England into the Christian epic of *Paradise Lost* (1667) and the burlesque epic of *Hudibras* (Part I, 1663; II, 1664; III, 1678).[1]

Remarking on Garrick's brilliance as an actor, Hannah More once wrote: 'I should have thought it as possible for Milton to have written *Hudibras*, and Butler *Paradise Lost*, as for one man to have played Hamlet and Drugger with such excellence'.[2] I have no intention of implying here that Butler and Milton might have exchanged works.[3] Milton's note on 'The Verse' with its rejection of 'the jingling sound of like endings' could hardly find a more extreme anti-type than Butler's burlesque rhyme. These metrical extremes clearly enough express the extremes of tone, of decorum. But I want to suggest that these extremes find common middle-ground in the heroic tradition that both poems are reacting against, and that their grounds of rejection are similar.

For both poems include explicit rejections of the heroic code. Milton's is well known and often commented on. It finds its major expression in the invocation to book IX when Milton announces he is about to deal with the Fall.

> Sad task, yet argument
> Not less but more Heroic than the wrauth
> Of stern *Achilles* on his Foe persu'd
> Thrice Fugitive about *Troy* Wall; or rage
> Of *Turnus* for *Lavinia* disespous'd,
> Or *Neptunes* ire or *Juno's*, that so long
> Perplexd the *Greek* and *Cytherea's* Son;
>
> *   *   *
>
> Since first this Subject for Heroic Song
> Pleas'd me long choosing, and beginning late;
> Not sedulous by Nature to indite
> Warrs, hitherto the onely Argument
> Heroic deemd, chief maistrie to dissect
> With long and tedious havoc fabl'd Knights
> In Battels feignd; the better fortitude
> Of Patience and Heroic Martyrdom
> Unsung; or to describe Races and Games,
> Or tilting Furniture, emblazond Shields,
> Impreses quaint, Caparisons and Steeds;
> Bases and tinsel Trappings, gorgious Knights
> At Joust and Tournament; then marshald Feast
> Serv'd up in Hall with Sewers, and Seneshals;
> The skill of Artifice or Office mean,
> Not that which justly gives Heroic name
> To Person or to Poem.
>
> [IX, 13-19, 25-41][4]

And the rejection of 'Warrs, hitherto the onely Argument/ Heroic deemd' is repeated later in the account of the Giants when Adam is shown:

> Cities of Men with lofty Gates and Towrs,
> Concourse in Arms, fierce Faces threatning Warr,
> Giants of mightie Bone, and bold emprise;
> Part wield thir Arms, part curb the foaming Steed . . .
>
> [XI, 640-643]

The consciously inflated manner, the vocabulary of Spenser, and the Latinate 'part . . . part . . .' construction echoing Virgil establish the epic note. Then we see the heroes in action, seeking forage and driving

> Ewes and thir bleating Lambs over the Plain,
> Thir Bootie; scarce with Life the Shepherds fly,
> But call in aid, which makes a bloody Fray;
> With cruel Tournament the Squadrons join;
> Where Cattel pastur'd late, now scatterd lies
> With Carcasses and Arms th' ensanguind Field
> Deserted: Others to a Citie strong
> Lay Siege, encampt; by Batterie, Scale and Mine
> Assaulting; others from the wall defend
> With Dart and Jav'lin, Stones and sulphurous Fire;
> On each hand slaughter and gigantic deeds.
>
> [XI, 649-659]

It is a sophisticated passage in its interplay of noble terminology and brutal action. The 'Ewes and thir bleating Lambs' represent not only the slaughter of animals to feed the marauding army but also the loss of the shepherds' livelihood and also, metaphorically, the mothers and children suffering before the army, just as we see the shepherds flee. The pastoral 'Where Cattel pastur'd' is superseded by 'th'ensanguind Field'; and the cattle, unawares awaiting their later slaughter, their later shift into carcasses, are identified with the slaughtered men whose carcasses we see: men are driven as beasts to the slaughter in this world. The most striking phrase is the collocation of 'slaughter and gigantic deeds', insisting on their identity and making us aware of the nature of the actions denoted by such heroic, endorsive phrases as 'gigantic deeds'. Michael interprets the episode to Adam:

> Such were these Giants, men of high renown;
> For in those dayes Might onely shall be admir'd,
> And Valour and Heroic Vertue calld;

To overcome in Battel, and subdue
Nations, and bring home spoils with infinite
Man-slaughter, shall be held the highest pitch
Of human Glorie, and for Glorie done
Of triumph, to be styl'd great Conquerors,
Patrons of Mankind, Gods, and Sons of Gods,
Destroyers rightlier calld and Plagues of men.

[XI, 688-697]

Butler's rejection of the heroic ethos is expressed throughout *Hudibras*, though never in such sustained passages. The most explicit statement occurs in the description of Talgol, the butcher, whose military prowess is associated with his civilian occupation. The same language is applicable to both his activities, and the descriptions of him are skilfully ambiguous. Butler may be equally well talking about his peacetime trade as a butcher or his military skill: that we cannot distinguish which, makes its simple, telling moral point:

Yet *Talgol* was of Courage stout,
And vanquish'd oftner then he fought:
Inur'd to labour, sweat, and toyl,
And, like a Champion, shone with Oyl.
Right many a Widow his keen blade,
And many Fatherless, had made.
He many a Bore and huge *Dun Cow*
Did, like another *Guy*, o'rethrow.
But *Guy* with him in fight compar'd,
Had like the Bore or Dun Cow far'd.
With greater Troops of Sheep h' had fought
Then *Ajax*, or bold *Don Quixot*: . . .

For he was of that noble Trade
That *Demi-gods* and *Heroes* made,
Slaughter, and knocking on the head;
The Trade to which they all were bred;
And is, like others, glorious when
'Tis great and large, but base if mean.
The former rides in Triumph for it;
The later in a two-wheel'd Chariot,
For daring to profane a thing
So sacred, with vile bungleing.

[I, ii, 299-310, 321-330][5]

Like Milton, Butler gets his effects by interweaving the elevated terms of militarism's social acceptance – 'noble', 'glorious', 'sacred' – with the reductive language of the brutal action – 'knocking on the head', 'trade', 'slaughter'. Both insist on the analogy of 'heroism' with slaughtering animals. But Butler's most telling stroke is his indication of how murder when performed on a large scale becomes sacred. Civilian murderers go to the gallows not for taking human life but for taking insufficient life, for failing to perform the rite with full military amplitude.

And Butler has an attack on the martial heroism of traditional epic in his own voice, paralleling Milton's invocation to book IX, with his opening of the second canto of book I:

> There was an ancient sage *Philosopher*,
> That had read *Alexander Ross* over,
> And swore the world, as he could prove,
> Was made of *Fighting* and of *Love*:
> Just so *Romances* are, for what else
> Is in them all, but *Love* and *Battels*?
> O'th' first of these w' have no great matter
> To treat of, but a world o'th' later:
> In which to doe the Injur'd Right
> We mean, in what concerns just fight.
> Certes our Authors are to blame,
> For to make some well-sounding name
> A Pattern fit for modern Knights,
> To copy out in Frays and Fights,
> (Like those that a whole street do raze,
> To build a Palace in the place.)
> They never care how many others
> They kill, without regard of mothers,
> Or wives, or children, so they can
> Make up some fierce, dead-doing man,
> Compos'd of many ingredient Valours,
> Just like the Manhood of nine Taylors.
> So a wild *Tartar* when he spies
> A man that's handsome, valiant, wise,
> If he can kill him, thinks t'inherit
> His Wit, his Beauty, and his Spirit:
> As if just so much he enjoy'd
> As in another is destroy'd.
> For when a Giant's slain in fight,
> And mow'd orethwart, or cleft downright,

It is a heavy case, no doubt,
A man should have his Brains beat out,
Because he's tall, and has large Bones;
As men kill Beavers for their stones.

[I, ii, 1-34]

The satiric note is dropped here for a direct statement. Burlesque rhyme, and the reductive images, remain; but they remain to reinforce the bitterness of the attack, are used to deflate the idea of the Romance glorification of battles, of 'Warrs hitherto the onely Argument / Heroic deemd'.

The dramatic enactment of the inadequacy of military heroism, its wrongness, and the reasons for its inadequacy and wrongness, is in *Paradise Lost* the war in Heaven. Satan shows his evil throughout the poem; but his attack on mankind is by 'false guile' (III, 92); his use of force occurs in the war. Arnold Stein in his analysis of this episode has indicated how 'the invention of artillery is an attempt to usurp ultimate moral might by means of matter'.[6] Satan is attempting to usurp God's moral authority by means of force. The 'confusion of spirit and matter' here is indicative of Satan's own mental and moral confusion. It is for just such confusions that Butler derides Hudibras and his fellow-Presbyterians:

> For his *Religion* it was fit
> To match his Learning and his Wit:
> 'Twas *Presbyterian* true blew,
> For he was of that stubborn Crew
> Of Errant Saints, whom all men grant
> To be the true Church *Militant*:
> Such as do build their Faith upon
> The holy Text of *Pike* and *Gun*;
> Decide all Controversies by
> Infallible *Artillery*;
> And prove their Doctrine Orthodox
> By Apostolick *Blows* and *Knocks*;
> Call Fire and Sword and Desolation,
> A *godly-thorough-Reformation* . . .
>
> [I, i, 187-200]

The ironic collocations of 'Infallible *Artillery*' and of 'Apostolick *Blows* and *Knocks*' express succinctly the moral confusions that we see enacted by Satan in the war.

Rejecting then a certain code of behaviour, Milton and Butler are led to question the literary forms that ennoble that code. Butler wrote in his Note-books, 'Heroicall Poetry handle's the slightest, and most Impertinent Follys in the world in a formall Serious and unnaturall way: And Comedy and Burlesque the most Serious in a Frolique and Gay humor which has always been found the more apt to instruct, and instill those Truths with Delight into men, which they would not indure to heare of any other way'.[7] Both Milton and Butler recognize the ethical importance of literature and both are concerned that the false ethic of military heroism should no longer be spread. The original ethical impulse of the epic no longer remains, Butler believes: both the message and the medium are unacceptable. The old impulse must deliver its new message through new forms: and he describes the new form oddly in terms of the old knight-errant going forth: 'A Satyr is a kinde of Knight Errant that goe's upon Adventures, to Relieve the Distressed Damsel Virtue, and Redeeme Honor out of Inchanted Castles, And opprest Truth, and Reason out of the Captivity of Gyants or Magitians.'[8] The old heroic code, then, is to be extirpated and superseded by the new heroism of satire.

Milton's rejection of the traditional heroic, his identification of the 'destroyers' with Satan the destroyer, his giving Satan the heroic accoutrements, have often enough been remarked and documented.[9] His size, his strength, his shield, his spear – all these have their Homeric and Virgilian counterparts. At the same time Satan's corruption, degradation, and evil are emphasized in his shield, compared to a spotty moon, in the fading glory of his appearance, in the comparison of him and his followers to Eastern tyrants and to barbarian hordes. From the beginning of the poem Satan is both the traditional hero and the embodiment of evil: and the two qualities are shown to be inseparable in him and in all heroes. Military valour results inevitably in destruction: 'For onely in destroying I find ease' [IX, 129].

The cruel destruction men wreak on each other in the world is clearly enough seen to result from the Fall; the military heroic is a direct result of the evil of Satan, himself embodying that heroism. Images of waste and destruction abound – the military devils are like locusts, barbarians, heroes of epic and romance.

They are much more splendid indeed than earthly heroes: they could not be surpassed:

> though all the Giant brood
> Of *Phlegra* with th'Heroic Race were joind
> That fought at *Theb's* and *Ilium*, on each side
> Mixt with auxiliar Gods; and what resounds
> In Fable or Romance of *Uthers* Son
> Begirt with *Brittish* and *Armoric* Knights;
> And all who since, Baptiz'd or Infidel
> Jousted in *Aspramont* or *Montalban*,
> *Damasco*, or *Marocco*, or *Trebisond*,
> Or whom *Biserta* sent from *Afric* shore
> When *Charlemain* with all his Peerage fell
> By *Fontarabbia*.
>
> [I, 576-587]

And their achieved aim is the destruction of man, the reduction of the richness of Paradise to:

> an Iland salt and bare,
> The haunt of Seals and Orcs, and Sea-mews clang.
>
> [XI, 834-835]

Butler's rejection of the heroic is achieved by a quite different procedure. Hudibras and Ralph are supremely incompetent. Hudibras has the will to destroy, of course: at the end of the battle into canto two of the first book, Hudibras:

> star'd about, and seeing none
> Of all his foes remain but one,
> He snatch'd his weapon that lay near him,
> And from the ground began to rear him;
> Vowing to make *Crowdero* pay
> For all the rest that ran away.
>
> [I, ii, 1025-1030]

Ralph prevents him, but the will was there.

Whether, even so, Hudibras could have killed Crowdero is doubtful. Butler heaps ridicule on his competence as a warrior, and on his physical qualities. Satan's size is emphasized by

Milton; he transcends the dimensions of any conventional hero:

> he above the rest
> In shape and gesture proudly eminent
> Stood like a Towr.
>
> [I, 589-591]

Quite the reverse is Hudibras, with neither the size nor the phallic symbolism of Satan. The Lady calls him 'a *Roan-Guelding*, twelve hands high' [II, i, 694]. For this non-equestrian age Zachary Grey's note provides a gloss: 'This is very satyrical upon the poor Knight, if we consider the significa-tion of That Name; and from what the Widow says, we may infer, the Knight's Stature, was but Four foot high'.[10] Hogarth's engravings portray Hudibras as a humpbacked dwarf. When Hudibras approaches battle Butler comments:

> For as our modern wits behold,
> Mounted a Pick-back on the Old,
> Much further off; much further he
> Rais'd on his aged Beast could see:
> Yet not sufficient to descry
> All postures of the enemy.
>
> [I, ii, 71-76]

Perched on his horse, his vision is still circumscribed – unlike Satan. The description of the towering Satan is an echo of a description of Turnus in the *Aeneid*.[11] That it is of Turnus, not Aeneas, qualifies the endorsive nature of the allusion of course; but it still allows Satan to be a dignified hero, ennobled by a literary tradition. By contrast the Virgilian allusion used to characterize Hudibras is wholly belittling:

> For as *Æneas* bore his Sire
> Upon his shoulders through the fire:
> Our Knight did bear no less a Pack
> Of his own Buttocks on his back:
> Which now had almost got the upper-
> Hand of his Head, for want of Crupper.
> To poize this equally, he bore
> A *Paunch* of the same bulk before:
>
> [I, i, 287-294]

Derision is Butler's weapon. The traditional heroic gestures are reduced to the derisory in his two heroes, brought to the contemptible.

Milton treats Satan in this way when he has finished with him. After the Fall, when the notes change to tragic and the emphasis is shifted on to 'the better fortitude / Of Patience and Heroic Martyrdom' in Christ and Adam, then Satan's heroism is reduced to a tawdry thing. He shares Hudibras' shiftiness and evasiveness when, after Eve has eaten the apple, he 'slunk' away. And derision is heaped on him upon his return to Hell:

> a while he stood, expecting
> Thir universal shout and high applause
> To fill his ear, when contrary he hears
> On all sides, from innumerable tongues
> A dismal universal hiss, the sound
> Of public scorn.
>
> [X, 504–509]

This contemptuously comic treatment of the hero as he and his audience are turned to serpents is most unheroic. But it is similar to the treatment meted out to Hudibras. And there is a Hudibrastic note earlier in *Paradise Lost* in the description of the Paradise of Fools. The pilgrims wandering there find that:

> . . . now Saint *Peter* at Heav'ns Wicket seems
> To wait them with his Keys, and now at foot
> Of Heav'ns ascent they lift thir Feet, when loe
> A violent cross wind from either Coast
> Blows them transverse ten thousand Leagues awry
> Into the devious Air; then might ye see
> Cowls, Hoods and Habits with thir wearers tost
> And flutterd into Raggs, then Reliques, Beads,
> Indulgences, Dispenses, Pardons, Bulls,
> The sport of Winds: all these upwhirld aloft
> Fly ore the backside of the World farr off . . .
>
> [III, 484–494]

The 'backside' is a familiar part of the Hudibrastic burlesque note and the banana-skin action is like Hudibras mounting his horse. This passage is related to the anti-heroic theme, for at the

Paradise of Fools the first arrivals were the warriors of book XI:

> First from the ancient World those Giants came
> With many a vain exploit, though then renownd.
> [III, 464-465]

Such burlesque action is the basis of *Hudibras,* though rare in *Paradise Lost.* But occasionally, amidst being hailed with cudgel-blows and rotten eggs, Hudibras ventures a rare, traditionally heroic action, suitably described:

> He drew up all his force into
> One Body, and that into one Blow.
> But *Talgol* wisely avoided it
> By cunning sleight; for had it hit,
> The Upper part of him the Blow
> Had slit, as sure as that below.
> [I, ii, 819-824]

Had he hit – but of course he misses. In the next battle he ventures a similar blow of which Montague Bacon, quoted in Zachary Grey's additional *Notes to Hudibras* (1752),[12] remarked, 'This is very like *Milton*', quoting:

> Together both with next to Almightie Arme
> Uplifted imminent, one stroke they aimd
> That might determin, and not need repeat.
> [VI, 316-318]

The passage in *Hudibras* referred to is this:

> The *Knight* with one dead-doing blow
> Resolving to decide the fight,
> And she with quick and cunning slight
> Avoiding it, the force and weight
> He charg'd upon it was so great,
> As almost sway'd him to the ground.
> No sooner she th'advantage found,
> But in she flew, and seconding
> With home-made thrust the heavy swing,
> She laid him flat upon his side . . .
> [I, iii, 844-853]

Certainly the opening two lines are heroic in a way comparable to Milton's account. But in context the heroic is tarnished with

H

absurdity: for the blow is a failure, overtopples Hudibras, and causes his defeat. Moreover he is attacking a woman, a most unheroic, unchivalrous action. Before this final blow we have seen how he:

> rain'd a storm
> Of blows so terrible and thick,
> As if he meant to hash her quick.
>
> [I, iii, 836-838]

Grey cited a parallel to this description from *The Faerie Queene*. As with the heroic note above, such a parallel serves only to contrast the heroic with the actualities of the situation – Hudibras' attack on a woman. This reflects ill enough on our hero and on heroism; worse though is the fact that he is *defeated* by a woman. He is both cruel and unchivalrous, and weak and incompetent.

Although incompetence and absurdity characterize Hudibras and Ralph, the moral outrage of Milton's account of the wrongness of traditional heroic values is present just as strongly in *Hudibras*. We do not need L'Estrange's unconvincing *Key to Hudibras* to be reminded that contemporary readers read *Hudibras* in the full context of the civil wars and the regicide. Hudibras and Ralph are buffoons and 'bumkins'; at the same time they are figures from a recent all-too-real political experience. The reader laughing at the fight over the bear would remember without mirth the bloodshed of Worcester, or Dunbar. For all their absurdity, Hudibras and his fellows had done enough damage. Hudibras on horseback provokes Butler's comment:

> So have I seen armed heel,
> A Wight bestride a *Common-weal*;
> While still the more he kick'd and spurr'd,
> The less the sullen Jade has stirr'd.
>
> [I, i, 917-920]

Hudibras hiding under a table to avoid capture by the tormenting devils at the Lady's house is dragged out from his security in a way recalling a famous incident in the civil wars:

> And as another of the same
> Degree, and Party, in Arms, and Fame,

That in the same Cause, had ingag'd,
And War with equal conduct wag'd,
By vent'ring only but to thrust
His Head, a Span beyond his Post:
B'a *Gen'ral* of the *Cavalliers*
Was drag'd, through a window by th'Ears:
So he was serv'd in his Redoubt,
And by the other end pull'd out.

[III, i, 1137-1146]

These detailed allusions to events of the Civil War spread of
course throughout the poem, while the second canto of book III
is unconcerned with the adventures of Hudibras and Ralph and
consists of a long digression about the end of the Interregnum.

The hideousness of civil war was vividly present for both
Milton and Butler. Milton's theme, though precluding a specific
treatment of recent British history, dealt with the archetypal
civil war that Satan provoked in heaven. Michael rebukes
him:

. . . how hast thou disturbd
Heav'ns blessed peace, and into Nature brought
Miserie, uncreated till the crime
Of thy Rebellion!

[VI, 266-269]

Yet after the abortive Rebellion, at least the devils can manage
to live in peace – so different from the multiplication of divisions
and sects that occurred in Britain after the War. The poet's own
voice utters a cry of anguish in his description of Hell:

O shame to men! Devil with Devil damnd
Firm concord holds, men onely disagree
Of creatures rational, though under hope
Of heav'nly Grace: and God proclaiming peace,
Yet live in hatred, enmitie, and strife
Among themselves, and levie cruel warrs,
Wasting the Earth, each other to destroy:
As if (which might induce us to accord)
Man had not hellish foes anow besides,
That day and night for his destruction wait.

[II, 496-505]

Hudibras himself utters a similar plea against dissension in his first speech in the poem:

> There is a *Machiavilian* Plot,
> (Though ev'ry *nare olfact* it not)
> A deep design in't, to divide
> The well-affected that confide,
> By setting Brother against Brother,
> To claw and curry one another.
> Have we not enemies *plus satis*,
> That *Cane et angue pejus* hate us?
> And shall we turn our fangs and claws
> Upon our own selves, without cause?
>
>   [I, i, 735-744]

It was a sad enough irony that Milton should lament over man's inability to agree, while describing the devils who, though initiators of discord, at least held agreement amongst themselves. But Butler's irony is more bitter still; for Hudibras who makes this plea for concord is (in Butler's view) the poem's representative of one of the major causes of faction, one of the Presbyterians largely responsible for the Civil War. Declaiming against the conflict of a bear-baiting, Hudibras is oblivious of the larger conflict he is participant in. Indeed the suppression of bear-baiting was one of the Cromwellian actions against the old order – one of the continual trivial acts of faction. A note in Grey's edition records how 'some of Colonel *Cromwell's* Forces coming by accident unto *Uppingham* Town in *Rutland* on the *Lord's Day*, found these Bears playing there in the usual manner: and in the height of their sport, caused them to be seiz'd upon, tied to a tree and shot'.[13] Whatever the developing complexities of irony that open in the knight's speech, the sad question, 'Have we not enemies *plus satis*?' stands, like Milton's 'as if . . . Man had not hellish foes anow besides', as a desperate, haunting lament.

What both *Paradise Lost* and *Hudibras* remarkably have in common are heroes of appalling degradation. We have already seen their commitment to violence. Their utter dishonesty must also be stressed – a quality so basic to both of them that it can easily be missed as not worthy of comment. Satan's dishonest rigging of the debate, his lying comment on his return to Hell

that Night and Chaos 'fiercely oppos'd / My journey strange'
[X, 478-479], and his lies to Eve, pretending to be a serpent,
pretending to have eaten the apple himself, these are central to
his character. His deceitfulness is utter: he deceives Uriel with a
show of sincerity, and Milton comments:

> So spake the false dissembler unperceiv'd;
> For neither Man nor Angel can discern
> Hypocrisie, the onely evil that walks
> Invisible . . .   [III, 681-684]

These qualities are fully shared by Hudibras who lies to the Lady
that he has undergone punishment, who pours forth hypocritical
professions of his love for her.[14]

Corrupt from the outset, Satan and Hudibras are both heroes
who yet degenerate into greater corruption. From his original
heroic speeches (which none the less from the beginning provide
clear evidence of his corruption) Satan follows a progressively
downward course. His moments of nobility become fewer.
He bravely sets off alone to Earth (though to do so he has to
fix the debate) and we soon see him in the postures of an
heroic confrontation for single combat: but his antagonist is his
own son whom he fails to recognize and the posture issues in no
fight. After the first two books he is reduced to using a series
of degrading disguises and he achieves his destruction of man
not by heroic grandeur but by singling out a woman alone and
lying to her. Hudibras' similarly unchivalrous attack on a
woman (and his worse defeat at her hands) has been noted. And
Hudibras' knight-errantry is diverted from its public concerns in
part one to besieging the Widow to gain her property at the
poem's end – a similar decline from true heroic and romantic
pretentions. From the speeches Hudibras began with in canto
one, speeches that bore at least some relationship to heroic
utterance, he has degenerated to mere quarrels with Ralph, to
logic-chopping, to the tortuous justification of lying:

> Is't not *Ridiculous*, and *Nonsense*,
> A *Saint* should be a slave to *Conscience?*
>   [II, ii, 247-248]

Just as Satan, the warrior-hero, is reduced to deceit, to lies, to
speeches rather than action, so Hudibras, the so-called knight,

engages in no action in part III; heroic combat gives way to argument and lies. And like Satan, the lies are to the woman. From the beginning, of course, Hudibras has preferred words to deeds: but action has been forced on him by the bear-baiting crowd who respond to his harangue with blows. By the poem's end he is, like Satan, utterly discredited as a hero. For a second time he is defeated by a woman when the Widow traps and exposes him and foils his attempt to marry her. Satan likewise is rewarded for attacking a woman by receiving his defeat ultimately from the woman. Adam says to Eve, recalling God's plan:

> . . . thy Seed shall bruise
> The Serpents head; pitteous amends, unless
> Be meant, whom I conjecture, our grand Foe
> *Satan*, who in the Serpent hath contriv'd
> Against us this deceit: to crush his head
> Would be revenge indeed.
>
> [X, 1031-1036]

The final failure of both Hudibras and Satan singles them out from the ranks of other heroes. We must not forget that at the end of *Paradise Lost* Satan has not effected any successful revenge on God but has succeeded only in heaping worse punishment on his own head. Hudibras similarly has utterly failed to impose his puritanical discipline on the bear-baiting or the skimmington, has left Sidrophel not (as he thinks) dead but perfectly well, and has failed to win the Lady.

It is important to note that for all their rejection of the traditional heroic ethos both Milton and Butler judge their heroes from that ethos as well as from their other value schemes. Although concerned to dismiss the heroic code Butler and Milton are concerned to show how their 'heroes' fail both by that code and by their own more humane one. Attacking women, being defeated by women, failing in their quests – these are all offences under the old code. Hudibras goes to great lengths to avoid the pain of the beating he has vowed to undergo. Vows should mean everything and pain nothing to the proper hero, of course. But neither Satan nor Hudibras are proper heroes. We are left wondering whether it is likely that the great figures hallowed in literature were either.

The hero of the epic poem traditionally provided an ideal of behaviour. This presented problems for early critics of *Paradise Lost* for how could Satan be such a hero? By a terrible irony, though, he is: Satan, for fallen man, is indeed the ideal of behaviour, the model observed. This hero is not someone who ought to be, but someone who regrettably is, admired. The qualities most admired in the world are Satan's qualities: we see him compared to military heroes, adventurous seafarers, scientific inventors, classical orators. And so it becomes Milton's concern to show the evil of those qualities – to show how bravery or eloquence can so readily be used for evil ends. He underlines the false-heroic by creating the Christian heroes Christ and Adam. This new heroism, 'the better fortitude', supersedes the old.

Butler's method is less complex by far. He simply inverts the traditional heroic. The old hero was everything admirable: Hudibras is everything contemptible. There is no fear the reader will admire him or Ralph. The danger is, of course, that Hudibras will be seen as contemptible only in his incompetence in fulfilling the heroic code, in having a rusty sword rather than a bloodstained one. Butler, however, avoids this danger. He avoids it partly by allowing no positives to creep in at all: there is no 'good hero', either of the supersessive sort (Christ or Adam), or of a traditional sort. Butler's new knight-errant is satire itself. Amongst the cast of the poem the hopelessness of Hudibras and Ralph is the total picture; their opposition, whether the mob or Sidrophel or Whackum, is equally disreputable. (The Lady alone is exempted from this degradation; but she represents nothing positive herself.) Implicitly, everyone in the civil wars was the same. It is important to note that, although Butler was hailed by the Royalists at the Restoration and has always been seen as a partisan writer, he does not introduce a 'good Royalist' to set against Hudibras and Ralph or the mob. There is not much evidence that he had time for either side: his views on the Restoration court are as contemptuous as his views on the Cromwellian Commonwealth.

Not only are no positives allowed in, Butler also devalues not only his epic hero but the epic conventions. Milton was concerned to surpass pagan epic: he summoned the 'Heav'nly Muse' [I, 6]. He will 'soar|Above th' *Aonian* Mount' [I, 14-15],

Mount Helicon; he replaces the pagan mount of the Muses with three Biblical mountains, *Oreb*, *Sinai*, and *Sion* Hill: three to one. And having shown the Bible richer in places of inspiration than the classical world, he then emphasizes that the Christian muse does not depend on the superstitions of place at all but flourishes in 'th'upright heart and pure' – it is above geographical restriction.[15]

Butler observes the conventions too and invokes a muse – though somewhat grudgingly:

> We should, as learned Poets use,
> Invoke th'assistance of some *Muse*;
> However Criticks count it sillier
> Then Juglers talking t'a Familiar.
> We think 'tis no great matter which:
> They'r all alike: yet we shall pitch
> On one that fits our purpose most,
> Whom therefore thus do we accost.
>
> Thou that with Ale, or viler Liquors,
> Didst inspire *Withers*, *Pryn*, and *Vickars*,
> And force them, though it were in spight
> Of nature and their stars, to write;
> Who, as we find in sullen Writs,
> And cross-grain'd Works of modern wits,
> With Vanity, Opinion, Want,
> The wonder of the Ignorant,
> The praises of the Author, penn'd
> By himself, or wit-ensuring friend,
> The Itch of Picture in the Front,
> With Bays, and wicked Rhyme upon't,
> All that is left o'th' forked Hill
> To make men scribble without skill,
> Canst make a Poet, spight of fate,
> And teach all people to translate;
> Though out of Languages in which
> They understand no part of speech:
> Assist me but this once, I 'mplore,
> And I shall trouble thee no more.
>
> [I, i, 631-58]

While Milton is trying to elevate and Christianize the muse Butler is deliberately reducing it to the lowest: he introduces it late, complains at the necessity, casts doubt on its value, reduces it to charlatanism with the mention of 'Jugglers', and puts its power down to ale. The twin peaks of Parnassus are degraded to the image of serpent duplicity.

Butler's particular degradations of his chosen form show his intention at its clearest. Instead of Virgil's *'Arma virumque. . . .'*, instead of the nobility of Milton's

> Of Mans First Disobedience, and the Fruit
> Of that Forbidden Tree. . . .

Butler opens:

> When *civil Dudgeon* first grew high,
> And men fell out they knew not why;
> When hard words, *Jealousies* and *Fears*,
> Set Folks together by the ears,
> And made them fight, like mad or drunk,
> For Dame *Religion* as for Punk . . .
>
> [I, i, 1-6]

The vocabulary destroys any dignity. Noble combat is 'Dudgeon', it is motiveless, causeless; the issues are no more significant than petty quarrels. In the revised text of the poem 'Dudgeon' is replaced by 'Fury', ennobling the opening at the expense of this contemptuous note, but the analogy of fighting for religion 'as for Punk' remains to reduce the combat to the most vulgar and trivial. Grey's edition notes: 'Sir *John Suckling* has express'd this Thought a little more decently, in the *Tragedy* of Brennoralt.

> *Religion now is a young Mistress here,*
> *For which each Man will fight, and die at least;*
> *Let it alone awhile, and 'twill become*
> *A kind of married Wife, People will be*
> *Content to live with it in quietness.'*[16]

But Butler's indecency is crucial, for in this conflict there was no decency. The poet is concerned to show the degradation of the times, to show that there is no place for the noble here. Such set pieces of epic poetry as the description of dawn are reduced to the contemptible in *Hudibras*. Milton still retains an epic dignity:

> Now Morn her rosie steps in th' Eastern Clime
> Advancing, sowd the Earth with Orient Pearl . . .
> [V, 1-2]

Not so Butler:

> The Sun had long since in the Lap
> Of *Thetis*, taken out his *Nap*,
> And like a *Lobster* boyl'd, the *Morn*
> From *black* to *red* began to turn.
> [II, ii, 29-32]

The intervening deities, those stock characters in epic, provided a problem for the seventeenth-century poet. Both Milton and Butler reject the traditional use of them. Milton reduces and Christianizes them by making their role to some degree the allowable but limited role of the angels, guarding Eden at night, expelling Satan, and instructing Adam. Butler dismisses them even more fully from his epic. He rationalizes, trivializes, and vulgarizes divine intervention; when Hudibras is about to shoot Talgol:

> But *Pallas* came in shape of Rust,
> And 'twixt the Spring and Hammer thrust
> Her *Gorgon*-shield, which made the Cock
> Stand stiff as if 'twere turn'd t'a stock.
> [I, ii, 781-784]

With the absurdity of the modern hero, Hudibras, and the reduction of the epic set-pieces to the trivial or vulgar, critical attention is readily directed towards the traditional epic heroes. Butler looks afresh at events of the past the muse has celebrated and doubts their nobility. When Orsin throws a stone at Hudibras the action seems most unheroic. But Butler draws a classical parallel. This is not, however, to ennoble Orsin but to reduce the past to the same vulgar level. The stone is

> not so huge a one
> As that which *Diomed* did maul
> *Æneas* on the Bum withall.
> [I, iii, 492-494]

The Homeric heroes may have been bigger and better than the moderns and thrown larger stones; but 'maul' and 'Bum' put them in their proper context. Similarly the siege of Troy is reduced to:

> . . . when the restless *Greeks* sate down
> So many years before *Troy* Town.
>
> [I, ii, 424–425]

The reduction of besiege to 'sat down', and the ironic juxtaposition to it of 'restless', economically make their point.

Amongst these deviations from the expected practice of epic and romance, perhaps the most remarkable feature shared by *Paradise Lost* and *Hudibras* is their lack of action. The major activity in *Paradise Lost* occurs in the war in Heaven – and this is told in retrospect, the result already determined, and told with a satirical note. At its high point the war becomes comic, absurd. The puns with which Satan introduces his cannon, the angels' reaction of throwing back mountains, and the conclusion:

> So Hills amid the Air encounterd Hills
> Hurld to and fro with jaculation dire,
> That under ground they fought in dismal shade:
>
> [VI, 664–666]

are incidents worthy of *Hudibras*. Some of the same bad puns about cannon and breaches indeed occur in *Hudibras*:

> And *Cannons* shoot the higher pitches
> The lower we let down their breeches . . .
>
> [II, i, 263–264]

The Angels' response to Satan's artillery with mother earth is paralleled in *Hudibras* when '*Colon* chusing out a stone, / Levell'd so right, it thumpt upon' Hudibras who was gripping his pistol [I, iii, 519 ff.]. But to force particular parallels is not the point; it is the spirit behind the portrayals of military engagements which is significant. For, contrasted with the expected, traditional epic note, there is a striking similarity of attitude to the military set-pieces.

The battle apart, there is little action in *Paradise Lost*. The story was so well known that there could be no surprise or suspense. There is little narrative interest. Adam and Eve can only wait, doing nothing except cultivate their garden. God's foreseeing the Fall prevents any surprise. Satan's preparation and carrying-out of his campaign is the main narrative impulse, but this is deliberately frustrated by our being shown God's prescience. When one of the characters of the poem is omniscient the narrative can hardly provide a major impulse in the poem. When we reach the Fall the action takes only two lines.

Hudibras has even less coherent action than *Paradise Lost*. There is the first battle with the bear-baiting crowd, the second battle, the stocks; and the wooing of the Lady. The encounter with Sidrophel provides a diversion only tenuously related to the main narrative lines. But those narrative lines themselves are never fulfilled. Hudibras is diverted from his public duties to wooing the Lady, and a digression on the Interregnum disrupts for an entire canto the small amount of narrative impulse his wooing might have had. The incidents are few and the note is bathetic throughout. Hudibras does not win the Lady, he does not conquer the crowd but is put in the stocks by them, he does not kill Sidrophel. Sidrophel's excitement at the star of omen he detects epitomizes the bathetic mode of the poem's action and expectations; the star is in fact a child's kite.

Predominantly *Hudibras* is concerned with arguments, with incessant talking and quarrelling. Before the first incident Hudibras announces:

> now the Field is not far off,
> Where we must give the world a proof
> Of Deeds, not Words, and such as suit
> Another manner of Dispute.
>
> [I, i, 859-862]

But it is of the words that the reader remains most conscious:

> For *Rhetorick*, he could not ope
> His mouth, but out there flew a Trope:
>
> [I, i, 81-82]

And the Lady recognizes Hudibras in the stocks, she says,

> Not by your Individual Whiskers,
> But by your Dialect and Discourse; . .
>
> [II, i, 155-156]

Similarly in *Paradise Lost* we remember the debate in Hell, the debate in Heaven, the dialogue on astronomy, the argument between Adam and Eve about gardening alone, the serpent's rhetorical seduction, the long speeches of quarrel and reconciliation, the final books of instruction from Michael. Satan introduces his cannon with a punning attack of words, and Arnold Stein has noted the significance of the devils being driven to Hell by verbal abuse 'When the fierce Foe hung on our broken Rear / Insulting' [II, 79-80].[17]

And perhaps this can be related to the age. There were battles enough in the Civil War. But there were also floods of pamphlets, disputes, controversies. After all, the winning side was Parliament – the forum for discussion, for speeches, for words.

It is with such debates and disputes that both poems are mainly concerned. Milton's proclaimed intention to 'justifie the wayes of God to men' is an explicitly disputatious one, with centuries of argument behind it. And the debate in Hell has always and inevitably been seen in relationship to the political debates of the Interregnum. In *Hudibras*, indeed, that aspect bearing a particularly realistic relationship to the Interregnum is the argument between Independent and Presbyterian, the argument conducted with abstruse evidence and doubtful logic, the shifts and dishonesties. Even in the stocks Hudibras and Ralph while away time not by planning how to escape (as Milton's devils do in Hell) but in further ideological dispute (like the philosophizing devils after the debate). Deeds give way to words in these two parliamentary epics.

We are familiar with the reaction of disillusion, with the rejection of the old ethos after the First World War, in the writing of Frederick Manning, R. C. Sherriff, Robert Graves, and in so many of the poets. It is likely that something similar happened after the Civil War. The case that Milton's disillusionment with his countrymen in the Interregnum and with the Restoration prevented his writing the planned patriotic epic has often been advanced. But the shift in *Paradise Lost* was not only away from the patriotic to the supranational but from the epic ethos to a new Christian epic, to 'Patience and Heroic Martyrdom', to the quietism and pacifism that many of the Puritans came to adopt.[18] He would not sing the praises of the old military heroic. Montague Bacon's 'Dissertation Upon Burlesque Poetry', included in Zachary Grey's additional *Notes to Hudibras* (1752), suggests an interesting parallelism of attitude between Milton and Butler. Discussing Butler's burlesque style he writes:

> I am endeavouring to shew why He chose This Style – He who, as Mr *Dryden* observes, was capable of Any.
>
> I shall quote two unexceptionable Authors for this: In the first Place, *Milton*, who, in his History of the Times before the *Conquest*, says, That the Reason of his employing himself in Things so remote was, to chase out of his Thoughts the present Times, which were not worthy of his Pen: Their Actions, he says, were so *petty*, so beneath all History, that he could not bear to treat of them. Sir *William Temple* too says, That the publick Affairs before 1660 were so full of Madness, that he could not think of engaging in them.
>
> Now, if, by the Testimony of these two Authors, which no Party will refuse upon this Occasion, the Times we are speaking of were so *petty*, so *beneath all History*, so full of Madness, were they not a fit Subject for a *Travestie*? Were they not the proper Object of Burlesque? Was it not a proper Burial for a Scene of *Pettiness, Putidness* Madness and Inconsistency?[19]

The times were too contemptible for heroic treatment. Butler wrote in his Note-Books, 'if any man should but imitate what these Heroical Authors write in the Practice of his life and Conversation, he would become the most Ridiculous Person in the world, but this Age is far enough from that, for though none ever abounded more with those Images (as they call them) of Moral and Heroicall Virtues, there was never any so opposite to them all in the mode and Custome of Life'.[20] Milton withdrew from the present into history, and later again into *Paradise Lost*, showing a better ethic than the one man had followed. Butler dealt with the times – but dealt with them in their contemptibility. He offered no better ethos, but was concerned to show the absurdity of the existing one. Butler claimed, after all, that the basic incident of *Hudibras* was true: 'As for ye Story I had it from ye Knts owne Mouth, & is farr from being feign'd, yt it is upon Record, for there was a Svite of Law upon it betweene ye Knt, & ye Fidler, in wch ye Knt was overthrowne to his great shame, & discontent, for wch he left ye Countrey & came up to

Settle at London'.[21] If the event was true that was comment enough on the degeneration of the times: that was one reason why the traditional heroic was no longer a possible form. Heroes were never of any real ethical worth according to Butler; but by the seventeenth century even the small distinction they had was lost: 'A Hero was nothing but a fellow of a great Stature, and strong Limbes, who was able to carry a heavier Load of Armes on his Back, and strike harder Blows, then those of a lesser Size. And therefor since the Invention of Guns came up, there can be no true Hero in great Fights, for all mens Abilitys are so leveld by Gun-shot, that a Dwarf may do as heroique Feats of Armes that way as a Gyant. And if he be a good Markesman, be too hard for the stoutest Hector and Achilles too.'[22] Judged by the old code the present times are contemptible; but the old heroic code is, judged by the realities of the recent war, contemptible too. Milton and Butler seem to have been in accord on these positions.

An essential part of Milton's critique of the traditional heroic was the provision of an alternative. Christ provides the example for Adam to follow. In the concluding books Michael offers Adam instruction. Is *Hudibras* in contrast utterly negative? In allowing Hudibras and Ralph no redeeming features and in introducing no acceptable new heroism is Butler offering nothing?

In the public field he certainly offers nothing. Butler's view of the public world, Interregnum or Restoration, seems to have been one of sardonic despair. Yet the final impression of *Hudibras* is not one of utter nihilism. For what comes through, despite Hudibras's maraudings, is an impression of the richness of everyday, private life, the rich texture of rural life. Where else in English literature of this period do we find so full an awareness of the nature of everyday life, of the popular diversions and amusements, of the rich store of proverbial wisdom, of the traditional balladry? Sir Philip Sidney mentioned *Chevy Chase*: Butler paraphrases a couplet from it and his mention is perhaps only the second mention in literary contexts of that famous ballad.[23] Grey's notes show a whole range of popular ballads and ditties and stories that Butler alludes to. He alludes also to a huge wealth of popular amusements: besides bear-baiting there are mentions of mountebanks, travelling monsters at fairs, football, kite-flying, whipping-tops, puppet plays; such games as blindman's buff, ducks-and-drakes; such customs as the skim-mington; there is the traditional lore and superstition about animals – hares changing sex, crows smelling powder, foxes weighing the geese they carry; and the continual animal imagery goes to establish a full, rich, rural England, a hinter-land of reference behind the Hudibrastic absurdities; there are the traditional superstitions about astrology, witchcraft, will-o'-the-wisps; and there are the innumerable proverbs. Especially noticeable are the foods – *Hudibras* is a culinary repository of the seventeenth century, the best indication of what was eaten – porridge, plum porridge, black puddings, mincepies, custard, toasted cheese, lobster, bacon, leeks, onions, bread-and-cheese, white-pot, buttermilk, curds, ale.

It is this everyday, rural England that Butler cumulatively establishes; and much of his hostility to the Puritans comes from their attempts to suppress and reform tradition, their dictator-ship of foods:

> Quarrel with *minc'd Pies*, and disparage
> Their best and dearest friend, *Plum-porredge*;
> Fat *Pig* and *Goose* it self oppose,
> And blaspheme *Custard* thro' the *nose*.
>
> [I, i, 225-228]

their dictatorship of holidays:

> And some against th' *Ægyptian Bondage*,
> Of *Holy-days* . . .
>
> [III, ii, 285-286]

He is opposed both to the silliness of proscribing certain foods and to the limiting and narrowing of the richness of the tradi-tional life.

Butler's positive values are only implicit. But it is this rich texture of rural life he draws on for his imagery, for the establishment of his world. It is the private, non-political, domestic life. Not the self-conscious Horatian retirement of Marvell and Cowley but the non-aristocratic, rural world of the small farmer, the private world of domesticity. Just as Milton's epic rejects the heroic grandeur of Satan's Hell in favour of the domestic simplicities of Adam and Eve, so Butler rejects the heroic values. Milton establishes Adam and Eve in a bliss of simplicity; in our first encounter with them we see them pick fruit:

> The savourie pulp they chew, and in the rinde
> Still as they thirsted scoop the brimming stream;
> [IV, 335-336]

The famous comment, 'No fear lest Dinner cool', is a positive note in the establishment of this domestic simplicity. And although the Fall has changed things considerably these private, domestic values remain with Adam and Eve. Michael tells Adam he will find 'a paradise within thee, happier farr' [XII, 587]. Paradise is to be sought privately, individually: it is not to be imposed on others by military tyranny or any other coercion but to be sought by the individual within himself. For both Milton and Butler, happiness came to be seen as residing not in military glory, noisy public splendour: nor in literary 're-tirement'; but in the everyday, the domestic. The epic had to be wrenched from its old ethos for this view to be expressed. Nor did it revive again in England. Others wrote, or began, epics – Blackmore completed some fourteen. But none ever achieved the success, none ever achieved the vast readerships, of *Paradise Lost* and *Hudibras*. The two most popular, most read, epic poems in English both rejected the old epic values.

NOTES

1. The fullest consideration of Milton's rejection of the epic values is John M. Steadman, *Milton and the Renaissance Hero* (Oxford, 1967). This theme is also discussed in T. J. B. Spencer, '*Paradise Lost*: The Anti-Epic', *Approaches to 'Paradise Lost'*, ed. C. A. Patrides (London, 1968), pp. 81-98. The studies of Davis P. Harding and Arnold Stein cited below support this general argument.

John Wilders in his recent edition of *Hudibras* (Oxford, 1967) complains that 'in *Hudibras* both epic and romance are parodied in-discriminately' [p. xxxiv]. But Steadman points out that 'Renaissance heroic tradition comprised the romance as well as the epic. . . . Literary frontiers had yet to be definitively drawn, and the question of their demarcation was provoking acrimonious debate among such theorists as Pigna and Giraldi, Tasso and Scaliger. . . . Thus, for many critics, the epic tradition embraced the romance tradition almost in its entirety' [Steadman, op. cit., pp. 109, 110]. In attacking the values of the heroic tradition it is appropriate that Milton and Butler should refer both to epic and to romance.

2. Quoted in Austin Dobson, *Eighteenth Century Vignettes: Third Series* (London, 1923), p. 19.

3. Butler has an attack on Milton in 'Fragments of an Intended Second Part of the Foregoing Satire' (i.e., 'Satire upon the Imperfection and Abuse of Human Learning'), ll. 141-152. Butler satirizes Milton's emphasis on his opponent's errors of Latin style rather than concern with the theme of regicide in his controversy with Salmasius. (In Butler's *Poetical Works*, ed. G. Gilfillan [Edinburgh, 1854], II, 235; and *Milton: The Critical Heritage*, ed. J. T. Shawcross [London, 1970], p. 76.)

William Somervile attempted a burlesque juncture of the two styles in a brief poem 'Hudibras *and* Milton *reconciled*' (in his *Occasional Poems, Translations, Fables, Tables,* &c [London, 1727], pp. 93-96). The poet writing random octosyllabics of scatological analogies to the difficulty of writing poetry is disturbed, at one in the morning, by a Miltonic, blank-verse thunderstorm; and then returning to octosyllabics,

> I piss'd, thrice shook my giddy Head,
> Let a great F—t, and went to Bed.

4. All quotations from Milton are from the text of B. A. Wright, *Milton's Poems* (Everyman Library, 1956).

5. All quotations from *Hudibras* are from the text of John Wilders (Oxford, 1967). References to 'Grey' are to the two-volume edition of Zachary Grey (Cambridge, 1744).

6. Arnold Stein, *Answerable Style* (Minneapolis, 1953), p. 37.

7. Samuel Butler, *Characters and Passages from Note-books*, ed. A. R. Waller (Cambridge, 1908), p. 278.

8. Butler, p. 469.

9. See, for instance, John M. Steadman, *Milton and the Renaissance Hero*, Davis P. Harding, *The Club of Hercules: Studies in the Classical Background of 'Paradise Lost'* (Urbana, 1962), Michael Wilding, *Milton's 'Paradise Lost'* (Sydney, 1969).

10. *Hudibras*, ed. Zachary Grey (Cambridge, 1744), I, 339, n.

11. *Aeneid*, VII, 783-784; see Davis P. Harding, *The Club of Hercules*, p. 45.

12. Zachary Grey, *Notes to Hudibras* (London, 1752), p. 31. I have normalized the quotation from *Paradise Lost* to B. A. Wright's text.

13. Grey, *Hudibras*, I, 78.

14. E. C. Baldwin in 'A Suggestion for a New Edition of Butler's *Hudibras*', PMLA, XXVI (1911), 528-548, sees hypocrisy as the central topic of the poem. Butler 'scourged hypocrisy of every form . . .' [p. 531]; 'that the *Hudibras* is a satire upon hypocrisy exemplified in typical representatives of the society of the seventeenth century, rather than merely an attack upon an already vanquished political party, is clearly shown by even a casual reading of the *Characters*' [p. 533].

15. See David Daiches, 'The Opening of *Paradise Lost*', in *The Living Milton*, ed. Frank Kermode (London, 1960, p. 63).

16. Grey, *Hudibras*, I, 2, n.

17. Stein, op. cit.

18. Milton's turning in *Paradise Lost* to the 'paradise within' has been often enough remarked – e.g., E. M. W. Tillyard, *Milton* (London, 1930), pp. 292-293. Milton's pacifism in *Paradise Lost*, however, has been obscured by the assumption that the indubitably Old Testament and militaristic *Samson Agonistes* was written afterwards. Consequently the pacifist themes have been neglected in favour of others that seemed to show a continuity with *Samson Agonistes*. But, as W. R. Parker argues in his *Milton: A Biography* (Oxford, 1968), 2 vols., 'not a scrap of evidence has ever been published to show that it [i.e., *Samson Agonistes*] was written late in Milton's life. Late *publication* proves nothing, suggests nothing; other early works . . . were published late' (pp. 903-904). Parker's suggested date of 1647 for the commencement of the poem (pp. 313, 903-917) accords with the development of Milton's ideas.

An incipient distaste for war and military methods emerges strikingly in Milton's two sonnets to military commanders. He addresses Fairfax in 1648:

> For what can Warr but endless warr still breed,
> Till Truth and Right from Violence be freed;

and in 1652 he addresses Cromwell:

> yet much remaines
> To conquer still; peace hath her victories
> No less renownd than warr.

Neither of these sonnets rejects a military solution. Such a rejection
did not come easily to Milton. But both of them offer a qualification.
The process of thought leading to *Paradise Lost* is developing.

Much later, the item in the errata of the first edition of *Paradise
Regained* (London, 1671), 'for "destroy" read "subdue" ', catches the
Christian quandary and Milton's post-Restoration sensitivity to
violence. Christ is explaining his youthful sense of vocation:

> yet this not all
> To which my Spirit aspir'd, victorious deeds
> Flam'd in my heart, heroic acts, one while
> To rescue *Israel* from the *Roman* yoke,
> Thence to subdue and quell ore all the earth
> Brute violence and proud Tyrannic power,
> Yet truth were freed, and equity restor'd:
> Yet held it more humane, more heav'nly first
> By winning words to conquer willing hearts,
> And make persuasion do the work of fear;
> At least to try, and teach the erring Soul
> Not wilfully misdoing, but unware
> Misled: the stubborn only to *destroy*.
>
> [I, 214-226]

'*Destroy*' is the word of Satan the 'destroyer', the word of military
solutions. Milton replaces it. The whole passage walks on a tightrope,
trying to stress how Christ will end military tyrannies, yet trying to
avoid the impression that he destroys them by similar, military means.
Perhaps the temptation to respond to 'brute violence' by brute
violence led the old regicide into letting Christ offer to 'destroy'.
Whatever the cause, however, Milton then took pains to *correct* the
line. The alteration to 'subdue' is an alteration by a man who has
grown very sensitive to the issues of war, of militarism, to the dangers
of enforcing the morally right by evil means.

19. Grey, *Notes*, pp. 4-5.

20. *Characters and Passages from Note-books*. p. 278.

21. See Ricardo Quintana, 'The Butler-Oxenden Correspondence',
in *Modern Language Notes*, XLVIII (1933), 1-11, 486.

22. *Characters and Passages*, p. 468.

23. I, iii, 95-96.

Thomas Traherne:
Intellect and Felicity

FRANCIS KING

> I saw moreover that it did not so much concern us what Objects
> were before us, as with what Eys we beheld them; with what
> Affections we esteemed them, and what Apprehensions we had
> about them.
>
> [*Centuries*, III, 68]

> When you think not of these Things you are in the Dark.
>
> [*Centuries*, IV, 94]

Traherne's originality is not originality of thought but of procedure – he does not carry ideas forward to a new synthesis or a
deeper analysis but uses them, as they are, as the stuff of
spiritual experience. He does not move beyond the ideas of
God and the world already available to him, yet he has the
freedom of those ideas, transforming all in an intellectually
irresponsible but spiritually accurate way into the house of
felicity. 'You never Enjoy the World aright, till you see all
things in it so perfectly yours, that you cannot desire them any
other Way' [*Centuries*, I, 38].

The main recent critical activity has been to trace parallels
between Traherne and the intellectual tradition on which he
draws. The more one reads in this tradition, the more hypnotic
this finding of parallels becomes; Traherne's mind moves
through the recollected statements of a very wide range of
Philosophers and Divines and proceeds by familiar patterns of
argumentation and meditation until one seems to be moving
around a whispering gallery of familiar voices.

Yet it is surprisingly difficult to pin him down to any particular source. In *The Paradise Within*, Louis L. Martz makes illuminating parallels between Traherne's *Centuries* and Augustinian theme, style, and method of meditation, but ends tentatively: 'One can say no more than this: the principles of Augustine seem to have formed the nucleus around which all the literature of Platonism, pagan and Christian, gathered to help Traherne create his own original exploration of the mind'.[1] And, turning to St Bonaventura's handbook for clear patterns of meditation, he says: 'Used with caution, the *Itinerarium* can throw considerable light upon the progress of the *Centuries*' – as indeed it does.

Similarly, after her detailed comparison between the ideas of Traherne and of the Cambridge Platonists, Carol L. Marks ends her gathering of parallels by saying: 'Just when he seems like a typical Christian Platonist, he overleaps the boundary with a fit of idiosyncratic daring. . . . The impress of his personality, of his informed intuition, is such that the portrait of his intellect evades labels. He remains what he was: an original.'[2]

What therefore seems worth attention, now that the main parallels have been clearly drawn, is Traherne's imaginative process; and that, for all its careful orthodoxy of ideas, follows its own laws and 'evades labels', digesting all into the action of felicity. It is this that makes him an original in the only sense a mystic might allow – not one who has produced a new idea, a new shadow, but one who has raised all thinking into a conversation with the divine.

Miss Marks, in her final paragraph, presents the curious picture of Traherne 'arriving at his personal philosophy through youthful reflection', then, in his mature years, reinforcing 'his early intuition' with study. I can see no reason to think Traherne arrived at any 'personal philosophy' separately from his learned studies, which began early enough, and the 'fit of idiosyncratic daring' which makes her paint this picture, is the claim, in *Sight*, that the inward eye

> . . . . can pry
> Into the End
> To which things tend,
> And all the Depths descry
> That God and Nature do include.

> By this are view'd
> The very Ground and Caus
> Of sacred Laws.
>
>   [ll. 63-70]

This is not a personal intuition, a piece of philosophical daring reaching to the edge of heresy – it is a commonplace of mystical literature, typical of the stage of Illumination[3] in which Traherne mainly rests.[4] Miss Marks is right in saying that his 'informed intuition . . . evades labels' but it is not by inventing any new idea that carries him beyond the particular intellectual system we have found him using. Personal intuition has priority over learning not in the sense of youthful and original ideas controlling and superseding mature study but in the way the pressing mystical intuition, the Infant Eye, uses with abandon a variety of orthodox ideas, not to their usual end of defined belief but as the material for rebuilding divine Knowledge. 'My Knowledg was Divine; I knew by Intuition those things which since my Apostasie, I Collected again, by the Highest Reason' [*Centuries*, III, 2]. The highest reason is the tool of divine recollection, the world of intellect is subjected, not to its own laws but to the rebuilding of the Infant Eye.

The common critical comment on Traherne's possible heretical tendencies is a misunderstood reaction to this thoroughly unorthodox use to which he subjects the respectable and carefully-hedged world of ideas. It is the imaginative and spiritual process of his 'informed intuition' that I want to investigate more closely, both on the autobiographical journey from Apostacy to Felicity and in the present circle of his joys.

I think we may take it as a fact of Traherne's development – and not *just* a projection onto childhood of a spiritual theory – that his early experience of everything 'at rest, Free, and Immortal' was either unusually powerful or (if we all trail clouds of glory) less overlaid by the acquired ignorance that accompanies the child. At any rate, the child's experience of unity with the known remained more operative in him than in most of us; even in his 'Apostasie', it operated close to consciousness as the cause and end of desire. The question Traherne asks, at the beginning of the *Centuries*, of 'the friend of my best friend', 'Do you not feel your self Drawn with the Expectation and Desire of som Great Thing?' is clearly a reflection of his own experience. (At the beginning of the third Century, he tacitly admits that the 'Divine Light wherewith [he] was born' was an unusual privilege, when he exhorts Mrs Hopton to 'Pray for (Those Pure and Virgin Apprehensions) earnestly'. We may all have the desire of happiness but the urgency and all-pervasiveness of Traherne's 'Desire of som Great Thing' is clearly his special 'Gift of God'.) Even when, 'Swallowed up . . . in the Miserable Gulph of idle talk and worthless vanities . . . [he] lived among Shadows', he would, he says in *Centuries*, III, 15, 'com a litle to my self · so far as to feel I wanted som thing, . . . to long after an unknown Happiness'.

But the vague longings of subconscious memories of felicity do not carry us, or him, very far towards his characteristic mature vision. Though they come first in time and priority, they would not achieve maturity or even recover effectiveness without taking thought. Clearly enough Traherne turned to the traditional spiritual teaching of his time – or, rather, since he began so early, the tradition he knew offered concepts for fulfilment which the memory could adopt or censor. 'Once I remember (I think I was about 4 yeer old, when) I thus reasoned with my self . . . If there be a God, certainly He must be infinit in Goodness. And that I was prompted to, by a real Whispering Instinct of Nature.' The piece of ratiocination embedded in the reminiscence is the voice of the author rather than that of the '4 yeer old' but to put it this way shows a sure instinct. A post-Romantic might claim that 'a real Whispering Instinct of Nature' showed the child God's nature – 'God being with thee when we know it not'. Traherne, more plausibly, I think, implies that the traditional formulation of a truth is the pre-requisite, to be ratified by the recognition given by intuition. The instinct may prompt, as a desire for some unknown thing, but the formulation, offered by the ratiocinative mind and its accumulated tradition, must be produced for intuition to re-cognize itself or even to become aware that Instinct *is* Whisper-ing. To whisper, even instinct must be given words, agents not created spontaneously by need but given meaning by the tradition of intellect.

Yet the overt statement in the above quotation is, at first

glance, the Romantic claim that nature whispered the goodness of God, even though that information comes across in a thoroughly traditional piece of reasoning. This ambivalent presentation of the logical order of events reigns over the whole of Traherne's meditational work. The sentence I have already quoted – 'I knew by Intuition those things which, since my Apostasie, I Collected again, by the Highest Reason' – only carries the meaning I have given it, that is, the priority of intuition in the process of recollection, when it is seen in the context of the previous meditation: 'Those Pure and Virgin Apprehensions . . . attended me into the World and . . . I remember them till now . . . without them all other Gifts had been Dead' [*Centuries*, III, 1].

Without this initial statement that childhood was a continuing influence, the second meditation would, in fact, deny the influence of the original Intuition in the process of Recollection and suggest that the independent process of the Highest Reason collected again those things which constitute Divine Knowledge. The two attitudes to Recollection, the priorities of 'Intuition' and 'Reason', seem to exist side by side, logically distinct yet handled without apparent awareness of contradiction.

This ambivalence is perhaps further evidence of Traherne's debt to St Augustine. M. J. Charlesworth says: 'Augustine did not want to be a "rationalist" denying the proper autonomy of faith, any more than he wanted to be a naive fideist denying the autonomy of reason, and the strain represented by "crede ut intelligas" and that by "intellige ut credas" exist together in his thought in an unresolved or ambivalent state'.[5] The early memory and later felicity seem for Traherne to displace or swallow up faith (that 'sure foretaste of truth not yet manifested'[6]) but the parallel remains.

For Traherne at least, however, the unresolved presentation of the priority of 'Intuition' and 'Reason' is not a fault but a characteristic. What we find in his imagination is a practical co-operation of the two faculties in a union that sidesteps the whole perennial controversy. (It says something for his essential balance in an unbalanced age that, in spite of his demands for 'more evident results from the grace of God than we others', he nevertheless neatly fits Ronald Knox's description

of the 'ordinary believing Christian' in whom 'the two principles
of reason and revelation are interlocked'. 'The theologian',
Knox continues, 'will sort them out and delimit their spheres for
you, but in everyday life there is an unconscious give and take
which regulates your thought without friction.'[7])

Traherne's work is a fulfilment of the promising four-year-
old's procedure. The autobiographical element suggests that,
from that early age, the same pattern persists: 'in the midst of
dreams', coming a little to himself, he would turn to the common
thoughts and theological doctrines about God for truths in
which he might recognize the Truth known by him in Infancy.
The most commonplace cliché could become agent for the
recollection of himself into Angel Infancy. The 'Pure and
Virgin Apprehensions', remaining operative though unknown,
would choose whatever dead statement offered passage into
consciousness: 'without them all other Gifts had been Dead'.
But the statements must be found by study, by the intellect,
though felicity was the impetus, the 'Infant Ey' the judge of
what found statements were useful.

Of course, the process of reawakening was gradual – the brief
tentativeness of its beginnings is caught in the sentence 'Yet
sometimes in the midst of these Dreams, I should com a litle to
my self'. But the procedure did operate even before felicity was
achieved; we are presented with the picture of Traherne, even
in the 'Miserable Gulph', being guided to those beliefs necessary
for the eventual possession of God in the world even when they
did not demonstrate their truth by the immediate achievement
of felicity. In meditations 17 and 18 of the third Century, for
example, we find the still un-recollected Traherne suddenly im-
pelled to the kind of meditations on the World and on Creation
which later were to be the most complete and transparent
mediums of the achieved felicity. 'Som times I should be alone,
and without Employment, when suddainly my Soul would
return to it self, and forgetting all Things in the whole World
which mine Eys had seen, would be carried away to the Ends
of the Earth: and my Thoughts would be deeply Engaged with
Enquiries, How the Earth did End? Whether Walls did
Bound it. . . . Little did I think that the Earth was Round, and
the World so full of Beauty, Light and Wisdom.' We sense
clearly in the autobiographical passages a profound impulsion

to reach a particular but as yet unknown vision of the Universe, an impulsion issuing in a deep engagement of Thought in Enquiries that may find out the concepts capable of releasing the satisfying Enjoyment. The end of such Enquiries is implied in Traherne's continual juxtaposition of these memories of desolate searching with the later satisfied vision that fulfills them; the last sentence of the above passage recalls us to the present of the *Centuries*, and the apparently factual enquiries (the beginnings of the thread of scientific investigation that runs through Traherne's vision of the world), exhaust themselves into the regained knowledge of an Earth that is not only round but 'full of Beauty, Light and Wisdom'. 'When I saw that, I knew by the Perfection of the Work there was a GOD, and was satisfied, and Rejoyced'. Despite the form of his thinking, Traherne was engaged not in scientific enquiry but in the compulsive search for material for felicity: these questions are answered not by mere roundness but by perfection and satisfaction.

A later stage of the process of finding the forms for felicity appears in his early *Meditations on the Six Days of Creation*. One must agree with Miss Wade in saying this was 'written before felicity was attained'[8] – it lacks the ringing, musical tone that penetrates the *Centuries* like the sound of the numinous and is written from the point of view of faith and hope, not felicity. But its relationship with the regained vision is close – it is like the ground-plan and detailed drawings about to be executed. 'Consider how poor and naked the World and thou hadst been without these Treasures, and value them accordingly. Never therefore behold it, but with Wonder and Gratitude, presume not to enjoy it till thou first prize its infinite Value; and offer thy Thanksgiving for it. Look upon it with Delight, consider it with Wisdom.'[9] The process of enquiry has found the form and detail most closely suited – though it had to fetch them from afar, the Hexaemeron being a rare oddity in the seventeenth century.[10] Miss Marks, at the beginning of her article referred to above, remarks on his 'eclectic intellect and – more important in shaping Traherne's persistent individuality – original, highly personal feelings'. The two elements of his individuality should be much more closely associated than such a statement implies, since the eclecticism of such a choice of literary kind is what finds a voice for and offers self-knowledge to the felicity-directed feelings. The choice of the Hexaemeron, a form that sets his imagination in exactly the stance for the 'Enjoyment' of the world, is an interesting example of the way 'the first Light which shined in my Infancy in its Primitive and Innocent Clarity' sought for expression, even in remote countries of learning and even when still engulfed in forgetfulness.

The end of this process is not instant ecstasy, that is to say, silence. In *Centuries*, IV, 11, Traherne writes: 'That Maxim also which your Friend used, is of very Great and Divine Concernment: *I will first spend a great deal of time in Seeking Happiness, and then a Great deal more in Enjoying it*'.

So far I have been extracting the autobiographical element from the *Centuries*, the search for felicity and the curious process by which the lost childhood and the labours of intellect 'interinanimate' each other on the long climb from the gulf. But the *Centuries* are written from the point of view of achieved Happiness; in all the major works, the autobiography of search is contained within the activity of Enjoyment. From having been, in actuality, a thing of infinite difficulty, the laborious study becomes, as a retrospect, part of the activity of Happiness: 'To be satisfied in God is the Highest Difficulty in the whole World. And yet most easy to be don. To make it possible that we should be satisfied in GOD was an Attchievment of infinit Weight, before it was attempted, and the most difficult Thing in all Worlds before it was Attchieved. . . . But it is most Easy at present, becaus GOD is' [*Centuries*, III, 63].

Though there is a radical change when we expand our view from the remembered past to the writer's present – the change from the activities of longing to satisfaction – the enjoyment of Happiness is also an intense mental activity and of the same kind.

Traherne's stress on the soul as 'all Act' appears ubiquitously:

> My Naked Simple Life was I.
>   That Act so Strongly Shind
> Upon the Earth, the Sea, the Skie,
> It was the Substance of My Mind.
>
> ['My Spirit', ll. 1-4]

But this is the pure spiritual Act of Infancy, the Act whose glorious memory and potentiality lead him to study Divinity, as we have seen. The action of continued enjoyment of Happiness is different. The 'Act' of 'Simple Life' needs no contribution from learning – Traherne compares it explicitly in the same stanza of 'My Spirit' to the 'Deitie', who can hardly be thought to indulge in scholarship or even to search (the prerogative of man in the great chain of being). And it would be not unreasonable to expect the labour of recollection to issue, on its successful resolution, into such pure apprehensiveness. The 'Ease' of the 'Attchievment', we might expect, would be the pure, effortless Infant Eye regained, and, at his worst, Traherne does try to give a direct expression of that state, un-distanced by transference to childhood or by mature thought:

> Ah me! tis all the Glory, Love, Light, Space,
>   Joy Beauty and Varietie
> That doth adorn the Godheads Dwelling Place.
>
> ['The Vision', ll. 3-5]

Though we may suppose Traherne had such moments (notoriously difficult to describe and conducive to banal commonplaces of language), and though they remained the central life of his sphere of joys, without which all other gifts had been dead and his writing barren of the accents of felicity, the *activity* of felicity is an intense and learned activity, rather than pure Act. Like the search for happiness, its practice depends on conventional intellectual material and patterns of thought to maintain the stance of Felicity: hence the literary product.

For example, the quality of the description of the 'Naked Simple Life' quoted above, lies in its intellectual and imaginative precision, the concentrated product of conceptual thought working on living memory. It is this conjunction that radiates felicity, not the flaccid exclamations about Glory, Love, Light, Space, which seem a betrayal of the act of 'Life'. It is the continuing process of ranging thought that seems to provide the proper vehicle for continuing 'Happiness' – what was essential to the finding remains essential to the keeping. 'To be satisfied in GOD is [not "was"] the Highest Difficulty in the whole World. . . . But it is most Easy at present, because GOD is'.

Traherne, at times, talks as though it is just the regaining of the 'infant Ey' that the adult needs (it is a parallel confusion of ideas to his ambivalence over 'Instinct' and 'Reason'). But clearly, in practice, once the infant's completely unself-conscious, that is, unverbal identification with, and hence spiritu-alization of the world, is gone into the 'Gulph of Idle Talk', it is only the labour of self-consciousness, operating through the tools of intellect, learning to control 'Talk', that can find and hold the stance that practises happiness. One instance in which he does clearly recognize the distinction between infant and adult per-ception of the eternal is the rather bad poem 'The Improvment' (and bad without his brother's help). At the end, however, the poem shows Improvment when he comes a little to himself and admits that in childhood he

> had not yet the Eye
> The Apprehension, or Intelligence
> Of Things so very Great Divine and High,
>
> .   .   .   .   .
>
> All these were unperceivd, yet did appear:
> Not by Reflexion, and Distinctly known,
> But, by their Efficacy, all mine own.

This addition of self-conscious intellect, of reflection and distinct knowledge, to the 'Infant Ey' is no slight thing. The 'Naked, Simple Life', by becoming sharply thoughtful, is quite trans-formed. The 'Infant Ey' is not relationship but identity; once this stage is lost, any felicity must depend on right relationships, and it is the basic principle of Traherne's recovered felicity that perfect enjoyment is a deliberate relationship with God, a co-operation in the circle of gifts and praises. It is not just that maturity adds the distinct knowledge of 'Things so very Great Divine and High' to their 'unperceivd' efficacy, but that the adult must construct and adopt and maintain a conscious imaginative stance – that is, a relationship – before the circula-tion of felicity can begin. In 'The Circulation', though the theme is primarily the slightly 'daring' idea that 'Who blesseth must be Blest', there is implied the necessity for continued circulation – we cannot be Blest unless we learn to bless. (To put it in more orthodox terms, true happiness depends on loving the world for God's sake, a learnt qualification of our natural tendency to seize it for ourselves.)

> The Soul a Vessel is
> A Spacious Bosom to Contain
> All the fair Treasures of his Bliss
> Which run like Rivers from, into the Main,
> And all it doth receiv returns again.

It is by our recognition of and conscious colloquy with the source that things again become 'Divine'.

The passage I have quoted earlier from the *Meditations on the Six Days of Creation* makes the principle even clearer. The early experience must become conscious valuation and thanksgiving before you can enjoy the world again. For Traherne, the practice of orthodox Christian thought gave the material, the stance for this active spiritual life.

I have been stressing the importance of thought and learning in Traherne's spiritual organization while trying to bring out the peculiar function it has for him. The spiritual state characteristic of Traherne is so vivid and dominating that it embraces and transforms the ratiocination on which it depends; and when the system of ideas suffering transformation is a carefully orthodox Christian belief, the unorthodoxy of his treatment of the intellectual tradition gains contrast. What was designed in full belief becomes just a useful imaginative tool.

If his thinking had been a vague, eclectic spume blowing on the ghostly paradigm of his engulfed 'childhood', as on a Platonic Idea, until it became visible and therefore consciously operative, we might easily accept its content just as transparent metaphor rather than belief; Yeats's intellectual system was clearly a self-defining fantasy of this sort, the creation of a 'Vision' of things that could hold his imagination in the stance he needed. Traherne, however, is treating the formulations of strict belief, the Truths for whose truth men defined and died, with the same intellectual irresponsibility as Yeats his personal fancies.

Again, if he had turned for models to more typically mystical literature, the rhapsodists of Illumination, we could easily accept such a symbolic handling of customary Christian language.

In their descriptions of experience, the criteria of objective truth, and the language and forms of thinking for belief, are patently transcended as being, for the moment, irrelevant. Traherne, however, typically turns to this language and these forms – the language and forms of belief and its ramifications in theology and ethics – but with his mind on, as it were, the 'Beatifick Vision'. The whole process has a transparency which at its best opens our eyes to the orient and immortal world; at its worst, it results in empty Christian cliché, vacant panes. (How conscious Traherne was of this peculiar use of belief is a difficult question to answer; and whether Traherne would have realized a more literal substance in his statements about God if he had attained the further mystical stage of union, must remain an hypothesis.)

In *Centuries*, III, 59, we see a striking example of this double process – an ostentatiously rationalizing scholastic manner wrapping up ideas about God in the forms of logical satisfaction and somehow thereby releasing the mind into spiritual satisfaction at the same time. (Earlier in the third Century, Traherne has spoken of 'These Liquid Clear Satisfactions . . . the Emanations of the Highest Reason'. The word 'Satisfaction' is useful to him, since it applies ambivalently to the conclusion of a logical process and to an emotional state. The 'Highest Reason' comes to seem like ordinary logic working miracles.)

> The Image of God implanted in us, guided me to the maner wherin we were to Enjoy · for since we were made in the similitud of God, we were made to Enjoy after his Similitude. Now to Enjoy the Treasures of God in the Similitud of God, is the most perfect Blessedness God could Devise. For the Treasures of GOD are the most Perfect Treasures and the Maner of God is the most perfect Maner. To Enjoy therfore the Treasures of God after the similitud of God is to Enjoy the most perfect Treasures in the most Perfect Maner. Upon which I was infinitly satisfied in God, and knew there was a Dietie, becaus I was Satisfied.

In *Centuries*, III, 60, Traherne refers to this 'Satisfaction' as a 'Spectacle', a 'Sight of Happiness', and 'a Great Part of the Beatifick Vision'. It marks, I think, the point of conversion from 'Difficultie' to ease, from Apostacy to Felicity; it seems to me typically queer that such a piece of reasoning should be blessed with spiritual power, should open the mind to the 'conversation of God'.

Nicholas of Cusa, in *De Docta Ignorantia*, says: 'The relationship of our intellect to the truth is like that of a polygon to a
circle; the resemblance to the circle grows with the multiplication of the angles of the polygon; but apart from its being
reduced to identity with the circle, no multiplication, even if it
were infinite, of its angles will make the polygon equal the
circle'.[11] Nicholas of Cusa shows a process similar to Traherne's
continual reasoning in the presence of God, but as this quotation
shows, it is always a reasoning that seeks to defeat itself by
pointing to the leap of ignorance necessary to make the circle. In
Traherne there seems to us a curious disparity between the
labours of intellection and the satisfaction that is a 'Great
Part of the Beatifick Vision' but it is not the gap that needs a
leap. The patterned arguments about 'similitudes' and 'maners'
lead him directly into his happiness. The disparity is not the
traditional incongruence between the labouring intellect and the
felicitous soul, but a difference between the kind of knowledge
such argument proves in its own terms and the kind of knowledge into which, by his special use, it releases Traherne.

The diffuseness of effect which we find so distracting or
anaesthetizing in reading Traherne at length[12] comes from this
disparity between the not very impressive intellectual proceeding we are asked to go through and the sense of a potent
spiritual calling trying to transform this proceeding into a
different kind of experience, a literal one, and succeeding only
fitfully. For Traherne, in actuality, it may have been true that
'Having these Principles, nothing was more easy then to enjoy
the world . . .'.[13] but we are more likely to agree with: 'One
thing he saw, which is not commonly discerned; and that is,
that God made Man a free Agent for his own Advantage; and
left him in the hand of his own Counsel, that he might be the
more Glorious. *It is hard to conceiv* [my italics] how much this
tended to his Satisfaction.'[14]

It is difficult to conceive until one realizes that, for Traherne,
argumentation is not a separate, solid thing that can even be
thought to prove the truths of the spirit (as it still can in
Nicholas of Cusa, since he denies it). The remembered experience pressing for fulfilment, the present felicity, do not
demand proof but a form in which to acquiesce and find themselves. Traherne is 'satisfied in God' because he has discovered

K

the formula which conforms his mind to the stance of blessedness, and the element of conventional belief operating in such a passage as meditation 59 is just the final layer of mind finding its appropriate transparency.

One cannot but feel that, however much the *Centuries* are 'Augustinian, in theme, in style, in method of meditation',[15] there is little of the rigorously demanding understanding that hounded St Augustine on his journey towards and his exploration of his faith. The arguments that satisfy Traherne are not proofs, either in the sense of patent demonstration or in the sense of tests; if they are proofs, it is only in the sense of 'the proof of the pudding is in the eating', as the proof of the above passage lies not in the intellectual conclusiveness of the demonstration but in the satisfaction into which he is released by 'believing'. Though for St Augustine intellection was ultimately support for the faith, it was much more of a load-bearing member of the structure, in its own terms of reasonable demonstration. The gaps of logic and the triteness of the forms of reasoning in Traherne, which nevertheless led by understandable motions of the spirit to the knowledge that God exists, are foreign to St Augustine.

A good example of Traherne's way with beliefs is to be found in his discussion of 'Whether it be the Soul it self, or God in the Soul, that shines by Lov, or both', in *Centuries*, IV, 83-85. He completes that opening question by saying 'it is difficult to tell: but certainly the Lov of the Soul is the sweetest Thing in the world'. And his subsequent exploration of the two, to-the-reason mutually exclusive possibilities does not try to resolve the question but rather to explore the sweetness to be extracted from the temporary assent to each proposition. And, in continuing to play with the idea in meditations 86 and 87, he produces the delightful but hardly definitive resolution of the puzzle in the image of human souls as mirrors with eyelids: 'And were they Mirrors only that return his Lov, one would think it impossible, while he shines upon them, to forbear to shine · but they are like the Ey, Mirrors with Lids, and the Lid of Ignorance or Inconsideration interposing, they are often times Ecclypsed, or shine only through som Cranies'. In 87 he calmly says, 'In the Estate of Misery . . . a Soul lovs freely and purely of its own self, with Gods Lov, things that seem un-capable of Lov, Naught and evil'. By this time he has moved on, in his undefined, undefining way, beyond the problematical opposition of the two possibilities to the unification that is our experience of them. In a sense, the 'mirror with lids' has resolved the problem by carrying us back to our experience where the functioning of the soul is ours *and* divine *and* no problem.

Margaret L. Wiley's description of a 'dominant thought-pattern of many outstanding thinkers of the Late Renaissance'[16] may light up the principle behind this practice of Traherne. 'What one could not rationally puzzle out (because of man's inescapable nescience) might be lived out, and by doing, one might come at last to know' (the original formulation being left as a paradox). I quote from her chapter on the Cambridge Platonists who, like Traherne, play down the bitterness of 'man's inescapable nescience' and of the sting of paradox. Miss Wiley goes on to speak of their 'diminished awareness of and lamentation concerning man's nescience and a strong tendency when reconciling dualisms to end up with something less tense and quivering than paradox. In other words, the conflicts and stresses within man's soul and between him and God are some-how mitigated and glossed over.'[17] This is a fine description of Traherne's way with ideas as I have been examining it, but the weakness we feel in the philosophers, their 'diminished awareness', their glossing-over of stresses, is no weakness in Traherne since the required rigour of thought that is necessary to make valid even the Cambridge Platonists' kind of philosophy is simply irrelevant to Traherne's purposes. His end is achieved when we have a stronger taste of the sweetness of the 'Lov of the Soul'. Man's nescience is not painful to one already resting in felicity – it is, if anything, part of the infinite space within, available for the act and praise of God.

> My Soul doth there long Thoughts extend;
> > No End
> Doth find, or Being comprehend:
> > Yet somwhat sees that is
> > The obscure shady face
> > > Of endless Space,
> > All Room within; where I
> Expect to meet Eternal Bliss.
> > > ['Insatiableness', ll. 23-30]

His treatment of formulated beliefs reminds one of John Smith's famous description of religious truth as 'something rather to be understood by a *Spiritual sensation* than by any *Verbal description*'.[18]

A neat example of Traherne's disarming of paradox is in his conversion of the tense phrase *Docta Ignorantia*, which embodies Nicholas of Cusa's curious stretching towards divine ignorance through subtle thought, into 'A learned and a Happy Ignorance' in the poem 'Eden'. The joined opposition of the phrase is separated or relaxed by the felicity that makes of paradox an easy spiritual performance.

And what does Traherne mean when he says he 'knew there was a Dietie' because he was 'satisfied'? Visionary satisfaction in all the works and contexts of human life was the End for Traherne and it is not only the argumentation but even the dogmas themselves that seem rhetorical tools. In the first sentence of the passage from *Centuries*, III, 59, quoted earlier, he claims that the image of God, implanted in his mind, guided him: a thoroughly orthodox (even Augustinian) statement. But the phrase 'the Image of God' is glossed by its use in the previous meditation, *Centuries*, III, 58: 'In Discovering the Matter or Objects to be Enjoyed, I was greatly aided by remembering that we were made in Gods Image'.

Felicity is Traherne's occupation; beliefs, like the ratiocinative process, are great aids and their meaning is their function. To remember the concept, that we are made in God's image, is to put the faculties in the right stance for Enjoyment. So, in the opening of meditation 59, Traherne is not stating an objective belief but saying effectively, 'to think of myself as the "Image of God" and to let myself enjoy the world through this sense of being "the similitude of God" produced that satisfaction, that "sight of happiness" [*Centuries*, III, 60] which is the only purpose and "proof" of beliefs'. 'Upon this I began to believ . . . that evry Creature is indeed as it seemed in my infancy. . . . Evry Thing being Sublimely Rich and Great and Glorious' [*Centuries*, III, 62] – and we see where all thoughts tend. To know there is a Deity because he is satisfied is to have found an idea that works; the question of the reality of these ideas, which so bothered St Augustine, is not here aroused.

The Christian terminology thus loses its particularity and

weight when even God becomes merely a function of Felicitous human vision. Similarly, when we compare Traherne with other poets, even with such poets as Vaughan and Herbert who have obvious links with him but do not speak from felicity, much of the language and imagery seems transparent. He was conscious of this in the introductory poem found in Philip Traherne's MS.:

> The naked Truth in many faces shewn,
> Whose inward Beauties very few hav known,
> A Simple Light, transparent Words, a Strain
> That lowly creeps, yet maketh Mountains plain,
> Brings down the highest Mysteries to sense
> And keeps them there; that is Our Excellence:
> At that we aim; to th' end thy Soul might see
> With open Eys thy Great *Felicity*,
> Its Objects view, and trace the glorious Way
> Wherby thou may'st thy Highest Bliss enjoy.

Traherne, in his best passages, shows an excellence that justifies this boast – the well-known passages and even passing images that concentrate the tensions and rhythms and accumulated connotations of poetic language into a spiritual sensation:

> I within did flow
> With Seas of Life, like Wine . . .
> ['Wonder', ll. 21-22]

Here the highest mystery is strongly brought to sense in a compression of meanings that is quite startling in one who could emptily go on about tracing 'the glorious Way / Wherby thou may'st thy Highest Bliss enjoy'.

As with the theology so the poetry: it is as though his eye is on the Beatifick Vision from the beginning and does not need the kind of commitment, whether to theological or poetic exploration, that fuses language and thought into something capable of supporting the full weight of the searching imagination. Vaughan and Herbert (and St Augustine) are quite differently dependent on what they can *make*, from the mystical Traherne. Undigested and vapid clichés, descriptive or exclamatory catalogues, hardly-fitted versification, and unassimilated

'Thought' seem to work his end, of supporting felicity, where less 'elevated' writers would flop. The passages of high quality come to seem accidental felicities on the path to Felicity (usually when the argument brings him around to childhood) rather than the climactic moments of meditational advance, as Martz implies.[19]

The radical difference between Traherne and such thinkers as St Augustine is the difference between one who speaks from the heart of light and one who looks towards it in hope. It is not a question of which was closer to salvation – no doubt the saint has the greater claim to that problematical privilege – but of which knew 'the real Joy and Glory of the Blessed . . . the Enjoyment of the Whole World in Communion with God, not this only, but the Invisible and Eternal' [*Centuries*, IV, 9]. Though the saint, like Traherne, had his earlier vision to convince him and give him the upward weight of love, it is only a past, brief thing, and he is left with only earthly equipment, the longings, struggles, and failings of prose, rational man. His joy is 'the joy of hope that comes from faith'.[20] Traherne, however, always speaks as if from the heights, not just of hope and faith, but of felicity.

He was not, of course, always on the heights, even after de-apostacizing himself. 'I speak not His Practices but His Principles . . . his Practices are so short of these Glorious Principles, that to relate them would be to his Shame' [*Centuries*, IV, 30]. But:

> For Man to Act as if his Soul did see
> The very Brightness of Eternity . . .
> For Man to Act even in the Wilderness,
> As if he did those Sovereign Joys possess . . .
> It doth increase the Value of his Deeds,
> In this a Man a Seraphim exceeds.[21]

Traherne maintains the imaginative elevation and took it as a maxim of his spiritual imagination, as of his moral conduct, 'That he never allowd himself in Swerving from any of these [principles]. And that he repented deeply of evry Miscarriage: and moreover firmly resolved as much as was possible never to erre or wander from them again' [*Centuries*, IV, 30]. His principle is always to speak as from a strong tower of achieved felicity, wherever he may actually be in his conduct or visionary acuity.

The attitude may be illustrated by the opening sentence of *Centuries*, IV, 39 – 'Thus He was Possessor of the whole World, and held it his Treasure'. He does not distinguish between the belief he holds, that the world is his Treasure, and the actual experience of possessing it, as though principle and practice were congruent. 'Having these Principles nothing was more easy then to enjoy the world' [*Centuries*, IV, 41].

Similarly in *Centuries*, IV, 38, he gives what we feel to be an admirable list of the difficulties of achieving heaven, thoroughly orthodox and ostentatiously so by the conventionality of the phrases and the echo of *Romans*, Chapter 12: 'Lov God Angels and Men, Triumph in Gods Works, delight in Gods Laws, Take Pleasure in Gods Ways in all Ages, Correct Sins, bring good out of evil, subdue your Lusts order your sences, Conquer the Customs and Opinions of men, and render Good for evil'. But Traherne is speaking as from the top of this impossible stairway: he looks down on these steps as passed and simply concludes, 'you are in Heaven evry where'. The complete omission of the formal elements of that sentence (the appalling 'If' which, in view of the judgement 'If we say that we have no sin, we deceive ourselves and there is no Truth in us', would postpone heaven permanently), is a reflection of Traherne's peculiar adoption of perfection as the natural resting-place or throne of man.

Similarly, in *Centuries*, IV, 41, he is speaking as from habitual perfection: the world being enjoyed, 'he had nothing more to do, then to spend his Life in Praises and Thanksgivings'. Though things may in actuality be amiss, this is only something wrong with himself, not with the perfection which is his natural habitation and in which, so far as he clings to his principles, he *is*. 'If any thing were amiss, he still would have recours to his own heart, and found nothing but that out of frame · by restoring which al things were rectified, and made Delightfull.' This is an echo of *Centuries*, III, 60: 'All Things were well in their Proper Places, I alone was out of frame and had need to be Mended · for all things were Gods Treasures in their Proper places, and I was to be restored to Gods Image. Wherupon you will not believ how I was withdrawn from all Endeavors of altering and

Mending Outward Things. They lay so well methoughts, they could not be Mended: but I must be Mended to Enjoy them.'

Already here the process of mending is begun simply by adopting the Wellness of all things – the final mending of his own heart is similarly performed by ceasing the endeavour of altering and Mending and simply adopting the natural end of his faculties, perfection: 'All Objects are in God Eternal: which we by perfecting our faculties are made to Enjoy. Which then are turned into Act [i.e., God's Image] when they are exercised about their objects · but without them are Desolat and Idle; or Discontented and forlorn' [*Centuries*, III, 68]. The soul is perfected by allowing it to be what it is, all Act, exercised about its Objects. This once seen, the only tactic is to be what you are, a tactic performed by precisely the imaginative stance of Traherne – 'act as though you are in Heaven, because you are'. The basic principle of Traherne's imagination is the adoption of perfection, felicity, as point of view of all his utterance.

It is from this centre, this 'Sphere of Joy', that Traherne's peculiar qualities radiate: it reorientates all the material he handles. In his use of theological and meditational thought, it is not a question of building a ladder up which one may climb either for the clear sight of God or for the jump in the dark – such a ladder has to be made with a greater rigour and con- sistency of thought to support the full weight of rational man. The intellectual acuity and persistence of St Augustine comes near to that construction but still does not serve to lift his head with any permanence into the realm of 'Reall Joys'. For Traherne, broken shards of that theology are sufficient to dazzle one with flashes of the light that radiates from the felicitous soul (at least when they do manage to catch the light).

Consequently, however much Traherne was immersed in St Augustine, there is not the urgency of direction that shapes even the self-acknowledged gropings of the latter – the sense of a powerful intellectual process moving *towards* comprehension. Traherne is far less clear as to where any of his discourse is going, either in the repetitive gropings of the individual meditation or in the overall progress of the *Centuries*. If the work is based on such a pattern as is to be found in St Bona- ventura's 'Augustinian journey' (and Martz is properly cagey about that too),[22] it is more as a purely formal structure than as the informing spirit. The pose of achieved felicity gives to his thought the pattern not of waves pressing onwards towards the shore of God but of waves reaching up to catch on their crests the divine light. The wave motion is learned, perhaps, from St Augustine – Martz's demonstration of likeness is admirably clear.[23] But the 'darting hither and thither' of the mind that 'comes upon what we know and takes form from it receiving its likeness at every point'[24] is *not* essentially, for Traherne, part of a 'movement of passage'. His dominant image is not the stair but the sphere: ' . . . an interminable Sphere, which as som say of the Sun, is infinities infinita, in the Extention of its Beams, being equaly vigorous in all Places, equaly near to all Objects, Equaly Acceptable to all Persons, and equaly abundant in all its Overflowings' [*Centuries*, IV, 66]. Even the Augustinian metaphor of the weight of love, in the *Confessions*, which Martz shows is echoed by Traherne,[25] is altered in this way. St Augustine says, 'We are inflamed by thy gift, and are carried upwards', while Traherne says, 'If Love be the Weight of the Soul, and its Object the Centre . . .'. Martz sums up St Augustine's efforts by a quotation from *De Trinitate*, 8.13: 'We have found, not the thing itself, but where it is to be sought; and that will suffice to give us a point from which a fresh start may be undertaken': Traherne's characteristic writing takes its peculiar tone from the sense, the resolutely maintained sense, of having found and being possessor of 'the thing itself'. His explorations are not search, but realization. That it 'mine should be, who nothing was, / That Strangest is of all, *yet brought to pass*'[26] [my italics].

Again, it is because he is 'concentred on a Sphere of Joys' that Sin is displaced from its more orthodox role in meditation as the dark side of longing, the equipoise of Christ. For one at home in felicity, sin is only a blurring of the eye. It is real enough and movingly 'breeds a long Parenthesis in the fruition of [his] Joys' – that is, in the third Century, from meditations 47 to 51. But it is only a parenthesis and a parenthesis with the implications of 'a passage introduced into a context with which it has no connexion' (*OED*, 1, b) or 'a sentence so included in another sentence as that it may be taken out, without injuring the sense of that which encloses it' (Dr Johnson). Sin is no essential part of the meaning of earthly life and it is for this reason that Christ, though present frequently and at some length as the optician (and as a central element of the orthodoxy on which Traherne draws), carries little emotional weight and seems to attain little of the reality and significance as an essential part of the Trinity that He has for those bound to the body, longing for the resurrection and the life everlasting. Traherne's principle is expressed in the preface 'To the Reader' in *Christian Ethicks*:

> *I do not speak much of Vice, which is far the more easie Theme, because I am intirely taken up with the abundance of Worth and Beauty in Vertue, and have so much to say of the positive and intrinsick Goodness of its Nature. But besides, since a strait Line is the measure both of it self, and of a crooked one, I conclude, That the very Glory of Vertue well understood, will make all Vice appear like dirt before a Jewel, when they are compared together.*

NOTES

1. *The Paradise Within* (New Haven, 1964), pp. 54–55.

2. Carol L. Marks, 'Thomas Traherne and Cambridge Platonism', *PMLA*, LXXXI (1966), pp. 521–534.

3. See Evelyn Underhill, *Mysticism* (London, 1930), pp. 254 ff.

4. See K. W. Salter, *Thomas Traherne, Mystic and Poet*, (London, 1964), pp. 46 ff.

5. Introduction to *St Anselm's Proslogion* (Oxford, 1965), p. 21.

6. St Bernard, *On Consideration*, trans. G. Lewis (Oxford, 1908), V, iii.

7. R. A. Knox, *Enthusiasm* (Oxford, 1950), p. 586.

8. Gladys I. Wade, *The Poetical Works of Thomas Traherne* (London, 1932), p. xii, quoted by G. R. Guffey in the Introduction to his facsimile edition of the *Meditations* (Los Angeles, 1966), p. ii.

9. Ed. Guffey, p. 32.

10. See Guffey, p. vii.

11. *Of Learned Ignorance*, trans. Fr Germain Heron (London, 1954), p. 11.

12. See Martz, *The Paradise Within*, p. 44: ' . . . mental fatigue is perhaps at first the most notable effect of any effort to read Traherne's *Centuries* steadily for any considerable length of time'.

13. *Centuries*, IV, 41.

14. *Centuries*, IV, 42.

15. Martz, p. 54.

16. Margaret L. Wiley, *Creative Sceptics* (London, 1966), pp. 118-119.

17. Wiley, p. 120.

18. John Smith, *Attaining to Divine Knowledge*, Section I; in E. J. Campagnac, *The Cambridge Platonists* (Oxford, 1901), p. 80.

19. Martz, p. 49.

20. *Confessions*, trans. R. S. Pine-Coffin (Harmondsworth, 1961), VI, 6, p. 119.

21. *Christian Ethicks* (London, 1675), p. 344.

22. Martz, p. 57. The first half at least of the fourth Century seems to me to be, not a conscious abstraction of divine principles from experience, on a Platonic ladder of love, but simply the description of the ways of 'Activ Happiness', in opposition to the contemplative occupation; this is an equally valid interpretation of the first meditation of the Century which Martz quotes to *his* purpose. The whole Century moves around the question, not merely of Principles but of Practice, the continuing light of every day, the persistence of happiness by activity, after its attainment by the meditative ascent. There is a sense of progression in the first three Centuries but this is as much a function of Traherne's story of his reattainment of felicity as of the present purpose of the work. Is a possible explanation of the unfinished fifth Century Traherne's recognition, forecast in the sudden summary of IV, 100, that there *is* further to go than he had thought, steps yet unachieved?

23. Martz, pp. 43-54.

24. St Augustine, *De Trinitate*, 15, 25, quoted by Martz, p. 49.

25. Martz, p. 40.

26. 'The Salutation', ll. 41-42.

Rochester and the
Traditions of Satire

HAROLD LOVE

I

Rochester began to write verse satire at a time when the genre
was at an extraordinarily interesting stage of its development.
The full blossoming of the Restoration libel industry with its
bureaucracy of procurers, copyists, and distributors was still a
decade distant,[1] neither perhaps had the time quite come when
a letter to a friend in the country would be incomplete without
the latest lampoon. Yet the new mode of topical, clandestine
satire, which was to find its monuments at the turn of the
century in the various 'State-Poems' collections, had already
made its influence felt in most areas of literary and social life
and had produced, in Marvell's 'Last Instructions to a Painter',
its first masterpiece. To write satire in this new idiom was as
natural for the aspiring wit, and even for the courtier or professional man who did not consider himself a wit, as to dabble
in chemistry or to drink coffee, and it is probable that the
operation was generally undertaken in much the same spirit.
There is little evidence of aspiration towards art: the vast
majority of lampoons were written about current happenings
and for immediate consumption. Their occasions might be to
hurt an enemy, to entertain a friend, or in very rare instances to
instruct society at large in the principles of virtue, but more
often simply to display and request approbation for the author's
wit on a level only slightly higher than that of the *bon mot* or
impromptu simile.

Satire of this kind is really a branch of what Johnson in his
life of Rochester calls 'colloquial' – that is, 'conversational' –

wit[2] rather than of literature as we normally understand the word. Sir Fopling's poetical essays in *The Man of Mode* are an unforced expression of his 'parts', an expression which could just as easily have taken the form of a dance, a new system of cravat-tying, or a repartee. In each case (And is it significantly different for Dorset and Rochester as their contemporaries saw them?) it was the parts which were the real object of public interest, not the particular manifestation. There were, of course, satirists working within the tradition who were seriously, often perilously, concerned with major public issues and who had every reason for not wishing the natural sprouts of their wit to be laid too close to their own doors. Yet even these give little sign of being aware of any public beyond the immediate one. Even more significantly, if we consider the self-conscious moralism of the satire of the succeeding half-century, we find that the lampooner has little interest in ethical issues as such; his assault is partisan, personal, and particular. He is speaking his own mind on his own behalf; not – as Pope was generally able to assume – society's mind on society's behalf. As a consequence of this he is rarely found capable of drawing a distinction between personal antipathy and political or moral disapproval; indeed the presence of one will unfailingly generate the other. One has to search through a great many pages of the main repositories of the genre[3] before discovering a good word, however severely qualified, for a victim.

Satire, in short, by the early 1670s was a genuinely popular art. In so far as it relied heavily on in-group scandal for its material, full comprehension of particular poems will often have been restricted to a fairly limited body of readers; however, its forms and its language were universally accessible and its practice seems to have been established in all literate sections of the community and in all parties of Church and State. When it married itself to music it was to the most widely current of all genres, the street ballad and the playhouse song.[4] Such popularity is not without its surprising element. Satire of the type we are concerned with had been written in England only since the turn of the century, and its earliest stage had seen it very much a possession of the *avant-garde*, of inns-of-court literati, over-educated but under-beneficed clergymen, private-house dramatists, and the like. This first phase had also seen it rough to the point of uncouthness in rhythm, labouredly recondite in expression, obscene with a calculatedness far removed from the quite routine indecency of its Restoration descendant, and so repugnant to conservatives that on one famous occasion they had it consigned to the flames as a genre by the common hangman.[5]

Exactly what happened to satire between the days of Marston, Hall, and Donne and those of the lampooners, and how the coterie experiment became a major medium of public communication, are questions which still have to be properly investigated, but that it was basically the same form involved seems reasonably clear. The Elizabethan and Jacobean satirists, under the firm impression that they were creating an exact English equivalent of the satire of the Romans, Horace and Juvenal, had in reality been developing an original form of satire distinct from its supposed models both in tone (this partly the result of the misapprehension that the satirist should be a *satyr*, that is, a splenetic, foul-mouthed, whip-wielding railer 'lashing the lewdness of Britannia'[6]) and equally in structure. Where Roman satire, and its inspiration, the cynic diatribe,[7] had generally presented their satiric portraits as *exempla* within a general moral argument, the new satire of the 1590s was conceived as a series of virtually independent satiric epigrams (another classical form which was being revived in the same circles at roughly the same time), sometimes dignified by a sketchy introduction, sometimes, though more rarely, with a loose, semi-dramatic frame, but with little real pretension to thematic unity and none at all to the moral seriousness of the Roman satirists. John Peter has suggested that its real progenitor both in manner and form is Martial.[8]

By the time this model reached the hands of the Restoration poets certain fundamental changes had taken place. Satire had become topical – unimaginably so by earlier standards. It now dealt with living contemporaries rather than the grotesque type figures of the Jacobeans. At the same time its language had shed the 'spurious snotteries' of forced phraseology and recondite vocabulary which had provided Jonson with such excellent matter for ridicule in *The Poetaster* and become rawly quotidian. The snarling satyr-satirist has gone too: in his place as speaker of the satire comes the equally indecorous but much less frenetic figure of the Restoration debauchee, usually presented either directly or by implication as a lewd, no-nonsense claret-drinker:

> I who from drinking ne're could spare an hour,
> But what I gave to some obedient Whore,
> Who hate all Satyr, whether sharp or dull,
> From *Dryden* to the Governor of *Hull*;
> Provok'd at length to a Poetick Rage,
> Resolve to share in railing at the Age.
>
> ['Quem Natura negat'[9]]

> Fools must be medling in matters of State,
> While I drink my Botle, and sw—ve wth my Mate:
> The Morning's being cold, I sit by the Fire,
> And Scribble, while sixty swift Minutes expire.
>
> ['Satyr on the Ladys of Honor'[10]]

These are the differences. But more important things remain the same, among them the awareness that nearly all critics have shared in the case of Marston, that the satire is artistically as much about the satirist as it is about its ostensible subjects: about his indecency, his plain-man pragmatism, his virtuosity in invective, and the blatant insincerity of his professed horror at the vices he so lovingly flays. Quite as much as Will Kinsayder, the lampooner is 'playing the rough part of a satyrist'.[11] Structure too has largely remained constant over the century. The aggregation of loosely linked and perfunctorily introduced satiric epigrams, concluding abruptly as soon as the satirist had run out of victims, remains the favoured pattern, and elements of it are visible in even such more sophisticated lampoons as the various 'Advice to a Painter' poems[12] and Mulgrave's *Essay on Satyr*.[13] Satires such as these may pretend to the dignity of a formal ethical demonstration or a historical narrative, yet the differences are more often a matter of decoration than of essence: the main interest is still in the epigrams.

In any case, it was the lampoon tradition which provided Rochester with his model for 'Tunbridge Wells' which, if not the earliest of the long satires (his latest editor is uncertain on this point[14]), is certainly the most conventional in terms of the wider context of Restoration satire and may safely be taken as representing his point of departure as a satirist. Already, no doubt, he was aware of the other possibilities deriving from Berni and the drollery poets in one direction, and Horace and Horace's disciple Boileau, the first major seventeenth-century satirist to attempt a rigorous re-creation of classical models, in another, but when he first turned to the long satire it was in much the same spirit and with much the same improvisatory attitude towards form which he had already shown in his lighter stanzaic lampoons.[15] What remains astonishing and at the same time highly instructive about 'Tunbridge Wells' is that in this, Rochester's first extended essay at the couplet lampoon, he should have handled its techniques so well. There is even a sense in which he can be said to have exhausted most of the possibilities of the genre, making it inevitable that in his next major satire he would move beyond it.

The problem which confronts the writer of personal invective along the pattern favoured by the Restoration is that which confronts all users of the more primitive modes of satire: how to introduce an element of variety or climax into the repeated application of an identical stimulus – in this case the standard satiric 'epigram'. One way of doing this was a progressive intensification of the level of rant and salacity, a task at which most of the practitioners were sufficiently adept. The degree of formal subtlety required to operate at this level was not very great. The only essentials were an introduction and a list of victims, and the introduction need not be of any particular moment; indeed it was sometimes left out altogether:

> This way of writing I observe by some
> Is introduc'd with an Exordium.
> But I will leave to make all that adoe
> And in plain English tell you who fucks who.
>
> ['Satyr'[16]]

That interest of this kind could be maintained over even a longish poem is shown by the inexhaustible inventiveness in lubricity evident in the *Iliad* of the genre, Dorset's *A Faithful Catalogue of our Most Eminent Ninnies*.[17] However, the rigidity of the form could also be confronted in more positive ways. The satirists' problem was similar to that of mid-seventeenth-century musicians working in the fashionable ground-bass style

L

whose whole success depended on the fertility of invention a composer could bring to the embellishment of a simple, recurring sequence of harmonies. The better poets sought for every kind of contrast between component epigrams while at the same time searching for a greater overall complexity through the use of rhetorical or narrative frames and dramatic scenes. In 'Tunbridge Wells' Rochester is not yet concerned to transcend list structure, but he is using it like a virtuoso. The skill with which narrative and descriptive style are varied from portrait to portrait and the vivid realization of speaker and scene reveal an artist completely in command of the possibilities, albeit restricted, of his elected mode.

How unambiguously Rochester had committed himself to the lampoon style in this poem may best be seen through a comparison with a representative example written some seven years after his death when the form was at the peak of its popularity and even lesser practitioners were winning striking elaborations of the stand-'em-up-and-shout-'em-down pattern. Both 'Tunbridge Wells' and 'The Last Night's Ramble',[18] the work of an unknown author, are in essence strings of unrelated epigrams directed at a heterogeneous body of victims. The problem facing the satirist in each case is – to use a second analogy – precisely that which exercises the department-store window-dresser supplied with a number of saleable items and a number of dummies and having to combine them into a display which is at once natural, attractive, and persuasive. In the case of the satirist the first difficulty is to disguise the mechanical nature of the transitions from epigram to epigram. Rochester tries to achieve this by bringing his narrator and victims together for a morning-draught at the wells. The author of the 'Ramble' has disposed his around the premises of a bawdy-house. The exordia are in each case characteristically concise:

> At five this morn, when Phoebus raised his head
> From Thetis' lap, I raised myself from bed,
> And mounting steed, I trotted to the waters,
> The rendezvous of fools, buffoons, and praters,
> Cuckolds, whores, citizens, their wives and daughters.
>   My squeamish stomach I with wine had bribed
> To undertake the dose that was prescribed;
> But turning head, a sudden cursèd view

That innocent provision overthrew,
And without drinking, made me purge and spew.
[*'*Tunbridge Wells'*]

Warm'd with the pleasures, which Debauches yeild
Brain, stufft with fumes, Excess of Wine had fill'd,
I took last Night a Ramble being drunk
To visit old Accquaintance Bawd and Punk.
'Twas madam *Southcot* near old Dunkirk square, ⎞
That House of ease for many a Rampant peer ⎟
For only the lewd Quality f—k there. ⎠
[*'*The Last Night's Ramble'*]

The impress of what I have called the lampoon tradition is immediately evident in both cases through the informal rhythm, the idiomatic language, the casual indecency, and the immediate sense of a speaker – the 'claret drinker' – and of that speaker's delighted malice towards the rest of the human race. If there is any distinction in excellence evident at this stage it is probably in the greater rhythmic subtlety of Rochester's lines with the hint of mock-heroic bathos at the end of the first couplet and the dismissively slapdash jumbling together of the *dramatis personae* in the triplet which follows. But the idiom is recognizably the same, and recognizably different from that of English neo-classical satire as exemplified by Pope and Johnson.

Rochester's first victim has yet to be identified, but there can be no doubt that readers were expected to put a name to him.

From coach and six a thing unwieldy rolled,
Whose lumber, cart more decently would hold.
As wise as calf it looked, as big as bully,
But handled, proves a mere Sir Nicholas Cully;
A bawling fop, a natural Nokes, and yet
He dares to censure as if he had wit.
To make him more ridiculous, in spite
Nature contrived the fool should be a knight.
[How wise is nature when she does dispence
A large estate to cover want of sence?
The man's a fool, 'tis true, but that's no matter,
For he's a mighty wit, with those that flatter;
But a poor blockhead, is a wretched Creature.]
[Grant, ye unlucky stars! this o'ergrown boy
To purchase some inspiring pretty toy

That may his want of sense and wit supply,
As buxom crab-fish does his lechery.]
Though he alone were dismal sight enough,
His train contributed to set him off,
All of his shape, all of the selfsame stuff.
No spleen or malice need on them be thrown:
Nature has done the business of lampoon,
And in their looks their characters has shown.

[ll, 11-18 [+9], 19-24][19]

The chief point of stylistic interest in this passage is that the emphasis should lie so heavily on abusing the victim rather than presenting him. If we think of satire as working through the two distinct dimensions of telling (invective) and showing (distorted mimesis) we may feel surprise at the extent to which the passage is weighted towards the first and even more at Rochester's preference for the method of direct denunciation over the techniques of irony and understatement which have been the main resource of English satirists since the generation following his own. Physical detail of the victim is here restricted to the opening couplet: it is the speaker's attitude towards him – though we may initially think otherwise – which is the real substance of the passage. Certainly we find little evidence of the quality of satiric closeness to the object praised in Juvenal by John Peter (though, again, on a first encounter we may think we do):

> The Roman has a trick of bringing his subjects so close to the reader that their very proximity begins to be distasteful, intensifying the revulsion which his description of their conduct (bawling, simpering, panting, even vomiting) is in itself enough to call up. The whole force of his indignation makes itself felt, not in the generalizations that he from time to time permits himself, but in the unholy relish with which he examines the details of various pravities and affectations.[20]

But then this preponderance of the element of statement is another characteristic of the lampoon and perhaps another register of its comparatively primitive form. Its *raison d'être* is not to show but to taunt, either with straight-out abuse or the parading of unwelcome truths, usually of the 'who-fucks-who' variety. Its aim is to crush the victims by sheer weight of abuse – 'a sudden cursèd view', 'as wise as calf it looked' 'a bawling fop', 'more ridiculous', 'fool', 'blockhead', and so on – and in doing so to display its speaker as an object of at least equivalent interest to the victims. This may well have been the strain in the lampoon to which Dryden, whose own reaction from it was to lead to the ultimate understatement of mock-heroic, was alluding in a famous passage from the *Discourse Concerning the Original and Progress of Satire*: 'How easy it is to call rogue and villain, and that wittily! But how hard to make a man appear a fool, a blockhead, or a knave, without using any of those opprobrious terms! . . . A man may be capable, as Jack Ketch's wife said of his servant, of a plain piece of work, a bare hanging; but to make a malefactor die sweetly was only belonging to her husband' [II, 136-7]. To say that Rochester does not live up to Dryden's ideal is merely to say that he was writing something Dryden never attempted – satire of the first person in the popular mode. What comes through most strongly is not the object but the speaker's attitude towards the object and ultimately the speaker himself, querulous, foul-mouthed, and dyspeptic, and in no sense, needless to say, to be identified with his creator.

In emphasizing the slightness of the presentational element in the opening portraits of 'Tunbridge Wells' I do not wish to deny that Rochester can, when he wishes, present his characters to us in an extraordinarily vivid way. The passages of direct speech in the poem, the dialogue of squire and maid and the conversation of the two wives, do exactly this, as do some of the briefer, impressionistic phrases of visual description:

> From coach and six a thing unwieldy rolled, . . .
> [l. 11]

> Two rusty pistols, scarf about the arse,
> Coat lined with red, they here presume to swell:
> This goes for captain, that for colonel.
> [ll. 159-161]

– which is exactly, after all, how one does become aware of people in a crowd. But even when we encounter such intervals of pictorially effective presentation they are rarely left to speak for themselves. The narrator's attitude has to be expressed explicitly, usually at some length, although the object has already made the point by itself. The fop is the occasion for a generalized reflection on fops; the cadets an excuse for a disquisition on their bad habits as a class; the two wives, after their delightful conversation about the girl, have to be assailed all over again in a passage of invective that Pope for one would have seen no necessity for:

> Poor foolish fribble, who by subtlety
> Of midwife, truest friend to lechery,
> Persuaded art to be at pains and charge
> To give thy wife occasion to enlarge
> Thy silly head! For here walk Cuff and Kick,
> With brawny back and legs and potent prick,
> Who more substantially will cure thy wife,
> And on her half-dead womb bestow new life.
> From these the waters got the reputation
> Of good assistants unto generation.
>
> [ll. 139-148]

Rochester is perfectly aware that in most cases 'Nature has done the business of lampoon'; however, he is never tempted to follow the Horatian course of merely reproducing nature. And indeed why should we expect him to? His concern, as we have already seen, is as much with the speaker as with the victim, and it is in these passages of apparently gratuitous invective that the speaker is being most forcibly put before us. There is also a sense in which the speaker, like the title character of Wycherley's dramatic satire, *The Plain Dealer*, is himself another of the victims.

For the author of 'The Last Night's Ramble' things are a little simpler. His speaker is certainly identifiable as a character but remains primarily an agent for the reader, an observer, or perhaps we could more aptly say voyeur:

> The first divertisement I found was this,
> I heard the Treble note of yeilding Misse.
> Whisp'ring, Lord, S^r what pleasant Tales you Tell!
> You'l find th'Enjoyment worth your mony well.
> Then in Base viol voice I heard him swear
> Dam me a Guiney Madam's very fair.

The utmost Fee I ever gave to swive,
She answer'd, How d'ye think that we can live?
I'le swear Sr William R—ch s^r gave me five.
While thus I listned I observ'd at last,
Tho' she ask't more, she held the Guinea fast.

[ll. 8-18]

The method of this particular passage is entirely presentational; however the satirist is not aiming any more than Rochester or the lampooners in general had done at a sustained Juvenalian closeness to the satirised persons. Instead his poem proceeds through a succession of barely, though amusingly, narrated incidents which are developed no further than is necessary to sustain a simple emblematic function – as in the brief snapshots of the Bishop of Chester ('Who gravely was a fine young Whore confirming') and Lord Ranelagh, 'forty years worn out' who 'sweats and stinks for one poor single 'Bout', which while repulsive enough is a good deal short of the sustained kinetic assaults of a Juvenal.

A more fruitful point of comparison with Rochester is the handling of the basic problems of termination and transition. Here the author of the 'Ramble' begins with the advantage of a conclusion to work towards: once the victims have been dealt with he is free to put his speaker to bed at last and send him home – a nice touch – with his hair full of feathers. Rochester's poem, on the other hand, comes to an end simply because his list of victims comes to an end – an inherent flaw of the lampoon and one that such bolder spirits as Dorset in verse and Swift in prose preferred to meet with a flat *caetera desunt*.[21]

As far as the management of transitions is concerned, the author of the 'Ramble' has the simpler problem, in that having got his character inside the brothel all the old standbys of pornography are available – peeping through keyholes, overhearing conversations through walls, blundering into the wrong room and eventually into the wrong bed. But Rochester, although he moves with equal abruptness from topic to topic, has created an infinitely more realistic and lively scene and a much keener sense of the predicament of the narrator. Driven by an almost Gulliverian repugnance from the purge-swilling yahoos of Tunbridge, the claret-drinker flies from the pump to the lower walk, from the lower walk to the upper end, and from the upper end to the heart of the crowd, at each turn encountering new squadrons of fools. Everywhere there is a sense of movement, mirrored and reinforced by the splendidly flexible verse. Here at least there can be no dispute over excellences. The language of the 'Ramble' is so close to every-day speech as to be devoid of any intrinsic expressive power. What poetic life it does possess comes from a quality of stilted gravity, verging at one or two points on mock-heroic, with which the narration is endued by the wilful maladroitness of the couplets. Rochester, briskly moving from detail to detail, insult to insult, heaping up lists, now emphasizing, now tumbling over caesural and end-of-line pauses, laconically assiduous at all stages not to become too regular, achieves a rhythmic breath-lessness which is a perfect sound-image of the moral and physical predicament of his speaker. Indeed to a very large extent the speaker *is* the rhythm – as he should be. It is in the aural dimension, in other words, that we find a closeness to the material comparable to the visual closeness Juvenal gives us. But this is a closeness to the speaker and the speaker's reactions rather than to the objects which provoke these reactions. A good lampoon is first and foremost a performance.

The aims of my comparison of 'Tunbridge Wells' and 'The Last Night's Ramble' have been, firstly, to identify some of the predominant features of an important seventeenth-century satiric sub-genre, the couplet lampoon, and, secondly, to show what two poets were able to make of its somewhat meagre resources. It should also, I hope, have become clear that while Rochester when he wrote the poem was firmly in the lampoon tradition he was at the same instant close to exhausting it. It is not merely that he handles the formal problems, except that of providing a convincing termination, with such effortless assurance. We find over and above this a whole range of new interests invading the lampoon – an interest in character for character's sake, an interest in scene for scene's sake, a fondness for overt discursive moralizing as opposed to invective, any one of which needed only a little more emphasis to change the whole quality of the satiric enterprise. There is also clear evidence of a capacity for vivid presentation of speaker and victim which, given any more weight, would have made the moralizing as such irrelevant or superfluous. One feels simultaneously that there is little more left for Rochester to do with the lampoon and that it is already unstable in his hand, requiring only minor shifts in emphasis to make it something entirely different. Interestingly enough, one of these shifts can be seen taking place within the poem itself in the movement away from the satire on recognizable individuals of the opening lines – the unnamed but obviously identifiable knight and the future bishop, Samuel Parker – to the general satire on types with which the poem ends: the fop, the gallant and damsel, the two wives, and the cadets. In making this shift, which was to be taken further in his later satires, Rochester was moving against the whole tendency of native satire from Marston's day to his own. Yet he was also anticipating the course the Augustans were to follow towards a classically derived satire whose satirized figures were universal types of the vices and virtues, whose aim was the enunciation of universal ethical truths, whose structural basis was no longer the string of unrelated epigrams but the sustained moral argument, and whose speaker, if developed as a character at all, was to have a substantial, though not always unambiguous, degree of identity with the poet. But to follow Rochester further along this path it is first necessary to enquire into other than native models.

II

The satires in which Rochester explores alternatives to the lampoon ethos and epigrammatic structure are 'An Allusion to Horace', 'Timon', 'A Satire against Reason and Mankind', and 'A Letter from Artemisa in the Town to Chloe in the Country'. The first was a close imitation of Horace, the second and third free imitations of Boileau; only the last would appear to be entirely original. Of these four poems it is 'Timon' and 'Artemisa to Chloe' which will allow us the clearest notion of what Rochester gave to English satire. 'The Satire against Mankind', although probably the most admired today, is in a number of ways both more and less than a satire and might be more usefully described by the Popean, or, rather, Warburtonian, term 'moral essay'. The 'Allusion to Horace' is similarly of restricted relevance to the present discussion in so

far as all that needs to be said has already been admirably put
by Johnson:

> His Imitation of Horace on Lucilius is not inelegant or unhappy.
> In the reign of Charles the second began that adaptation, which
> has since been very frequent, of ancient poetry to present times;
> and perhaps few will be found where the parallellism is better
> preserved than in this.[22]

It is interesting and important that Rochester should have made
this experiment in close 'imitation' when he did. We might also
note that to the extent to which, as Vieth has suggested,[23] a
knowledge of the Latin original is necessary for full comprehension of the English imitation, it is the most prophetic
among his longer satires of the favoured methods of the succeeding half-century. But the very fact that this kind of thing
was to be better done by Pope and by Johnson himself makes it
of less interest to us than the things which were not to be
better done, and it is through 'Timon' and 'Artemisa to Chloe'
that we will come to the clearest understanding of what these
were. My thesis will be that in moving from native to neoclassical models Rochester was not abandoning one for the
other, but rather attempting to perfect a stance from which he
could draw on the resources of both traditions. In 'Timon' this
process was to lead to a highly effective fusion of lampoon and
neoclassical elements; 'Artemisa to Chloe', on the other hand,
represents a deliberate attempt to place the two traditions in
dissociative juxtaposition with each other.

In the case of 'Timon' we are dealing with a satiric theme
which has a very long history behind it. The *repas ridicule*,
originally, no doubt, a borrowing from the Hellenistic mime, is
used by Horace as the basis of the eighth satire of the second
book, by Lucian in 'A Feast of Lapithae', and alluded to in the
fifth satire of Juvenal. There is also the signal instance of the
Cena Trimalchionis. In the Renaissance it became a stock motif
of the tradition of satiric burlesque chiefly associated today
with the name of Francesco Berni. Rochester's immediate
though not necessarily sole model was the third satire of
Boileau, itself based on Horace's satire and on the tenth satire of
Mathurin Régnier, which was in turn indebted to Horace, to
Berni's 'Capitolo a Frascatoro' and Caporali's 'La Corte'.[24]

Both 'Timon' and Boileau's satire give accounts in the first person of an unwilling visit to a dinner-party. In each case the speaker is accosted by an unwelcome but insistent inviter – in Boileau a distant acquaintance and in Rochester a total stranger 'who just my name had got', and lured into attendance by the promise of good company. In Rochester's poem the promised guests are the poet's friends, Sedley, Buckhurst, and [Henry] Savile; in Boileau's, Molière and the musician, Lambert. Inevitably the inducements remain unfulfilled. Timon's company consists of four hectors – Half-wit, Huffe, Kickum, and Dingboy – and the host's wife ('A wife, good gods! a fop, and bullies too! / For one poor meal what must I undergo?' [ll. 45-46]); while Boileau's speaker finds himself confronted with a larger company including 'Deux nobles campagnards, grands lecteurs de romans', an author, and a parasite. Then follows, in each case, a tedious banquet rendered even more so by the naïve approbation of the other guests and arguments in the respective causes of national honour (Rochester) and literary excellence (Boileau), culminating in bouts of plate-hurling.

The outline just given will have made clear that 'Timon' is only in the most general sense a translation. Close comparison reveals that Rochester is using Boileau's satire in a highly self-aware way. His poem opens with a long account of a conversation in a coach between Timon and the bore which has no counterpart in his original, though it may easily draw, as Pinto has suggested,[25] on the opening of Horace's Satire I, ix. At the same time a passage of witty descanting by Boileau's interlocutor on the appearance of the returning diner has been silently passed over. Other major additions are the two delightful passages describing the host's wife and the insertion of quotations into the literary debate, which receives considerably more weight in the English poem; however, it is not this but a sudden switch to politics, again unique to Rochester, that sets the hectors to blows. There is also a general re-deployment of the satire away from food (at least a third of Boileau's poem being taken up with the anatomisation of various culinary monstrosities) towards the characters and their conversation. In fact, hardly an element of the original has escaped transmutation. As with the best Restoration translations of Molière – Shadwell's *The Miser* being a particularly good example – one has the sense of a completely deliberate selectivity resting on a sense of national and cultural identity quite as assured as that of the French writer. In Rochester's case this was also a consequence of his already being a practising satirist in a well-established native tradition. He is learning from Boileau but only as one master learns from another.

The point may be made more amply by a comparison of the opening lines of the two poems. After thirteen lines of introduction which Rochester reduces to four, Boileau's host breaks into a catalogue of enticements:

> Ah! monsieur, m'a-t-il dit, je vous attends demain.
> N'y manquez pas au moins. J'ai quatorze bouteilles
> D'un vin vieux . . . Boucingo n'en a point de pareilles;
> Et je gagerois bien que, chez la commandeur,
> Villandri priseroit sa sève et sa verdeur.
> Molière avec Tartuffe y doit jouer son rôle;
> Et Lambert, qui plus est, m'a donné sa parole.
> C'est tout dire, en un mot, et vous le connoissez. –
> Quoi! Lambert? – Oui, Lambert: à demain. – C'est assez.
> [ll. 20-28]

It is easy enough to conceive what a slightly later English satirist would have done with this; and, in particular, how lovingly he would have searched out the exact local counterpart to each of Boileau's allusions to the life of Paris. Rochester was himself to use such a technique in the 'Allusion to Horace' and Dryden in his revisions to Soame's translation of the *Art Poetique*. But Rochester is not merely translating from French into English or from Paris to London; he is also translating out of what we may loosely call a neoclassical mode of satiric discourse into the reigning native mode, lampoon, and in lampoon such playfully decorative allusiveness would be an irrelevancy. Instead we find ourselves flung straight at the bore to face the full bombardment of his importunity:

> At last I e'en consent to be his Guest.
> He takes me in his coach, and as we go,
> Pulls out a libel of a sheet or two,
> Insipid as the praise of pious queens
> Or Shadwell's unassisted former scenes,

Which he admired, and praised at every line;
At last it was so sharp it must be mine.
I vowed I was no more a wit than he:
Unpracticed and unblessed in poetry.
A song to Phyllis I perhaps might make,
But never rhymed but for my pintle's sake.
I envied no man's fortune nor his fame,
Nor ever thought of a revenge so tame.
He knew my style, he swore, and 'twas in vain
Thus to deny the issue of my brain.
Choked with his flattery, I no answer make,
But silent, leave him to his dear mistake,
Which he by this had spread o'er the whole town,
And me with an officious lie undone.
Of a well-meaning fool I'm most afraid,
Who sillily repeats what was well said.

[ll. 13-32]

This particular passage is a satiric epigram equivalent in effect
to those which are the building-blocks of 'Tunbridge Wells' and
'The Last Night's Ramble'. Equally characteristic of the lampoon manner are the colloquialness, the indecency, the high
proportion of directly pejorative words, the total absence of
irony, the undisguisedly personal tone of the criticism, and,
above all, the character of the narrator who, while slightly less
agitated about things than his counterpart in 'Tunbridge Wells',
is still recognizably close to the figure I referred to earlier as
the 'claret-drinker' – the Restoration counterpart to the snarling
satyrist of the Jacobeans. This last point is an important one
in that failure to recognize it will lead to an over-estimation
of the strength of the classical and equally of the autobiographical elements in the poem. Rochester, as a Restoration
peer, would hardly have been seized in the street, addressed in
the familiar form of the second person, and dragged off to
dinner by a down-at-heel ex-colonel whom he had never met
before; indeed it is to be doubted whether he would ever have
walked the park *in propria persona* unaccompanied by at the very
least a purse-bearer, a page, and a couple of footmen. (This
could easily have been the reason that induced writers of two
important manuscripts of the poem to attribute it to Sedley.[26])
We should also note how careful Timon is to stress that he is
not a writer of satire [ll. 20-24]. Rochester's friends would have

seen the point even if his twentieth-century readers have sometimes not.

'Timon', in short, is far from being wholly neoclassical in inspiration. Yet at the same time there is clear evidence of a desire on the writer's part to transcend the limitations of lampoon. We might note for a start the relative realism of the characterization, the detailed depiction of domestic *mores*, and the gently cumulative nature of the satiric exposé, all foreign to the native tradition. The abandonment of a fragmented for a continuous form, and the fact that the persons of the poem are not, as far as is known, portraits of living individuals, are equally evidence of an awareness of the ideals of the ancient tradition. But it is as yet *only* an awareness, for despite these things, and despite the fact that after the opening passage the hand of Jack Ketch's apprentice is considerably less in evidence than it had been in 'Tunbridge Wells', the speaker of the satire, specifically characterized in the opening lines as a gambler and a debauchee, can hardly claim to be speaking, as in neoclassical satire he ideally should, for the whole rational part of mankind. Timon's point of view remains that of a malevolent atom.

A new satiric mode has come into existence, a humanized lampoon, in which a fuller and more balanced concern with character has been secured without abandonment of the lancing, malicious invective characteristic of the popular tradition, and in which the satirist is still content to function as exposer, taunter, and entertainer rather than as civilizer, reformer, or advocate of moral positives. Rochester's cutting, throwaway colloquialisms: 'A song to Phyllis I perhaps might make, / But never rhymed but for my pintle's sake' [ll. 21-22], or 'Their swords were safe, and so we let 'em cuff' [l. 172], represent an inheritance from the lampoon which is alien to Boileau and to Pope (though not necessarily beyond the range of their master, Horace). Yet the subtlety of observation and the mobility of tone in the first account of the wife are equally outside the range of lampoon:

> In comes my lady straight. She had been fair,
> Fit to give love and to prevent despair,
> But age, beauty's incurable disease,

Had left her more desire than power to please.
As cocks will strike although their spurs be gone,
She with her old blear eyes to smite begun.
Though nothing else, she in despite of time
Preserved the affectation of her prime:

[ll. 47-54]

The new manner can move in the space of a couplet from the graceful understatement of 'prevent despair' and the almost elegiac cadence of 'age, beauty's incurable disease' to the brutal 'She with her old blear eyes to smite begun'; and in doing so it is able to sensitize the reader to a much wider range of responses to human realities than would have been possible within either of the two tributary modes. The complexity, or, rather, compound-ness, of tone established in the passage just quoted carries over to the subsequent

Falkland she praised, and Suckling's easy pen,
And seemed to taste their former parts again.

[ll. 107-108]

where it is impossible to be sure whether the dominant effect of the *double entendre* is one of malicious ridicule or amused sympathy. And what of the brief peep into Timon's subconscious we are offered when, after turning from the old blear eyes to his dinner, he finds that even the food has suddenly acquired an erotic aura, the side of beef recalling Mother Mosely, the bawd, being carried in a litter, and the carrots the Countess of Northumberland's dildo.[27] There are similar touches elsewhere: even the hectors almost manage to convince us of their reality, especially Huffe with his fondness for rumbling rhetoric, French arms, and blunt answers.

It is possible that if Rochester had lived longer and written more satire it might have emerged that the mode of 'Timon' was only a transitional stage between the lampoon and a much more 'neoclassical' Horatianism of the type foreshadowed in the 'Allusion'. But there can be no denying that the poem's effects are beautifully judged and that they work. We have to wait for the Swift of *Polite Conversation* and the *Directions to Servants* and, beyond him, Thackeray's Mr Wagg in *Pendennis* to encounter quite so devastating an observer of domestic deportment.

III

To turn from 'Timon' to 'A Letter from Artemisa in the Town to Chloe in the Country' is to re-encounter an issue bypassed in the earlier poem: the need for the writer of argued satire to camouflage the relatively crude patterns of contrast and summation which constitute the rhetorical basis of his discourse. It has already been shown in how acute a way this formal constriction had affected the lampoon. That it was also a problem to the writers of more elaborate kinds of discursive satire is evident from the peculiar textual history of Pope's *Epistle to Bathurst*.[28] Until 'Artemisa to Chloe' it was a problem that Rochester had not chosen to take seriously. In 'Tunbridge Wells' he had accepted the limitations of a simple epigrammatic structure as part-and-parcel of the mode he was working in. 'A Satire against Mankind' uses the *prolocutor-adversarius* pattern to soften a formality of exposition which is not in any case out of keeping with its aims. In the last of the major satires the issue was at last seriously acknowledged and in the same breath effortlessly transcended. 'Artemisa to Chloe' is certainly an argued satire but it is one whose rhetorical structure is an integral part of the poem's meaning rather than a mere scaffolding.

A look at the way in which this is achieved will also permit us to plot Rochester's attitude as an artist towards the rival modes. My feeling is that this new maturity of form reflects a new appreciation on Rochester's part of the relative advantages and limitations of the traditions of satire, and of the values and stances which each by its very nature imposed upon the writer using them. In fact, it is the differences between these traditions and the values which inform them that is, from one point of view, the real subject of the poem.

The first thing we need to note about 'Artemisa to Chloe' is that is is really two poems – a kind of literary counterpart to Sir William Petty's double-bottomed boat. More exactly, it is a lampoon within a satire of the neoclassical type. The opening lines involve a degree of preliminary feinting. After a lengthy introduction in which Artemisa acts as her own *adversarius* in a discussion of the folly of writing poetry which may owe something to Horace II, i, we are even, though entirely mischievously, given to expect a lampoon of the conventional kind:

> Y'expect at least to hear what loves have passed
> In this lewd town, since you and I met last;
> What change has happened of intrigues, and whether
> The old ones last, and who and who's together.
>
> [ll. 32-35]

But Artemisa is not this kind of satirist at all. Instead she proceeds on a very different tack to discuss the nature and benefits of love and to deplore the folly of modern attitudes towards it, especially on the part of women. It is only when she comes at length to her *exemplum* that we suddenly feel a breeze from the world of 'Tunbridge Wells':

> Where I was visiting the other night
> Comes a fine lady, with her humble knight,
> Who had prevailed on her, through her own skill,
> At his request, though much against his will,
> To come to London.
>
> [ll. 73-77]

After a further twenty-three lines describing the fine lady's entrance the newcomer embarks on a monologue which, with only one major interruption, continues until ten lines from the end of the poem. The overt aim of this monologue is to exemplify the criticisms of the sex made by Artemisa; however, after a while, and without sacrificing this function, it begins to impress us as a satire in its own right, directed not at the women but at the wits, and even going as far as to use the wickedness of the wits to justify the behaviour of the women.

During this process we are never, of course, allowed to forget that the speaker of the inner satire is primarily an object of criticism – loquacious, amoral, and affected:

> Here forced to cease
> Through want of breath, not will to hold her peace,
> She to the window runs, where she had spied

M

> Her much esteemed dear friend, the monkey, tied.
> With forty smiles, as many antic bows,
> As if 't had been the lady of the house,
> The dirty, chattering monster she embraced,
> And made it this fine, tender speech at last . . .
>
> [ll. 136-142]

Yet she is not without her own measure of satiric fervour, especially when, towards the end of her monologue, she does exactly what Artemisa is doing with her, in proffering a lengthy case-study, the history of Corinna. Even her moralizing, or, rather, anti-moralizing, can be granted a degree of positive effect. One will hardly respond as approvingly as Moll Flanders did to such sentiments as:

> A woman's ne'er so ruined but she can
> Be still revenged on her undoer, man;
> How lost soe'er, she'll find some lover, more
> A lewd, abandoned fool than she a whore.
>
> [ll. 185-188]

or the almost Popean:

> They little guess, who at our arts are grieved,
> The perfect joy of being well deceived . . .
>
> [ll. 114-115]

but one is pressingly aware of what the seventeenth century would have called the 'justness' of the observations and equally that they could never have been made in her own voice by Artemisa. Although the fine lady, like the claret-drinker, has no moral positives to put forward, hers is still an excellent point of vantage for a negative critique directed at the failings of others. She is distanced from the objects of her criticism only as far as is necessary for her to function freely as a critic: had she been any closer she would have become a case-study within her own satire much as she is within Artemisa's. The fact that we do not feel this of her helps to distinguish this kind of satire from the openly confessional type represented by Juvenal's ninth satire and Rochester's first-person satires against Mulgrave – 'A Very Heroic Epistle in Answer to

Ephelia' and 'An Epistolary Essay from M. G. to O. B. upon
Their Mutual Poems' – and yet there is at least an element
of the confessional, of gratuitous self-exposure, in this inner
satire of 'Artemisa to Chloe' as there is in 'Tunbridge Wells'
and the lampoon generally. The speaker is always recognizably
a part of the world she attacks in a way that is not true of
Artemisa, the balanced, humanely rational speaker of the outer
satire.

It should be clear already that this opposition of rhetorical
centres enables Rochester to dispose the matter of his argument
in a far more flexible way than was possible through the bare
list pattern of 'Tunbridge Wells'. The poem may be accounted
for in terms of traditional theory in so far as it uses a variant
of the *prolocutor-adversarius* pattern employed in 'Against
Mankind' in which the roles have somehow become reversed
so that Artemisa is the *adversarius* of the satirical fine lady at
the same time as the lady is hers. However, the pattern has
become much more than a convenient way 'to conceal the
bounds' of the argument.[29] In the conflict of points of view
Artemisa has the advantage of her rival's being included within
her field of attack, not to mention our natural preference for her
poignantly phrased idealism over the lady's uncharitableness
and worldly wisdom. And yet the fine lady's point of view
remains a cogent one. Moreover, she is able to qualify at least
some of Artemisa's arguments in a meaningful way and
possesses a far greater command of the rhetoric of deflation.

It will be helpful if at this stage we can look more closely
at what the two satirists stand for. It will also help if we can
bear in mind that the two ladies of the poem are in many ways
a reflection of the two selves of their creator, the affectionate
husband of Woodstock and the wild man of Whitehall (the
latter also, it would seem, a monkey-owner). The substance
of the debate is essentially that of Eliza and Olivia in Wycherley's
The Plain Dealer but the scales are more evenly weighted. The
position of the fine lady is Hobbesian and libertine (in the
seventeenth-century sense of the word): she preaches a moral
doctrine in which pleasure is the highest value and discretion
the most prized virtue, specifically the type of discretion
necessary to make a woman satisfied with a foolish lover
despite the superior attractiveness of a witty but more dangerous

one. Artemisa, on the other hand, speaks from a deeply-felt humanism, and in language which embodies the finest perceptions of the Augustan cult of good sense:

> Love, the most generous passion of the mind,
> The softest refuge innocence can find,
> The safe director of unguided youth,
> Fraught with kind wishes, and secured by truth;
> That cordial drop heaven in our cup has thrown
> To make the nauseous draught of life go down; . . .
> Is grown, like play, to be an arrant trade.
> The rooks creep in, and it has got of late
> As many little cheats and tricks as that.
>
> [ll. 40-45, 51-53]

The point of view criticized by Artemisa is, of course, exactly that maintained by the lady:

> How is love governed, love that rules the state,
> And pray, who are the men most worn of late?
> When I was married, fools were *à la mode*.
> The men of wit were then held *incommode*. . . .
>
> [ll. 101-104]

Yet the lady is able to justify herself in so far as her libertine point of view is a necessary one for inhabitants of a libertine world. Women must become jilts and dissemblers because men are worse. They must renounce love because it makes them vulnerable in a world whose idea of the sexual relationship is to make an instrument of another. The men of wit are

> Slow of belief, and fickle in desire,
> Who, ere they'll be persuaded, must inquire
> As if they came to spy, not to admire.
> With searching wisdom, fatal to their ease,
> They still find out why what may, should not please . . .
>
> [ll. 105-109]

In the light of this diagnosis (which Artemisa does not contest), it is the fool who will remain blind to women's pretences and infidelities who becomes the logical choice for a lover. The alternative is the fate of Corinna:

> Courted, admired, and loved, with presents fed;
> Youth in her looks, and pleasure in her bed;
> Till fate, or her ill angel, thought it fit
> To make her dote upon a man of wit,
> Who found 'twas dull to love above a day;
> Made his ill-natured jest, and went away.
> Now scorned by all, forsaken, and oppressed,
> She's a *memento mori* to the rest;
> Diseased, decayed, to take up half a crown
> Must mortgage her long scarf and manteau gown.
>
> [ll. 195-204]

The terms of the justification are not as broad as those of the condemnation, but they are terms whose validity we have to acknowledge.

Which is to say that the moral issue of the poem is in its confrontation of humanist and libertine platforms for human happiness; and that, while the superiority of the former is unquestioned, it is equally conceded that the latter may be the only basis for survival in the world the lady has to inhabit. The dilemma, to again refer to Wycherley, is exactly that posed by the vulnerable idealist, Alithea, and the triumphant realist, Horner, in *The Country Wife*. Anyone who wished to operate in this world where

> To an exact perfection they have wrought
> The action, love; the passion is forgot.
>
> [ll. 62-63]

will have to do so on a libertine basis or else risk the fate of Corinna or the equally horrible fate from which the over-trusting Alithea was only just saved by the intervention of Harcourt. But, having said this, one has still not accounted for the whole poem; and indeed it is doubtful whether the moral issue as articulated in the course of the debate is really the most important one. There are further dimensions to the debate which will not be perceived until we go beyond the circumscribed statements of Artemisa and the lady to the wider statement implied by the terms in which they conduct their respective sides of the debate and until we realize that the two debaters are being used by Rochester in entirely different ways, which are a consequence of the ways in which they have been used in separate traditions of satire with separate aims and separate concepts of the function of the satiric *prolocutor*. It is not merely a matter of opposed moral assumptions but of alternative methods of moral assertion which are not so much opposed as complementary and perhaps ultimately reconcilable.

I have already suggested that the real function of the lady is not to put positive recommendations, but rather to serve as a point of reference for a destructive critique of human behaviour. This permits us to link her with the kinds of satire created around the *personae* of the snarling satirist and the 'claret-drinker', the aim of which is similarly a negative criticism which may to some degree include the supposed propounder as one of its objects. (This is at any rate a pattern which recent writers have claimed to see in Jacobean satire[30] and which is sufficiently evident in the Restoration lampoon, though not always as blatantly as in the opening of 'Satyr Unmuzzl'd':

> Who'd be the man lewd libels to indite
> Yet fear to own what he ne'er fears to write?
> And meanly sneak his lampoons into th' world,
> Which are i'th'streets by porters dropp'd and hurl'd; . . .[31]

which turns out to be a sufficiently lewd libel – and anonymous.)

As well as opposing two sets of ethical assumptions, Rochester has also been opposing two different kinds of rhetorical strategy and ultimately two totally different traditions or sub-traditions of satire. The critique of the 'claret-drinker', like that of the lady, is a libertine critique: his aim is to expose the tyranny of appetite and the fragility of pretension. It is not his job to propose positives and it is rare for his approvable characteristics to extend beyond love of pleasure, hatred of sham, and the rather specialized kind of common sense essential for survival in a Hobbesian world. His positives, in fact, are determined in advance by the kinds of negatives he is being used to attack, and if he has to exemplify these negatives in his own person as well as in his ostensible victims it will certainly not damage, though it may complicate, the satire. We accept this position as a just basis for a destructive critique of certain kinds of human pretension, even while acknowledging that the positively asserted humanism of the neoclassical tradition was, at the time Rochester wrote, the only adequate basis for a satiric discourse which could deal with the potentialities as well as the actualities of life.

And so we return to the paradox that 'Artemisa to Chloe' is a satire within a satire; or, to put it more precisely, a lampoon within a satire. Although the inner satire lacks the epigrammatic structure which is the most consistent formal characteristic of the lampoon, it displays in very full measure the deflating rhetoric, the taunting, abusive tone, the eschewing of understatement, the sense of being presented with a speaker's opinions and sensations rather than an independent objective reality, the wholly partisan point of view, and the stance with regard to the world which we have previously characterized in terms of the *persona* of the 'claret-drinker' but which we can now define more generally as socially asserted libertinism. The world beyond Artemisa's front door is the world of 'fools, buffoons and praters' into which we ventured in 'Timon' and 'Tunbridge Wells', and the fine lady is the satirist of that world, a satirist, however, with no real hope or desire for a better. In opposition to her, the rational, measuredly idealistic tones of the outer satire, the tendency towards generalized reflective moralizing, the strong element of the ironical, the relative absence of unmediated invective, and the concern with positive recommendation as well as negative criticism, suggest increasingly the world of neoclassical satire and the satirically conceived lay-sermon or ethic epistle towards which it was eventually to evolve. Pope's approving quotation of one of Artemisa's best lines at the close of 'The Sixth Epistle of the First Book of Horace' makes the point sufficiently well.

I have already suggested that in 'Artemisa to Chloe' Rochester is writing about his own predicament both as a man and as an artist. The poem presents us with his two moral selves, country husband and London libertine, and simultaneously with two distinct visions of the satirist, claret drinker, and *vir bonus*. It is clear enough that by now he had strong reservations about the popular mode, especially about its narrow libertine basis and inability to generate meaningful communal positives. The day of the irresponsible censor, the malevolent atom, was passing: the satirist must learn to be an educator as well. And yet Rochester – and satire – still needed the lampoon manner. In

'Timon' we have seen him integrating the two traditions, in
'Artemisa to Chloe' just as carefully holding them apart – but
each is still essential if he is to say what he wants to say about
the world and his relationship to it. The difference is that in the
second satire the libertine satirist has to be hedged and qualified
by the presence and scrutiny of Artemisa.

The final stage in Rochester's rethinking of lampoon is found
in the last of the longer satires, 'An Epistolary Essay from M. G.
to O. B.'. The speaker of this poem, although intended as a
portrait of Rochester's enemy the Earl of Mulgrave, is still
recognizably a variant on the claret drinker. Tone and language
are exactly those of the customary lampoon exordium:

> I'm none of those who think themselves inspired,
> Nor write with the vain hopes to be admired,
> But from a rule I have upon long trial:
> T' avoid with care all sort of self-denial.
> Which way soe'er desire and fancy lead,
> Contemning fame, that path I boldly tread.
> And if, exposing what I take for wit,
> To my dear self a pleasure I beget,
> No matter though the censuring critic fret.
>
>   [ll. 12-20]

The case of 'M. G. to O. B.' is a particularly interesting one in
that until very recently it was believed to be a serious utterance
by Rochester in his own person,[32] a striking testimony to the
moral ambiguity of the lampoon *persona* and another hint why
Rochester was having progressively less use for it. As in
'Artemisa to Chloe' he is looking critically at what he himself
had been, and at a style that he had once used with complete
seriousness. But whereas in the earlier poem the assertions of
the lampooner are still, within their limits, meaningful ones,
now speech and mode are meant to provoke a wholly critical
reaction: the lampoon manner is being used in a spirit close to
that of parody. In doing this, Rochester is asserting the primacy
of his personality as poet over the *persona* of the satirist in a way
that we may think of as characteristically Augustan. He may
also be seen as foreshadowing the victory of collective values
and of the public voice over the partisan, individualistic values
and voices that satire had inherited from Marston, Cleveland,

Butler, and above all the lampooners. But Rochester did not explicitly proclaim this victory, and when it was proclaimed by others there were to be losses as well as gains.

NOTES

1. For detailed information, see George de Forrest Lord and others, edd., *Poems on Affairs of State* (New Haven, 1963), I, xxxii-xlii, and W. J. Cameron, 'A Late Seventeenth-Century Scriptorium', *Ren. and Mod. Studies*, 7 (1963), 25-52. The primary sources referred to by these writers may be taken as defining the limits of the particular tradition of satire here under discussion.

2. Samuel Johnson, *The Lives of the Poets*, ed. G. Birkbeck Hill (Oxford, 1905), I, 222.

3. It has been necessary in this article to generalize very broadly about the lampoon with only limited reference to particular examples. This has been done in the belief that the claims made are supported by a substantial body of the satirical verse contained in such printed collections as the Yale *Poems on Affairs of State* series referred to in note 1, in the numerous late-seventeenth and early-eighteenth-century publications under this and similar titles, and in the many manuscript anthologies of the period listed by the Yale editors and by D. M. Vieth (*Attribution in Restoration Poetry* [New Haven, 1963], pp. 493-496).
It should be understood that my immediate concern is with a particular tradition of popular satire using the pentameter couplet, which is to be seen as distinct from what we might loosely call the burlesque or Hudibrastic tradition, the drollery tradition (as represented in John Wardoper's anthology *Love and Drollery* [London: Routledge and Kegan Paul, 1969]), and the close imitations of classical satires, as well as from the vast and lively body of stanzaic lampoons stretching from the time of Suckling to that of Peter Pindar. I owe thanks to W. J. Cameron for indicating the necessity of such a statement of exclusions as one of a number of valuable comments on a draft of this paper. These also included a caution against excessively broad generalizing about 'traditions', which, I suspect, he would still feel to apply.

4. The tunes of the lampoons are given in Claude M. Simpson, *The British Broadside Ballad and Its Music* (New Brunswick, 1966),

and William Chappell, *Popular Music of the Olden Time*, 2 vols. (London, 1859; repr. New York: Dover, 1965).

5. See Arnold Davenport, ed., *The Poems of John Marston* (Liverpool, 1961), p. 3.

6. John Marston, 'Proemium in librum primum', 1. 2; in Davenport, p. 102. For further information on Jacobean satire and its prolocutor, see in particular John Peter, *Complaint and Satire in Early English Literature* (Oxford, 1956), pp. 104-186; Anthony Caputi, *John Marston, Satirist* (Ithaca, 1961), pp. 23-51; O. J. Campbell, *Comicall Satyre and Shakespeare's 'Troilus and Cressida'* (San Marino, 1938), pp. 15-53; and Alvin Kernan, *The Cankered Muse* (New Haven, 1959), pp. 81-140.

7. Cf. Mary Clare Randolph, 'The Structural Design of Formal Verse Satire', *PQ*, XXI (1941-42), 368-384.

8. Peter, pp. 155-156.

9. *Poems on Affairs of State*. Vol. III (London, 1704), p. 123.

10. Bodl. MS. Firth c. 15, p. 209. This manuscript has been chosen as the source for a number of poems not available in worthwhile printed sources because of its generally reliable text.

11. 'Satyra Nova', l. 14; in Davenport, p. 163. An additional link between Jacobean and Restoration practice is a fondness for heading poems with Latin tags. The four-volume *Poems on Affairs of State* (1699-1707) contains a number of titles of this kind, among them *Non ego sum vates, sed prisci Conscius Ævi* [I, 117], *Nobilitas sola atque unica virtus est* [IB, 33], *Barbara Pyramidum silent miracula Memphis* [IB, 35], and *Quem Natura negat dabit Indignatio Versum* [see note 9].

12. For some representative examples, see Yale *POAS*, I, 20-156. Further titles are given in Mary Tom Osborne, *Advice-to-a-Painter Poems* (Austin, 1949).

13. Yale *POAS*, I, 396-413.

14. The point is discussed by Vieth (*Attribution*, pp. 275-278), where after a careful consideration of the evidence he assigns both 'Tunbridge Wells' and 'Timon' to the spring of 1674. Of these two dates, it is that given to 'Timon', depending as it does on a reference to the Continental campaign of that year, which is most conducive to postponement. We have no reason to suppose that the hectors are any more up to date with current affairs than they are in their literary gossip. In fact, it could be argued that the reference would not have had real satiric point unless it was already stale at the time of writing.

15. As stated previously, this study makes no attempt to deal with this aspect of the lampoon tradition which is quite independent in its descent of Hall and Marston.

16. B.M. Harl. MS. 6913, fol. 132^r.

17. Yale *POAS*, III, 189-214.

18. The best text known to me is that in Bodl. MS. Firth c. 15, pp. 268-274. A diplomatic reprint of this text is included at the end of this volume (Appendix A).

19. This passage includes nine lines rejected by Vieth on the ground of uncertain authenticity.

20. Peter, p. 34.

21. See the conclusions of 'A Faithful Catalogue of Our Most Eminent Ninnies' (Yale *POAS*, III, 214) and *The Battle of the Books*.

22. *The Lives of the Poets*, I, 224.

23. *The Complete Poems of John Wilmot, Earl of Rochester* (New Haven, 1968), p. 120.

24. See Olga Rossettini, *Les influences anciennes et Italiennes sur la satire en France au XVIe siècle* (Florence, 1958), pp. 204-213.

25. V. de S. Pinto, *Poems by John Wilmot Earl of Rochester*, 2nd edn. (London, 1963), p. 197.

26. See Vieth, *Attribution*, pp. 281-292.

27. See Vieth, *Poems*, p. 68, n.

28. See *Alexander Pope: Epistles to Several Persons*, ed. James E. Wellington (Miami, 1963), pp. 3-7.

29.　　'He gains all points, who pleasingly confounds,
　　　　Surprizes, varies, and conceals the Bounds.'
　　　　　　　　　　　[Pope, 'Epistle to Burlington', ll. 55-56]

30. See, in particular, Kernan, *The Cankered Muse*, and, for a Restoration application, Rose Zimbardo, 'Structural Design in the *Plain Dealer*', *SEL*, I (1961), 1-18.

31. *POAS* (Yale), II, 209.

32. See Vieth, *Attribution*, pp. 103-136. Vieth was not aware of the poem's quasi-parodic relationship to the composite volume *Ovid's Epistles Translated* (1680). See also below pp. 284-5.

The Poems of John Oldham

HAROLD F. BROOKS

The poems of John Oldham, as Dryden reminds us in the noble
lines to his memory, are the work of a young man. He died at
thirty, in 1683, and wrote his poetry within the preceding
decade. The best of it still deserves to please. But the differences
between the best and the weakest of it cannot be properly understood apart from the poet's development and the genres he
attempted. As a practitioner of various genres, and in those of
the Augustan 'Imitation' and of heroic satire an important contributor to the form they afterwards assumed in the hands of
major poets, he is significant to the historian of literature. For
the social historian, he has a wealth of topical allusion and description: moreover, he both discusses the social position of the
man of letters and exemplifies it in his own career and in
the poems by which he hoped that career might be furthered.
Something should be said on these topics before concentrating
attention on his poetry as a source of more purely literary
pleasure.[1]

Much of Oldham's verse might bear the title he gave to a
fragment among his MS. drafts: 'Upon the Town and Times'.
To check and to realize its precise value for historical purposes,
the historian must consult all the relevant documentation he
can find in literature, diaries, memoirs, private correspondence
and archives, state papers, and the like. But the topicality has
its savour for the ordinary reader too. Especially 'in social and
moral satire' of this period, as Roger Sharrock has said, 'the
sense of vivid contemporary immediacy is often the chief
pleasure to be gained from the poem'.[2] To extend and sharpen
this sense in reading Oldham, an edition with full historical
notes is wanted.[3] Even without this, however, one excellent way

of enjoying his topicalities, his pictures of metropolitan life, and in particular his Imitation of Juvenal's third satire, is to treat them as part of a series which includes scenes from Restoration comedy, some of Dryden's prologues, Swift's 'Description of the Morning' and 'A City Shower', Gay's *Trivia*, and Johnson's *London*. On the prospects of educated men with their living to earn, whether as chaplains or as poor parsons, private tutors or schoolmasters, or precariously as dramatists and poets, Oldham is again making his own contribution to a traditional subject; and it is worth while to compare what he writes with Burton's 'Digression of the Miseries of Scholars', Joseph Hall's Satire VI, Book II, in *Virgidemiarum*, the opening episode of Jonson's *Poetaster*, Cowley's poem, 'The Complaint', and Eachard's *Grounds and Occasions of the Contempt of the Clergy*.

Oldham contributed to this tradition out of personal experience. When, after four years at Oxford, he returned home in 1674 to Shipton Moyne, it was to teach for a year or more in the school by keeping which his father, a minister deprived as a nonconformist, supplemented the income from a small private estate. His earliest extant poems were composed at this time: occasional pieces likely to recommend him to families of standing in the neighbourhood. Probably 'To Madam L. E.' is an instance. It is tempting to expand 'L. E.' as 'Lady Estcourt'; the Estcourts were seated hard by the Oldhams at Shipton Moyne and were patrons of the living Oldham's father had held at Long Newnton, on the further side of the Estcourt park. When Abraham and Joan Kingscote of Kingscote lost their eleven-year-old daughter, Oldham began an address to the mother, and wrote his completed lines, 'On the Death of Mrs. Katharine Kingscote'. Like those to 'L. E.' they are juvenilia; a conventional copy of verses. Both pieces derive closely from Waller's and Cowley's poems of compliment, and repeatedly borrow from them. The major work of these months in Gloucestershire was the elegy on Charles Morwent, Oldham's bosom friend at college. Elaborated on the largest scale, and with evident devotion, this ode is not without literary merits, to which we shall return. With the friendship it commemorates, it probably assisted Oldham's escape from provincial obscurity to the vicinity of the metropolis. For the headmaster at Whitgift School, Croydon, was a relative by marriage of Charles Morwent's father; and by 1676 the poet was usher (assistant master) under him.

At Croydon, he again pursued acquaintance with neighbouring gentry. His elegy on Harman Atwood of Sanderstead (d. 16 February 1677) eulogizes a pious benefactor of the Whitgift Foundation, whose niece the headmaster had married. The paraphrase on the 137th Psalm was written 22 December 1676 at Beddington; evidently Oldham was spending the Christmas season in the household of Sir Nicholas Carew.[4] He corresponded in verse and Latin prose with a half-cousin of the Carews, John Spencer. His 'Letter from the Country' (July 1678) was a reply to a verse-letter from Spencer (18 March 1678). Possibly a second Scriptural paraphrase, 'David's Lamentation' (September 1677), was written for a Carew audience.

Meanwhile, however, a more dazzling opportunity presented itself, as a result of Oldham's first satiric poem (July 1676), later christened, but not by him, 'A Satyr Against Vertue'. It was 'Suppos'd to be spoken by a Court Hector at Breaking of the Dial in Privy Garden'. This was a drunken exploit of Rochester's, and brought the satirist an appreciative visit from the Earl himself and some of his fellow-wits. In the sequel, Oldham appears to have composed several poems primarily for this circle: the obscene satires 'Upon the Author of the Play call'd Sodom' and 'Sardanapalus', intended to remain in MS., and 'A Dithyrambique on Drinking', 'Suppos'd to be spoken by Rochester at the Guinny-club' (5 August 1677). 'The Dream' (10 March 1677) and 'Upon a Lady: Out of Voiture' may also belong to this series. To anticipate, in more important poems than these Oldham came to profit from Rochester's literary example; and after Rochester's death (26 July 1680) he proclaimed the debt in a pastoral elegy, a version of Moschus' *Bion*. In 1676-7, he was cherishing hopes of notice at Court, from the household of James, the King's brother. Drafting a Latin letter, he refers to a lady who is coiffeuse to James's daughter Mary, and perhaps, he adds slyly, has charge of her rouge, too. This explains the name he bestows on 'Cosmelia', to whom he addresses love-verses in September 1676. Whether inspired by real emotion or not, poetically speaking these are mere *vers d'occasion*, no less derivative than the Kingscote elegy, from which indeed they borrow. The same woman is the imagined heroine of 'The Dream', which doubly distances, as wish-fulfilment and by pastoral convention, a scene of courtship ending in consummation. That November, Cosmelia assisted the poet in a major bid for Court favour, placing in the hands of Princess Mary (or more likely her mother) his ode upon her marriage to William of Orange. But, he comments, his pains were lost upon the recipient. They brought him, however, his first appearance in print: the poem, written 5 November (the morning after the marriage itself), was published within a few days by Herringman. Perhaps through this contact, Oldham seems to have got wind of a project Herringman did not publicly announce until February 1679: to bring out a new edition of Ben Jonson. For the Jonson ode, written at Croydon some time between 1 January and 24 March 1678, is optimistically entitled 'Upon the Works of Ben Jonson, reprinted'. Oldham wrote it, no doubt, in the hope of seeing it prefixed to the new edition.

October 1679 brought him a subject of passionate interest to the religious and political public of the whole nation. With the murder of Godfrey, following upon Oates's allegations of a Popish plot, the Popish Terror seized upon Tories as well as Whigs. Oldham determined to satirize the Jesuits, believed to be the arch-champions of counter-Reformation. After two false starts, he settled down to composing *Garnet's Ghost*. An early draft has a few heavily-deleted lines attacking the Catholic James, against whom it was part of the Whigs' Exclusion policy to direct the Terror. Sir Nicholas Carew was a strong Whig. But the completed satire and its three successors contain nothing to further party purposes: to suppose them Whiggish is absurd considering that they were published by Hindmarsh, bookseller under the patronage of James himself, and capable of being described as 'the notedst Tory in the town'. Oldham may have begun the series in the Whig ambience of Carew; he continued it in the Tory household of Sir Edward Thurland, who had been James's Solicitor-General. For on 1 March 1679 he left the Whitgift School to be private tutor to Thurland's grandson, at Reigate. As the months passed, Tories began to shrug off the Terror as a ploy of the Whigs, who were left the

only wholehearted believers in the plot: Dryden's verdict upon
it became possible:

Some truth there was, but dashed and brewed with lies.[5]

Oldham changed with the nation: as early as 9 March 1680, in
'The Careless Good Fellow' he treats the Terror with a
humorous detachment of which no Shaftesbury Whig would
have been capable; and in his 'Imitation of Horace, Satire I, ix'
(June 1681), the impertinent who 'begins to plague' his victim
'with the Plot', and demands 'are you not afraid of Popery?'
(under the King's successor), is coolly answered:

No more than my Superiors: why should I?

Oldham's horror of Catholic militancy and Catholic superstitions
and corruptions may have been first implanted by his upbringing
in his Presbyterian father's house; but even in the *Satyrs Upon
the Jesuits* his point of view, proper to an Oxford graduate, was
that of the Church-and-King men who condemned Papist and
Covenanting Puritan alike.

　　Piratically published almost at once (1679), the first Satyr
upon the Jesuits had a great success; and so, on their appearance
in the authorized edition of 1681, did the whole four with their
prologue. *A Satyr Against Vertue* was also pirated early in 1679;
the printer evidently Mary Clarke, who printed for Hindmarsh.
This piracy may have been what brought Oldham into touch
with Hindmarsh, who became his regular publisher. The
pirated text was reprinted by Hindmarsh in the authorized first
edition of *Satyrs Upon the Jesuits* – reprinted with most of its
corruptions uncorrected. Clearly it was this bad text which
provoked Oldham's satire entitled, in *Some New Pieces*, 'Upon a
Printer', but in the autograph, 'Upon a Bookseller'.[6] At that
time (Christmas 1680) Oldham was still a dependent tutor at
Reigate: but the double encouragement of having found in
Hindmarsh someone likely to go on publishing his work, and
of the success his anti-Jesuit satires had met with, no doubt
prompted his decision to come to London in the hope of paying
his way as an author. 'An Allusion to Martial' informs us that
he is living in a garret at the far end of Clerkenwell. *Some New
Pieces* came out by the end of 1681 and included his Imitation of
the *Ars Poetica*. This, he says, was a task imposed on him: in

N

answer, one may guess, to Sir William Soame's attack upon
him as 'the Author of Sardanapalus . . . and . . . other Writeings'.
Soame had adjured the 'School-Master'

> From the Boys hands, take Horace into Thine,
> And thy rude Satyrs, by his Rules, refine.[7]

A second edition of *Satyrs Upon the Jesuits* was called for *c.* May
1682. But to earn a competence by literary authorship, without
assistance from patronage or private means, was hardly in
Restoration times a practical proposition. Oldham had to turn
tutor again: his new pupil was the eldest son of Sir William
Hickes of Rookwood, at Low Leyton, Essex. Sir William had
an estate near the Oldhams in Gloucestershire: the poet's cousin
Mary had married into the Wickwar branch of the family, two
members of which had been his contemporaries and probable
acquaintances at Oxford. When Sir William's son was judged
ready to pursue his education by foreign travel, Oldham declined
the opportunity to accompany him: it is uncertain whether he
renewed his attempt at independence, or whether it was without
an interim that the young William Pierrepont, from June 1682
fourth Earl of Kingston, became his patron. He was invited to
the Earl's mansion at Holme Pierrepont, near Nottingham,
where just as his gift was maturing and his prospects brighten-
ing, he died of smallpox and was buried 7 December 1683.

Of his life from 1681 we know little. While at Rookwood, he
studied medicine with a distinguished physician, Richard Lower,
who figures as 'a Doctor, my deer Friend' in the Imitation of
Horace, Satire I, ix (June 1681), and is paid a compliment in the
Imitation of the *Ars Poetica*. In the poet's last year, perhaps in
his last fortnight, he wrote the ode to be set to music by Dr John
Blow for St Cecilia's Day 1684; the second of the annual
celebrations inaugurated 22 November 1683. It is in 1681-1683,
beginning with the 'Imitation' of Horace, that Oldham is
settling into his best vein. 'A Satyr . . . dissuading from . . .
Poetry', 'A Satyr address'd to a Friend . . . about to leave
the University', and the Imitation from Boileau's fifth satire,
'touching Nobility', can hardly be far in date from the Imitations
of Juvenal, Satires XIII and III, and Boileau, Satire VIII,
composed in April, May, and October 1682. One would have
liked more biographical information about Oldham's final period,

both because it was so fruitful and because if Dryden had any personal acquaintance with him it must have been at this time.

In this sketch of Oldham's career as a poet, we have seen him attempting different genres. Poets of the Restoration were much concerned with the tone and techniques proper to the genres their poems belonged to, deviated from, or sought to combine; that is, with the 'decorum' fitting for each 'kind' of poetry. To assess Oldham's work fairly and appreciate it fully, we need to look at it according to its 'kinds' and some of its antecedents. His short poems on several occasions of grief, congratulation, or compliment have already been dealt with. Other short pieces are translations from the classics, most of them amatory, but one of them bibulous, an Anacreontique successfully emulating Cowley's. This version of 'The Cup' has not, however, the memorable brilliance of Rochester's,[8] whose ear was finer, his imagination more lyrical, and who, by 'imitating' not translating, gave his poem a topical air. As a periphrastic translation Oldham's is more faithful, while running with the right ease and freedom. Sharing this quality, his 'Catullus Epigram VII Imitated' is again indebted to Cowley's Anacreontiques; and again, while retaining its own merit, pales beside the poem of a great lyrist; for Jonson's 'Kiss me sweet: the wary lover' is inspired by the same original.[9] But Jonson's 'Dialogue of Horace and Lydia' shows the disadvantages of his literalism (or 'metaphrase') in close translation. Neither he nor Herrick captures the gracefulness which makes the value of this slight ode in the Latin. Rightly, Restoration taste would reject Herrick's epithet 'love-cast-off Lydia' and Jonson's compound 'left-Lydia', such inversion for rhyme as Herrick's

> My heart now set on fire is,

and such phrases as Jonson's

> His arms more acceptable free,

and

> With gentle Calais, Thurine Ornith's son.

Despite a banal couplet,

> *Thyrsis* by me has done the same,
> The Youth burns *me* with mutual Flame,

Oldham's version has more 'decorum', and is preferable also to

Flatman's, where the pattern of rhyme lacks facility. This is not to say that either in the Oldham, or indeed perhaps in the Latin itself, we can find the fascination which made this lyric one of the most often translated in the seventeenth century. Ovid's *Amores*, and the Fragment then ascribed to Petronius, were favourites too, though not to the same degree. The 'Petronius' is echoed in Rochester's 'Platonic Lady'; and in Suckling's 'Against Fruition' on which Oldham drew in amplifying his paraphrase. Jonson's close version reads admirably, and, as paraphrase, Oldham's reads equally well, with the ready flow prized in such a genre by Restoration poets. Among the *Amores*, Rochester translated II. ix with concise felicity: Oldham chose lighter pieces and a lighter style. Not improbably it was Cowley's fantasia, 'The Inconstant', on the theme of II. iv that prompted him to try a direct rendering. In II. v, he is less elegant and tender than Sedley, whose narrative moves naturally where Oldham's seems forced and is sometimes clogged with tasteless ornament. Nevertheless, Oldham's is the more dramatic; he begins and ends with more sprightliness and vigour: he strives for effect, but sometimes obtains it.

It is not only in anacreontics and the *Amores*, and in the least mature of the occasional poems, that Oldham shows himself a disciple of Cowley, who in the earlier years of the Restoration had more prestige as pioneer and model than any other contemporary or recent English poet. As innumerable conscious and unconscious borrowings testify, Oldham knew 'the beloved Cowley'[10] by heart. With a very few exceptions, Oldham's poems are either in the heroic couplet, or are Cowleian Pindariques. The Pindarique appealed to baroque taste, and offered some escape from the reaction against every sort of 'enthusiasm', including *'furor poeticus'*, which was consequent upon the Civil War and went with the new stress on lucidity of expression and plain good sense. Though the regular structure of Pindar's own odes was recognized in the earlier and the later imitations of it by Jonson, Congreve, and Gray, Cowley ignored it. According to Cowley's 'Praise of Pindar', he is uncircumscribed, in virtue of his unique genius, either by Nature or by Art, and in the 'Ode.Upon Liberty' he is the type of liberty itself. From these poems, and from the preface and notes to the 'Pindarique Odes', we learn what Cowley finds in him: unexhausted abundance of invention; noble extravagance; an 'enthusiastical' manner, falling boldly from one thing into another with disregard of transition and a readiness to digress; all matched with an equal bravura in hyperbole, simile, and extended metaphor that partakes of simile. Similar qualities were seen, by such Orientalists as John Gregory, in Eastern poetry, and especially in the Hebrew poetry of the Bible. This perception, E. N. Hooker points out,[11] is significant for Samuel Woodforde's choice of Cowleian Pindarique for his paraphrases upon Psalms 18, 50, 68, and 104. 'The Psalms of David', writes Cowley, 'I believe to have been . . . the most exalted pieces of *Poesie*'; and again, 'the manner of the *Prophets* writing, especially of *Isaiah*, seems to me very like that of *Pindar* . . . '.[12] His own sequence of 'Pindarique Odes', which begins with Imitations of Pindar's Second Olympic and First Nemaean, ends with paraphrases on the 34th chapter of Isaiah and on the Biblical account of the Plagues of Egypt.

Perhaps it is only in contrast with the rival or complementary ideal so admirably embodied in the Augustan heroic-couplet styles at their best that Pindarique verse, as actually written by Cowley and Oldham, can claim the libertarian boldness promised by its inventor. We are acquainted with styles much bolder than the Pindarique both in technique and imagination. In their verse, Pindariques are free in so far as the lengths of stanza and of line, the disposition of the shorter and longer lines in the stanza, and the placing of the rhymes, are wholly at the discretion of the poet; the stanza need fall into no regular pattern, nor is one stanza to repeat the pattern of another. The metre, however, is consistently iambic. Significantly, too, in the odes from Pindar Cowley has a note: 'the Connexion of this *Stanza* is very obscure in the *Greek*, and could not be rendred without much *Paraphrase*', and other notes to similar effect.[13] In practice, that is, sharing the predominant tastes of his time, he supplies more logical progression than he finds in Pindar, taking away much of the abruptness that up to a point he admires. Something like that abruptness does appear with effect in 'The Resurrection', but the odes which have worn best, 'To Mr. Hobs' and 'To the Royal Society', appeal rather as essays in verse, firm in structure, on subjects of lasting interest. Cowley was at his best in the essay, not in metaphysical poetry, where he inherited an

ossifying tradition. For rhetorical heightening and ornamenta-
tion, Cowleian Pindarique is apt to rely on frigid conceits and
too-calculated hyperboles. Together with a prevailing dearth of
verbal music, these overworked conceits and hyperboles (often
trite to begin with), afflict the genre, as it proliferates among
imitators, with a mass of unnaturally inflated but incurably
prosaic verse.

Cowley uses the Pindarique for odes from Latin – from
Horace – as well as Greek; for paraphrases of sacred text; for
poems of moral reflection; for panegyric, in elegy and epithalamium, and in praise of originators in the arts of civilized life
and thought and culture: Bacon, Hervey, and Hobbes. In each
of these types, Oldham follows him. Specifically, too, 'The
Praise of Pindar' suggested 'The Praise of Homer'; and a note
to it, on Pindar's lost dithyrambiques and on two odes of
Horace that might have an affinity with them, gave the hint
for the 'Dithyrambique on Drinking'; while 'David's Lamentation' takes up Cowley's intention to have concluded *Davideis*
with a version of the same lament.[14]

In the earliest of Oldham's Pindariques, the elegy on Morwent,
he rises in at least one stanza[15] to the genuinely metaphysical:

> Thy Soul within such silent Pomp did keep,
> As if Humanity were lull'd asleep.
> So gentle was thy Pilgrimage beneath,
> Time's unheard Feet scarce make less noise,
> Or the soft Journey which a Planet goes;
> Life seem'd all calm as its last Breath.
> A still Tranquillity so husht thy Breast,
>   As if some *Halcyon* were its Guest,
>   And there had built her Nest;
> It hardly now enjoys a greater Rest.
> As that smooth Sea which wears the Name of *Peace*,
>   Still with one even Face appears,
> And feels no Tides to change it from its place,
> No Waves to alter the fair Form it bears;
>   As that unspotted Sky,
>   Where *Nile* does want of Rain supply,
> Is free from Clouds, from Storms is ever free;
> So thy unvary'd mind was always one,
> And with such clear Serenity still shone,
> As caus'd thy little World to seem all temp'rate Zone.

Though most of the comparisons are hackneyed, the rhetoric has melody, and the style looks back to the earlier and more living phases of the metaphysical tradition. The success, however, particularly of the first five lines, is in a vein from which Oldham, like the age, was moving away: it has no parallel in his subsequent poems. Yet even taking the elegy as a whole, the elaboration of its forty-three stanzas was evidently a labour of love; the borrowings are sought out from appropriate contexts and well woven together; and the progress of the poem, as Mr R. I. Mills has shown,[16] is strongly organized. These merits, as he insists, may account for Pope's listing it among 'The most Remarkable Works in this Author'.

The elegy on Atwood and the epithalamium for William and Mary, with the 'Counterpart to the *Satyr against Vertue*', are competent copies of verses, suited to their occasions. Among such things if they are a little above average, it is in virtue of Oldham's attention to structure, seen already on the larger scale of the Morwent ode. In the Atwood, for instance, he begins with two paradoxes concerning virtue: its mortality, and its exemplification in the person of a lawyer. Throughout, he continues to alternate topics which might serve in a hundred panegyrics, with topics particular to Atwood himself: his justice, his generous benefactions, and his piety, free from acrimonious party zeal. He concludes, conventionally, with Atwood's reception into Heaven, but accommodates his state of bliss to his profession, as 'the calm . . . Vacation of Eternity'. This wit may seem incongruous but was a decoration acceptable to baroque taste. The Atwood elegy, and more directly the palinode or 'Counterpart' to the *Satyr against Vertue* are poems of moral reflection: in this, and as another competent copy of verses, the paraphrase of Aristotle's ode upon Honour can be grouped with them.

The three 'sacred Odes' may be considered the weakest of Oldham's Pindariques. In 'David's Lamentation' and Psalm CXXXVII, amplification, which is all that he has to contribute, drowns the pathos of both originals and turns the fierce hatred at the end of the Psalm into a display of 'horrid' writing. If we allow that the original passion might be sacrificed for a different sort of effect, we are still disappointed by the mediocrity of the *amplificatio* itself, which employs with too little address the stock procedures of the school or college theme. This fault, making the poem too much of an academic exercise, extends also to the 'Hymn of S. Ambrose'. But since the original of that (the *Te Deum*) was already a public and declamatory poem, the *amplificatio* is at least not out of keeping. The 'Hymn' is more sounding than the two paraphrases from Scripture and the rhetoric is enlivened here and there: now by a Lucretian tag – 'the eternal flaming Jail', now by a Miltonic phrase – 'the bright Realms of everlasting day'; now by baroque conceits – 'an Angel-Laureat', the Prophets as 'Envoys extraordinary'; now by the quasi-dramatization of the Day of Wrath.

'The Praise of Homer' and the ode on Jonson owe part of their interest to their place in a tradition comprising two related 'kinds' of poetry. The first – to which, as I briefly indicated, the 'Homer' and 'Jonson' directly belong – eulogizes some original contributor to human culture, and is exemplified by Horace and Cowley on Pindar, and Cowley on Hobbes. The second sketches the progress of some art or craft, as, on the hint of Virgil in his first Georgic,[17] Dryden in *Annus Mirabilis* takes occasion to sketch the progress of navigation. This 'kind' culminates in Gray's 'Progress of Poesy'. The two are combined in Cowley's 'Ode To the Royal Society', which includes a 'praise of Bacon' within its 'progress of philosophy'; Gray's ode, also, mounts to its great eulogies of Shakespeare, Milton, and Dryden. And though Oldham is writing panegyrics, not 'progress poems', at the start he hails each hero as a founder: Jonson is the 'mighty *Founder* of our Stage'; Homer 'the unexhausted Ocean, whence / Spring first, and still do flow th'eternal Rills of sence'. Both these odes of Oldham's are constructed by using the recognized components of an academically-elaborated theme, from *exordium* to *conclusio*; but in each ode he moves freely between *narratio*, *confirmatio*, and *confutatio*, so that the sequence, though firmly controlled, is not too stereotyped.[18] In the Jonson, narration of the dramatist's achievement predominates; but in stanza 3 Oldham confutes the 'meer . . . Enthusiasts' who contemn the conscious artist, and in stanzas 9 and 10 those who charge Jonson with plagiarism and hold his slowness in composition to be a defect. That it was not so, is confirmed by comparison with the procedure of great painters and of God in creating the Universe. The favourite baroque analogy with the Deity is employed also in the *exordium* of The Praise of Homer. Homer's descriptive power is 'narrated' in stanza 2 and the inspiring prowess of his hero, Achilles, in stanza 3; but his greatness is affirmed chiefly by *confirmatio*: by what the *Iliad* meant to Alexander; by the consensus of nations and the universal currency of Homer's classical Greek in contrast with the English poets' vernacular; and by his power to confer a fame more lasting than any statue or royal palace. Following the *exordium*, Oldham confutes the tradition of Homer's blindness; and he begins the conclusion with another *confutatio*: Claudius' design of burning Homer's works only showed his own insanity. They are imperishable, until the general conflagration at Doomsday. Thus the poem is made to end as it began, with theological imagery. The same technique is used in concluding the Jonson ode: the image of travel transcending former limits, applied in the *exordium* to Jonson's dramatic art, is now applied to his more than solar glory. 'The Praise of Homer' is diversified by a profusion of rhetorical figures: parallel phrasing; the supposed vision; apostrophe, apologia, paradox, rhetorical question, carefully-chosen epithet, periphrasis, allusion, and analogy. The 'Jonson' has its share of these and both odes feature the topical conceit, as in the comparisons with contemporary finance, foreign trade, and religious extremists. Metaphor so deliberately extended that in effect it resembles simile appears several times in the 'Homer'; but in the 'Jonson' each stanza depends upon one or upon two such metaphors; the recurrence of this one figure strengthens the unity of the piece.[19] The workmanship of the 'Homer' extorts a certain admiration; but the 'invention' (or finding of material) draws mainly on commonplaces, and the qualities which for us give his epics their greatness are barely touched on. The 'Jonson' is much more interesting. Its topics again were commonplaces, most of them treated in *Jonsonus Virbius*; but Oldham has marshalled them in a verse-essay coherently summing-up admiration of Jonson as it stood in 1678.

Two Pindariques begin Oldham's career as a satirist. The 'Ode. Aude aliquid . . .' (*A Satyr against Vertue*) and 'A Dithyrambique on Drinking' again belong to a recognized 'kind' of composition: the ironic celebration of something which without irony would be denounced or scorned; or conversely the vituperation of something which without irony would be eulogized. The main line of the tradition, from ancient Greek and Roman times, has been very fully traced by H. K. Miller in his article 'The Paradoxical Encomium with special reference to its vogue in England from 1600 to 1800'.[20] If Erasmus, in *Encomium Moriae*, might praise Folly in prose, with all the more licence a poet might denigrate Vertue and incorporate in his *vituperatione* an encomium on Vice, employing an ostensibly grand Pindarique as his vehicle. Cowley had not turned the Pindarique to the purpose of satiric irony; Oldham's distinguished predecessor there was Samuel Butler in his *'Pindarick Ode' To the Memory of the Most Renowned Du Vall* (a notorious highwayman), published, as by the author of *Hudibras*, in 1671, the year following its 'hero's' execution. Oldham, at twenty-three, falls short of Butler.[21] Beside Butler's his irony shows laboured and too often obvious, and still more so perhaps when compared (as D. M. Vieth compares it) with Rochester's in 'A Very Heroical Epistle to Ephelia'.[22] In the comparison with Rochester, some allowance is to be made for difference of genre: lightness of touch is more requisite in an epistle, 'heroical' though it may be, than in an ostensible Pindarique. As in Pindarique eulogy, Oldham has a theme to amplify, and amplifies it by the stock rhetorical methods. The pedantry noted by Vieth comes then, in part, from the genre in which Oldham is writing; yet not wholly, since Butler can write his comparable Pindarique without it. Butler's satire, too, is complex and varied in its topical application; Oldham's topic of virtue and its opposite is conceived for the most part in such general terms as to constitute only the tritest of subjects. For Restoration amateurs of the paradox this would detract little from his performance: the wit they looked for was there in the sophistical attack on the impregnable and defence of the indefensible. This scholastic shadow-boxing, however, is not all that the poem amounts to. It is 'suppos'd to be spoken' by Rochester at the height of one of his more outrageous exploits, and is best when it best lives up to this pretence, satirizing attitudes that were genuinely part of the libertine tradition, and caricaturing sentiments which (as we know from his conversations with Burnet and from elsewhere) the Earl might indeed have uttered: for instance, the appeal from morals to Nature, since virtue is 'too difficult for Flesh and Blood', and the pride in an immoralism elegant, 'studied and elab'rate'. Rochester, for a time, fostered his own legend, as when he adjured Henry Savile to send wine 'as ever thou dost hope to *out-do Machiavel*, or *equal Me*':[23] and Oldham caught the spirit of it. Vieth rightly claims that he 'succeeds where all other satirists failed: he endows [his] mythic image of Rochester with some of the stature the man possessed in real life'.[24] The image is sustained in the 'Dithyrambique', which magnifies Rochester in a role the real man was to acknowledge (to Burnet) he had fallen into: 'the natural heate of his fancy, being inflamed by Wine, made him so extravagantly pleasant, that many to be more diverted by that humor, studied to engage him deeper and deeper in Intemperance'.[25] In its truth to this vein of extravagant fancy, the 'Dithyrambique' is genuinely amusing, and though I admit it has less range than its predecessor, I confess I read it with more pleasure. And though the libertine outlook offers a worthwhile target at certain periods and in certain circles (of which Rochester's was one), the false glory of intoxication, by whatever drug, is more widely and constantly in need of reduction to absurdity. One can see, though why it was the *Satyr against Vertue* that Pope listed among the 'most Remarkable Works in this Author'.[26]

The satires 'Upon a Woman' and 'Upon a Bookseller' are *dirae*: 'a maner of imprecation' (says Puttenham) 'such as Ovide [made] against Ibis',[27] the 'kind' by which (the story went) Archilochus drove Lycambus and his daughters to suicide. The two by Oldham are his first satires in the heroic couplet: apart from that, their interest lies chiefly in his pungent topical allusions, and his avowal, made also in the 'Apology' appended to the *Satyr against Vertue*, of a vocation as satirist.

> Had he a Genius, and Poetique Rage,
> Great as the Vices of this guilty Age . . .
> To noble Satyr he'd direct his Aim,

he declares in the 'Apology'. The times invite satire: and satire, he has begun to recognize, is his talent, the art in which he can shine. The bookseller was rash to provoke a poet who is not only

> Born to chastise the Vices of the Age,

but who seeks occasion for satire

> To shew my Parts, and signalize my Muse.

It was 'noble' satire that he aspired to write: what Dryden, distinguishing Boileau's *Lutrin* from Scarron's 'travestie' of Virgil, and his own *MacFlecknoe* or *Absalom* from Butler's burlesque *Hudibras*, calls 'manly' satire. The epithets designate a genre partaking of the grandeur of 'heroic poetry itself', of which (Dryden claims) 'the satire is undoubtedly a species'.[28] The first approach to this ideal was the mock-heroic; and in 1678 or 1679 Oldham transcribed *MacFlecknoe*, while in October 1678 he began a translation of *Le Lutrin*, completing the first canto in a style as lively as the original, if less polished.[29] Satire could be taken, however, beyond the comedy of mock-heroic and brought yet closer to epic. This was to be Dryden's achievement in *Absalom*, where, without forgoing the 'fine raillery' he admired in Horace, he combined his venom in greater earnest with the 'majesty' he found in Juvenal. Towards that ideal, Oldham in the *Satyrs Upon the Jesuits* made certain advances upon *MacFlecknoe* – which is not to pretend these *Satyrs* can compete with it as a work of art. No doubt it was in terms of this shared ideal of heroic satire that Dryden, characteristically generous, could write of the much younger poet,

> To the same Goal did both our Studies drive,
> The last set out the soonest did arrive.[30]

Oldham anticipated Dryden in taking for his subject the national crisis, and treating it with an elevation of style which is not (as in mock-heroic) merely assumed. Juvenal is his prime model; and as Dryden says of Juvenal, 'he could not rally, but he could declaim'.[31] In the first three *Satyrs* especially, the grandiose declamation animates his unnaturally imagined world of evil; the monotonous gloomy hyperbole, like Nat Lee's, creates an aesthetic effect. He treats the crisis of 1678-9 with some reference to the Popish Plot as Oates claimed to reveal it, but concerns himself chiefly with what he regards as its underlying cause: the unholy war of the Counter-Reformation against Protestantism, led by its shock-troops, the Jesuit Order. His attack faithfully reflects the mind of militant English Protestants, and the method of many anti-Catholic controversialists at the time, in concentrating on the bad principles attributed to the Papists, and the historical crimes for which these principles were held responsible; and in combining anti-clerical, anti-Papal charges as old as the Reformation or older with others drawn from the worst excesses of Jesuitism at the height of the Counter-Reformation crusade and from the Order's worst weaknesses, exposed by Pascal,[32] in its later-seventeenth-century period of decline. This generalizing method of his kept the *Satyrs* free from all admixture of lampoon. They were not even written for the sake of their effect in any conflict of Whigs and Tories: this is not political satire in the same sense as *The Medall* or Marvell's 'Last Instructions to a Painter': Oldham conceives himself as a national spokesman on behalf of Protestant England, which in the early days of the Terror even Tories believed to be threatened. Comparison with the 'Last Instructions' brings out how much the *Satyrs* gain from their unity of design, strengthened in three of the four by the device of quasi-dramatic monologue, in which the speaker (Garnet's ghost, Loyola on his death-bed, or one of his images) is made to incriminate himself or his votaries. The self-incriminating monologue was traditional: examples ranged from the Pardoner's Prologue in Chaucer to the latest broadside of a malefactor's penitent speech at the gallows. In Oldham, 'Loyola's Will' is as much an impenitent dying speech as a testament of policy bequeathed to his Order. The fictitious raising of an appropriate ghost, like Garnet's, to comment on the current situation has numerous precedents in the sixteenth and seventeenth centuries, some in popular and some in more formal literature; and there are several for the utterance of statues (Marvell's horses, for instance) or other inanimates (as in a dialogue between the Tower and Tyburn); though Oldham's immediate inspiration came from Sylla's ghost, prologue to Jonson's *Catiline*, and the monologue of Priapus' image in Horace. Behind 'Loyola's Will' he similarly acknowledges the *Franciscanus et Fratres* of Buchanan, and indeed more than one passage of his Satyr is translated from it.[33]

To have three of the *Satyrs* spoken, like his Rochester monologues, in a supposed situation, is as far as he goes toward providing a counterpart for the 'series of action' a satiric poem requires to make it epical or even mock-heroic.[34] The lofty subject, the national occasion of the *Satyrs*, was in truth a paroxysm of ignorant, cruel fear: even by March 1680 when he writes the rollicking 'Careless Good Fellow', Oldham will no longer see the Popish Plot through the miasma of the Popish Terror. His heroics are factitious, in a style resembling the rants in heroic plays; rants which he cites in his rough drafts. Juvenalian to a fault, the *Satyrs* have humour almost solely in their bite: even the fourth, mocking at superstition, has little of comedy in its effect.[35] Though they are Oldham's most celebrated pieces, they are not his best.

'Oldham has strong rage', said Pope to Spence, 'but 'tis too much like Billingsgate'.[36] The stricture applies principally to this first period of his as a satirist. Not improbably Dryden's friend Mulgrave had Oldham in mind when he wrote in 1682:

> Some think if sharp enough, they cannot fail
> As if their only business was to rail:
> Rage you must hide, and prejudice lay down,
> A Satyr's smile is sharper than his frown.

Oldham professed a theory of harshness in satire that went back to the Elizabethans,[37] and that Mulgrave rebukes:

> Of well-chose words some take not care enough
> And think they may be, as the subject, rough.
> This great work must be more exactly made,
> And sharpest thoughts in smoothest words conveyed.[38]

To 'a report that some persons found fault with the roughness of my Satyrs formerly publisht' Oldham had replied, justly, that his vocabulary *was* carefully chosen: 'I confess, I did not so much mind the Cadence, as the Sense and expressiveness of my words, and therefore chose not those, which were best dispos'd to placing themselves in Rhyme, but rather the most keen, and tuant, as being the suitablest to my argument'. Magnanimously, Dryden was to absolve the youthful satirist: 'Wit', he declares

> will shine
> Through the harsh cadence of a rugged line.[39]

Youthlike, Oldham was reluctant to accept a limitation in his potentialities, and despite his former dedication of himself to satire –

> my only Province and delight,
> For whose dear sake alone I've vow'd to write.[40]

resisted the idea that he was not gifted for more harmonious poetry. 'To shew that way [he] took', when writing satire, had been 'out of choice', and that he could compass a far different style, he made versions of two elegies, from Bion and Moschus, 'some of the softest and tenderest of all Antiquity'. He had translated, likewise, the passion of Byblis from the *Metamorphoses* in emulation of *Ovid's Epistles*, 1680. Practised in teaching translation with good heed to 'decorum' of vocabulary, he had small trouble in changing from his rich hoard of 'tuant' words to his hoard of 'soft' ones: but that did not re-tune his verse or alter his addiction to imperfect rhymes. 'Byblis' he confessed a failure: 'his vein (if he may be thought to have any) lying another way'. 'Delicacy and a good ear', Dennis was to pronounce, 'none but blockheads can grant him', though wit and genius 'none can deny him'.[41]

His genius found an apt vein in 'Imitations' of Horace, where the Roman allusions were altered to English ones such as Oldham might have made in an original poem, so that the Latin poet was given the air of writing in the times and circumstances of his translator or adaptor. Oldham had the theory of the form from Cowley and Dryden, and the practice chiefly from Cowley, Sprat, Boileau, and Rochester.[42] 'Imitation', as Miss Trickett observes, 'chastened and dignified' his 'violent style'.[43] Soame, we have seen, had advised him (in insulting terms) to refine his 'rude Satyrs' by the rules of Horace. Something like a Horatian phase in his work began with 'Ignatius His Image', partly modelled upon the eighth satire of Horace's first book and, in comparison with the other *Satyrs Upon the Jesuits* favouring him somewhat by its concern with follies, not crimes, and its lighter, more bantering manner.[44] Pope, ignoring the others, includes this in his list as 'Remarkable',[45] and indeed the last two of the five poems he names are also Horatian: Imitations of the next satire in Horace, I. 9, and of the *Ars Poetica*. The earliest of Oldham's 'Imitations', probably, was his refashioning of Moschus' 'Bion' into an elegy on Rochester;

but in two odes of Horace he succeeds much better. 'Quid dedicatum' with its theme – a favourite – of the happy man, and 'Eheu fugaces', with its moral sentiment of time and mortality, and its satiric phrase at the end, are congenial to him; and the acclimatization is agreeably managed by felicitous modern allusions and by casting the odes into Pindarique form, free, however, from the faults which spoil so many Pindariques: inept hyperbole and, contrariwise, a flatness of sense and sound. Oldham's cadences here, if not especially melodious, run fitly and pleasantly. But the masterpiece among his 'Imitations' of Horace is that of satire I. 9, on the impertinent bore. Sprat had written a lively Imitation of this,[46] and previously it had furnished the hint for Donne's first and fourth satires and for Marvell's on Fleckno. From comparison with these predecessors, Oldham's poem has nothing to fear: indeed, it is no mean forerunner of the Imitations of Horace by Swift and Pope. Needless to say, it has not the qualities which make Pope unique as a satirist: the nuance, fine sensibility, virtuosity of versification; the bloom of poetry and the sometimes intimate personal note. But it does not fall short of the Horatian original in humour, and evokes the world of Restoration London with no less sure a touch than Horace the world of Augustan Rome. Like Swift and Pope (nor should we forget Rochester, Boileau, even Sprat) Oldham can match the couplet to the rhythms of dialogue:

> 'Sir, I perceive you stand on Thorns' (said he)
> 'And fain would part: but faith, it must not be:
> Come, let us take a Bottle.' (I cried) 'No;
> Sir, I am in a Course, and dare not now.'
> 'Then tell me whether you desire to go:
> I'll wait upon you.' 'O! Sir, 'tis too far:
> I visit cross the Water; therefore spare
> Your needless trouble.' 'Trouble! Sir, 'tis none:
> 'Tis more, by half, to leave you here alone.
> I have no present business to attend,
> At least which I'll not quit, for such a Friend . . .'

Pope's colloquialisms owe something to Oldham's: when Pope writes

> The things, we know, are neither rich nor rare,
> But wonder how the Devil they got there,[47]

he is recalling the 'Imitation' of the *Ars Poetica*:

> When such a lewd incorrigible sot
> Lucks by meer chance upon some happy thought;
> Among such filthy trash, I vex to see't,
> And wonder how (the Devil!) he came by't.

Oldham is well suited by the recurrent mockery, in the *Ars Poetica*, of literary faults and fools: the satiric and the colloquial in his 'Imitation' are responsible for much of its raciness. Despite one howler, originally Dryden's, about *Gorboduc*, his allusions to English life and English and French literature are apt, as usual; and he imparts movement to the verse-paragraph. He worked from Jonson's very literal and Roscommon's freer translation as well the Latin, and drew on Boileau's *L'Art Poétique*: to follow his use of them enhances one's appreciation.

The Horatian middle style was proper for verse-epistles. 'A Letter from the Country', an earlier success of Oldham's, has affinity with his 'Art of Poetry' in tone, as in subject. Answering, closely at first, an epistle on poetry from his friend Spencer, he depicts himself in revulsion against his unprofitable Muse, but then reaffirms his inescapable passion for her. 'Transitions' is a memorandum in his notes for the *Satyrs Upon the Jesuits*, and skilful transitions help to give the 'Letter' its shape and easy progression.[48] As it comes to a climax, Oldham develops from a few phrases of Dryden's dedication to *The Rival Ladies*[49] a fine introspective account of his habits of composition, and asserts his vocation in ringing lines that Pope, again, remembered:

> In Youth, or Age, in Travel, or at Home,
> Here, or in Town, at *London*, or at *Rome*,
> Rich, or a Begger, free, or in the Fleet,
> What ere my fate is, 'tis my Fate to write.[50]

His vocation as poet or satirist is a subject on which he always writes well, as in passages of the 'Apology' for *A Satyr against Vertue*, 'Upon a Woman', and 'Upon a Bookseller'. He returns to it in 'A Satyr . . . dissuading . . . from . . . Poetry': the dissuader is Spenser's Ghost, and his argument the meagre prospects of a modern poet. The crowning infamy, denounced in a famous paragraph, has been the neglect of Butler,

> On *Butler* who can think without just Rage,
> The Glory, and the Scandal of the Age? . . .

'Spenser's Ghost' (as it may be called) is one of the six major and recently-written poems in the last volume Oldham lived to bring out. All are satires. Four are 'Imitations': two of Boileau, two of Juvenal. 'Spenser's Ghost' itself, and 'A Satyr address'd to a Friend' both have a precedent in Juvenal's Satire VII. With the 'Imitation' of Horace on the bore, they are Oldham at his best. He has discovered, it seems, the form he writes best in; and (although he will not refuse, of course, the commission for the St Cecilia Ode) he has settled down to write in it. Of the six satires, the 'Imitations' of Juvenal's XIIIth and Boileau's Vth ('A Satyr touching Nobility') are somewhat less interesting than the others. In these two, Oldham seems less closely engaged with his subject; or else it is the twentieth-century reader who is less engaged: Boileau's subject had had a fascinating history[51]; Oldham would be aware of its treatment by Juvenal (Satire VIII: Stemmata quid faciunt?) and by Joseph Hall (*Virgidemiarum* Lib IV. Sat. iii).

The remaining satires of the group are the triple peak of Oldham's achievement. Each is prompted by one of his strongest inspirations. Rochester had made a great impression on him, not least with 'A Letter from Artemisa' and 'A Satyr against Mankind'. He had transcribed them. And now he turned to the original of the 'Satyr', Boileau's Satire VIII, not to compete with Rochester but to furnish a close Imitation of what Rochester had transmuted. In the conduct of the debate, he matches his author, and his style is equal both to the set speeches and the quicker exchanges. What could be livelier than these lines? –

> 'Up!' (straight says Avarice) "tis time to rise.'
> 'Not yet: One Minute longer,' 'Up' (she cries).
> 'Th'Exchange, and Shops, are hardly open yet.'
> 'No matter: Rise!' 'But, after all, for what?'
> 'D'ye ask? go, cut the *Line*, double the *Cape*,
> Traverse, from end to end, the spacious deep:
> Search both the *Indies*, *Bantam*, and *Japan*:

Fetch Sugars from *Barbadoes*, Wines from *Spain*. . . .
And tho' you've more than B[*uckingha*]m has spent,
Or C[*layto*]n got, like stingy B[*ethel*] save.'⁵²

The Anglicizing topical allusions reflect, once more, his love-
and-hate for the town and times, which culminates in his com-
prehensive London satire 'In Imitation of the Third of Juvenal'.
There the evils prevalent in London as in ancient Rome – the
expense, the noise, the jerry-building, the dangers from traffic
by day and sons of Belial by night, the snobbery, the extorted
bribery, and the rest – are made vivid by modern particulars:
the poetaster Pordage in his wretched garret, for instance, or
the huge Portland stone impending from its vehicle in transit
to Paul's. The satire is often sharpened by the diction:

> What will you give to have the quarter-face,
> The squint and nodding go-by of his *Grace*?

It is never more heartfelt than when describing the contempt to
which poverty exposes a man in London, or keener than in
attacking sycophancy. Hatred of dependence, next to his vocation
as a poet, was Oldham's dearest passion; and he had found them
incompatible. He had tried and failed to live in London as a
poet without other employment and without a patron. In
'Spenser's Ghost' the scanty reward a poet might expect was
for him no merely traditional subject. He broadened it in the
third satire of the present trio, 'Address'd to a Friend that is
about to leave the University'. Here he surveys the possibilities
for a graduate now bound to support himself. Unemployment
faces the would-be parson, the ill-paid schoolmaster must 'beat
Greek, and *Latin* for [his] life'. Even a post in a noble household
offers nothing better than a humiliating existence (which
Oldham typifies by sharp detail of the lettered man's place
at mealtimes), and, after seven years' service, a miserable
chaplainship.

> For meer Board-wages such their Freedom sell,
> Slaves to an Hour, and Vassals to a Bell.

The spokesman's resolve for independence is pointed by a concluding apologue, the fable of the wolf and the dog from
Phaedrus. In this effective structural device Oldham is following

the satire (II. vi) that Horace ended with his fable of the Town and Country Mice; a satire Cowley and Sprat, between them, had 'imitated'.[53]

To earn a competence by literature alone, Oldham was born too early: but in his other great ambition he was not wholly thwarted. When, just after he had found himself as satirist and 'imitator', 'Fate and gloomy Night' encompassed him, he had 'established a Reputation', and as he rather wistfully phrased it, left behind him 'something to make me survive myself'.[54]

NOTES

1. The best short appreciations of Oldham are Miss Rachel Trickett's in *The Honest Muse* (Oxford, 1967), and Professor Roger Sharrock's (which he and I discussed) in 'Modes of Satire' (*Restoration Theatre*, ed. J. R. Brown and B. Harris, Stratford-upon-Avon Studies [London, 1965]).

2. Op. cit., p. 128.

3. The revision of my unpublished edition (D.Phil. thesis, Oxford, 1939; a microfilm copy is in the University of Adelaide) is now well advanced and has been accepted in principle by the Clarendon Press. Facts in the present essay are documented in the thesis and in the revised reprint (Kraus, Nendeln, Liechtenstein, 1969) of my *Bibliography of John Oldham* (*Oxford Bibliographical Society Proceedings and Papers*, V, i, 1936).

4. For confirmation of Oldham's contact with the Carews, which I deduced from his autograph MS. (Bodleian MS. Rawl. Poet. 123), see D. M. Vieth, 'John Oldham, the Wits, and *A Satyr against Vertue*' *PQ*, XXXII (1953), 91-93.

5. *Absalom and Achitophel* (London, 1681), l. 114.

6. See the note by Miss Leba Goldstein and myself, pp. 38 d, e, of the revised reprint of my Oldham bibliography, which supersedes what I wrote in the 1936 version.

7. B.M. MS. Harl. 7319, f.133, and (anonymously) *Examen Poeticum* (London, 1693), p. 328.

8. Which, however, though indirectly from Anacreon, are directly from Ronsard: see D. M. Vieth (ed.), *The Complete Poems of John*

Wilmot, Earl of Rochester (New Haven and London, 1968), p. 52, citing Curt A. Zimansky.

9. For this poem, and others cited in this paragraph, see *Ben Jonson*, ed. Herford and Simpson (Oxford, 1925-52), VII, 103; *The Poetical Works of Robert Herrick*, ed. L. C. Martin (Oxford, 1956), p. 70; *The Works of Sir John Suckling*, ed. A. Hamilton Thompson (London, 1910), p. 18; Abraham Cowley, *Poems*, ed. A. R. Waller (Cambridge, 1905), p. 133; Rochester, ed. cit., pp. 25, 35, 54; *The Poetical and Dramatic Works of Sir Charles Sedley*, ed. V. de Sola Pinto (London, 1928), I, 95; *Minor Poets of the Caroline Period*, ed. G. Saintsbury (Oxford, 1905), III, 396 (Flatman).

10. 'A Letter from the Country', l. 129.

11. 'The Early Poetical Career of Samuel Woodforde', in *Essays Critical and Historical Dedicated to Lily B. Campbell* (Berkeley and Los Angeles, 1950), pp. 100-102.

12. Ed. cit., pp. 156, 214.

13. Ed. cit., pp. 166, 168, 177.

14. Ed. cit., p. 11.

15. Stz. XXI.

16. In his thesis, accepted for the M.A. of the University of Adelaide. He is preparing, I understand, an article on this elegy.

17. Lines 125-149.

18. For theme-rhetoric, see T. W. Baldwin, *Shakspere's Small Latine & Lesse Greeke* (Illinois, 1944), pp. 281, 291, 327 ff.

19. As remarked by Mr R. I. Mills, op. cit.

20. *MP*, LII (1956), 145-178.

21. Cp. Alexander C. Spence (ed.), *Samuel Butler. Three Poems* (Augustan Reprint Society No. 88), 1961, and his unpublished London M.A. thesis, *Samuel Butler (1613-1680) Four Satires on Social Folly*, 1958, pp. 41-43, 206-235, especially 228.

22. *Attribution in Restoration Poetry: A Study of Rochester's 'Poems' of 1680* (Princeton, 1963), p. 185.

23. Letter I, John Hayward (ed.), *Collected Works of John Wilmot Earl of Rochester* (London, 1926), p. 251.

24. Loc. cit.

25. Gilbert Burnet, *Some Passages Of the Life and Death of . . . John Earl of Rochester* (London, 1680), p. 12.

26. See my Oldham bibliography (cp. note 3 above), No. II. 23 (Pope's copy).

27. George Puttenham, *The Arte of English Poesie*, ed. G. D. Willcock and A. Walker (Cambridge, 1936), pp. 57 f.

28. 'Discourse concerning . . . Satire', Watson, II, 147, 199.

29. Printed, from the autograph in MS. Rawl. Poet. 123, by A. F. B. Clark in his *Boileau and the French Classical Critics in England* (Paris, 1925).

30. *Poems*, ed. Kinsley, I, 389.

31. 'Discourse', Watson, II, 138.

32. In *Lettres Provinciales* (1656), which Oldham knew.

33. Cp. Andrew Marvell, *The Poems and Letters*, ed. H. M. Margoliouth (Oxford, 1952), pp. 179, 189, 191; *Rump Songs* (London, 1662), I, 340. Cp. also, but with caution, Weldon M. Williams, 'The Genesis of Oldham's Satyre upon the Jesuits', *PMLA*, LVIII (1943), 958-970, and 'The Influence of Ben Jonson's *Catiline* upon Oldham's Satyre upon the Jesuits', *ELH*, XI (1944), 38-62. This last receives needful qualification in C. H. Cable, 'Oldham's Borrowing from Buchanan', *MLN*, LXVI (1951).

34. Dryden ('Discourse', ed. cit., II, 143) quotes Heinsius' definition of satire as being 'without a series of action'.

35. R. I. Mills, op. cit., has made me more aware of the difference between this Satyr and the others (see further, below) but I do not go the whole way with him.

36. Joseph Spence, *Observations, Anecdotes, and Characters of Books and Men*, ed. J. M. Osborn (Oxford, 1966), I, 202 (No. 473).

37. Cp., e.g., J. B. Leishman, *The Monarch of Wit* (London, 1951), pp. 107-109.

38. 'An Essay upon Poetry', *Critical Essays of the Seventeenth Century*, ed. J. E. Spingarn (Oxford, 1908), II, 290.

39. *Poems*, loc. cit.

40. 'Upon a Bookseller'.

41. 'The Impartial Critick', in Spingarn, op. cit., III, 177.

42. Cp. my history of 'The "Imitation" in English Poetry, Especially in Formal Satire, before the Age of Pope', *RES*, XXV (1949), 124-140.

43. Op. cit., p. 102.

44. Cp. note 35, above.

45. Cp. note 26, above.

46. Oldham's attribution of this to Sprat, which I confirmed (coupling with it his part of Satire II. vi) in 'Contributors to Brome's

Horace', *Notes and Queries* (Vol. 174), 19 March 1938, was perfunctorily rejected by H. W. Jones and A. Whitworth in their checklist, *Thomas Sprat* (circulated in typescript, 1952). Since they relied on style alone, though without any other work by Sprat in this genre for comparison, and ignored both Oldham's testimony and my grounds of support for it, their rejection can be dismissed.

47. 'An Epistle . . . to Dr. Arbuthnot', ll. 171 f., *The Poems of Alexander Pope*, ed. John Butt (London, 1963), p. 603.

48. Regarding Augustan concern for transitions, cp. G. Tillotson, *On the Poetry of Pope* (Oxford, 1950), pp. 49-54.

49. Watson, I, 2.

50. Cp. in Pope, ed. cit., p. 630, the Imitation of Horace, Epistle I. i, l. 184.

51. See G. K. Hunter (ed.), *All's Well that Ends Well* (London, 1959), p. xxxviii, n. 1, and references there given.

52. Again Pope has echoes; cp. ed. cit., pp. 631, 633, Imitation of Horace, Epistle I, vi, ll. 38, 112.

53. See above, note 46.

54. The quoted phrases are from Dryden's memorial lines, ed. cit., I, 389, and 'A Sunday-Thought in Sickness'.

Two Restoration Prose–writers – Burnet and Halifax

K. G. HAMILTON

What follows has only a limited purpose – to examine some aspects of the prose-style of Bishop Gilbert Burnet and the Marquess of Halifax in the wider context of seventeenth-century writing. Its approach is primarily analytical and descriptive rather than appreciative, and the relative lack of overt response to the finer qualities, particularly of Halifax's prose, should not be taken as an indication that the writer believes that these are lacking.

A number of candidates have been suggested for the position of 'father' of modern English prose, from King Alfred in the tenth century, to John Wiclif in the fourteenth, to Sir Thomas More at the beginning of the sixteenth, to John Dryden at the end of the seventeenth. It is hardly my intention in this essay to put forward as rivals to this illustrious group either Burnet or Halifax – in the history of English prose writing neither is more than a minor figure. However, if by 'modern' prose is meant the impersonal, unobtrusive, flexible type of prose that can be readily adapted to suit a wide variety of subjects and purposes, then if Dryden is not the patriarch the title must go to the later seventeenth century more generally – to writers such as Burnet and Halifax and a host of others, who together evolved this type of prose from the more self-consciously oratorical, 'eloquent' prose of the earlier masters.

It should be made clear at the outset that to say that Dryden, or anyone else in the seventeenth century, wrote modern prose is not to be taken to mean that their kind of prose has remained unchanged since. Rather the seventeenth century provided a prose-style capable of a continuous, unobtrusive process of change and evolution that is still going on. Malory in his *Morte D'Arthur*, More in his *Richard III*, Ascham in his *Toxophilus*, Hooker in his *Laws of Ecclesiastical Polity*, Browne in his *Hydriotaphia* – all of these men wrote splendid prose: prose often far superior in its way to that of a Burnet or a Halifax. But each wrote a more-or-less specialist prose whose form, deliberately adapted to its particular purpose and largely unsuited to most other purposes, was with some exceptions more Latin than native English in origin and heavily influenced by the devices and forms of classical rhetoric. There was, indeed, plenty of good, straightforward, workmanlike prose written before the time of Dryden. But it was for the most part undistinguished, and without the support of self-consciously formal qualities usually tended to become rambling and shapeless. The achievement of the later-seventeenth-century prose writers was the extent to which they learned to avoid both shapelessness and a narrowly deliberate formality and to achieve instead a natural, conversational style, in which the thoughts expressed were, or seemed to be, themselves the main determinants in giving form and vitality to the utterance. English has, of course, continued to have its idiosyncratic writers who have developed more-or-less highly personal styles. But the seventeenth century showed that this was not necessary – that it was possible to write both well and unobtrusively.

If this development was thoroughly completed at all in the later seventeenth century it was in the prose of Dryden. In the work of most other writers of the period the process of development can be seen still at work, and it is often this that gives most interest to a study of the prose-style of writers such as Burnet and Halifax.

Gilbert Burnet, Bishop of Salisbury (1643-1715), was a voluminous writer on both political and ecclesiastical subjects, but he is most widely known today for his much-abused *History of My Own Time*. The two folio volumes of the original edition were published posthumously in 1724 and 1734, respectively. But the greater part of the work was first conceived as a series of memoirs, a 'private history' of the period, begun around 1683. The task of recasting the *History* in its present form was begun in 1702, but basically it is a work belonging to the later seventeenth rather than the early eighteenth century. The writings of Sir George Savile, first Marquess of Halifax (1633-1695), were first collected for publication in 1700 but were composed entirely within the period 1685-1689. Most of his work consists of political pamphlets, including the widely known *Character of a Trimmer* (1685, first published 1688) and a character of King Charles II (written shortly after the King's death but not published until 1750). There is also a delightful essay, *A Lady's Gift; or Advice to a Daughter* (1688), written for his own daughter and extremely popular in the eighteenth century.

Burnet's style in his *History* has inevitably suffered by comparison with the grandeur of Clarendon's *History of the Rebellion*, although it is a very different kind of book. Jonathan Swift, who was quite out of sympathy with Burnet's interest in the affairs of the Scotch – 'that beggarly nation' as Swift describes them, with their 'insignificant brangles and factions' – thought that his style was 'rough, full of improprieties, its expressions often Scotch, and often such as are used by the meanest people.'[1] He was particularly disgusted by Burnet's frequent habit of using a multiplicity of short sentences – 'pretty jumping periods' as he annotated this passage'[2]:

> Madame had an intrigue with another person, whom I knew well, the count of Treville. When she was in her agony, she said, *Adieu Treville.* He was so struck with this accident, that it had a good effect on him; for he went and lived many years among the fathers of the Oratory, and became both a very learned and devout man. He came afterwards out into the world. I saw him often. He was a man of a very sweet temper, only a little too formal for a Frenchman; but he was very sincere. He was a Jansenist: he hated the Jesuits, and had a very mean opinion of the king, which appeared in all the instances in which it was safe for him to shew it.[3]

The style that Swift objected to here is strongly reminiscent of one aspect of the prose of seventeenth-century character writers such as Bishop Hall, whom Milton, whose inclinations certainly lay in very much the opposite direction, accused of writing sentences 'by statute as if all above three inches long were confiscate'. And it is in the frequent character studies interspersed throughout the *History* that this abrupt, brief style is most apparent – in the character, for example, of Anthony Ashley

Cooper, Earl of Shaftesbury, the *Achitophel* of Dryden's poem:

> The man that was in the greatest credit with the earl of Southampton was sir Anthony Ashley Cooper, who had married his niece, and became afterwards so considerable, that he was raised to be earl of Shaftesbury. Since he came to have so great a name, and that I knew him for many years, and in a very particular manner, I will dwell a little longer on his character; for it was of a very extraordinary composition. He began to make a considerable figure very early. Before he was twenty, he came into the house of commons, and was on the king's side, and undertook to get Wiltshire and Dorsetshire to declare for him, but he was not able to effect it. Yet prince Maurice breaking articles to a town that he had got to receive him, furnished him with an excuse to forsake that side, and to turn to the parliament. He had a wonderful faculty in speaking to a popular assembly, and could mix both the facetious and the serious way of arguing very agreeably. He had a particular talent of making others trust to his judgment, and depend on it: and he brought over so many to a submission to his opinion, that I never knew any man equal to him in the art of governing parties, and of making himself the head of them. He was, as to religion, a deist at best. He had the dotage of astrology in him to a high degree: he told me, that a Dutch doctor had from the stars foretold him the whole series of his life. But that which was before him, when he told me this, proved false, if he told true: for he said he was yet to be a greater man than he had been. He fancied that after death our souls lived in stars. He had a general knowledge of the slighter parts of learning, but understood little to bottom: so he triumphed in a rambling way of talking, but argued slightly when he was held close to any point. He had a wonderful faculty at opposing, and running things down; but had not the like force in building up. He had such an extravagant vanity in setting himself out, that it was very disagreeable. He pretended that Cromwell offered to make him king. He was indeed of great use to him, in withstanding the enthusiasts of that time. He was one of those who pressed him most to accept of the kingship, because, as he said afterwards, he was sure it would ruin him. His strength lay in the knowledge of England, and of all the considerable men in it. . . . .[4]

But this abrupt, discontinuous style is not, I think, Burnet's normal or natural style. That he is making a special effort to conform to an accepted fashion for character writing, or is at least influenced by it in passages like this, is indicated by the looser, more freely flowing nature of his style elsewhere in the *History*. Here is the opening passage:

> I am now beginning to review and write over again the History of my own time, which I first undertook twenty years ago, and have been continuing it from year to year ever since: and I see some reason to review it all. I had while I was very young a greater knowledge of affairs than is usual at that age; for my father, who had been engaged in great friendships with men of both sides, living then retired from all business, as he took my education wholly into his own hands, so he took a sort of pleasure to relate to me the series of all public affairs. And as he was a man so eminent for probity and true piety that I had all reason to believe him, so I saw such an impartial sense of things in him, that I had as little reason to doubt his judgment as his sincerity. For though he adhered so firmly to the king and his side that he was the singular instance in Scotland of a man of some note, who, from the beginning to the end of the war, never once owned or submitted to the new forms of government set up all that while, yet he did very freely complain of the errors of the king's government, and of the bishops of Scotland. So that upon this foundation I set out first to look into the secret conduct of affairs among us.[5]

Burnet's sentence structure in passages like this gives the impression that he writes more or less directly as the ideas come to him, the sentence developing as the thought develops, one idea leading on to the next without any preconceived pattern or structure being imposed on its spontaneous development. That is, his prose might be described as 'natural' rather than 'artificial' in structure. In this respect Burnet's style has something in common with what I have described previously as the rambling, shapeless prose of some fifteenth- and earlier sixteenth-century writers. But because his thought itself is less random in its development it imposes a degree of form, of shape, on the sentence that is lacking in most earlier English prose that does not have form imposed on it from outside, as it were, either from the example of Latin or the devices of oratory. Compare Burnet's passage quoted above with, for example, this one which has been quoted as representative of a common type of sixteenth-century prose, and in which thought and expression wander at random together:

> The see of Rome being at that time voyde, the Cardinall, being a man very ambitious and desirous to aspire to that dignitie, wherein he had good hope and likelyhood, perceauing himselfe frustrate and eluded of this his aspiring expectation by the meanes of the Emperour Charles commending Cardinall Adrian, some-time his schoolemaster, to the Cardinalls of Rome, for his great learning, vertue and worthines, who therevpon was elected Pope (and comming from Spaine, whereof he had vnder the saide Charles the chiefe gouernment, before his entrie into the Citie of Rome putting off his hose and shoes and, as I haue hearde it credibly reported, bare foote and bare legged passed through the streetes towardes his pallace, with such humblenes as all the people had him in great reuerence) the Cardinall (I saie) waxed so wood therewith that he studied to . . ., &c.[6]

Burnet's narrative style, in fact, typifies in a relatively simple form what I have already suggested to have been the basic achievement of later seventeenth-century prose writers – the ability to allow the thought itself to give a natural order and shapeliness to prose. He is at the opposite extreme from the so-called 'euphuistic' prose of the sixteenth century in which the thought is consistently moulded to meet the demands of external criteria of form – criteria external, that is, to the thought itself. This passage, for example, from Lyly, in which the thought is basically simple but is continually complicated by the form in which it is cast:

> If therefore the Gods haue endewed hir with as much bountie as beautie. If she haue no lesse wit then she hath comelynesse, certes she will neyther conceiue sinisterly of my sodayne sute, neyther be coye to receiue me into hir seruice, neyther suspecte mee of lyghtnesse, in yeelding so lyghtly, neyther reiect me dis-daynefully, for louing so hastely. Shall I not then hazarde my lyfe to obtaine my loue? and deceiue *Philautus* to receiue *Lucilla*? Yes *Euphues*, where loue beareth sway, friendshippe can haue no shew: As *Philautus* brought me for his shadowe the last supper, so will I vse him for my shadow til I haue gayned his Saint . . .[7]

The two passages that have been quoted from Burnet's *History* – the opening paragraph and the selection from the character of Shaftesbury – could be taken as reasonably typical of the extremes of his style and conveniently designated as 'loose' and 'brief' respectively. Both would be in accord with the demand for a plain style, for a 'natural, naked way of writing' as demanded by the adherents of the Royal Society of London, of whom Burnet was one. But none the less his transitional position in the history of English prose style is evidenced by the fact that whereas his 'loose' style appears as a genuine development of a natural unobtrusive prose form, the plainness of his brief style is partly formal and artificial – the 'proper' style for a particular purpose.

A somewhat similar dichotomy between a brief and a more extended style is apparent in the writing of Halifax. Here are two passages, both taken from one of his political pamphlets, *A Letter to a Dissenter* (1687):

> This alliance between liberty and infallibility, is bringing together the two most contrary things that are in the world. The Church of Rome doth not only dislike the allowing liberty, but by its principles it cannot do it. Wine is not more expressly forbid to the Mahometans than giving heretics liberty to the Papists: they are no more able to make good their vows to you than men married before, and their wife alive, can confirm their contract with another. The continuance of their kindness would be a habit of sin, of which they are to repent, and their absolution is to be had upon no other terms than their promise to destroy you. You are therefore to be hugged now, only that you may be the better squeezed at another time. There must be something extraordinary when the Church of Rome setteth up bills, and offereth plaisters, for tender consciences: by all that hath hitherto appeared her skill in chirurgery lyeth chiefly in a quick hand, to cut off limbs; but she is the worst at healing of any that ever pretended to it. To come so quick from another extreme, is such an unnatural motion, that you ought to be upon your guard: the other day you were sons of Belial, now you are angels of light. This is a violent change, and it will be fit for you to pause upon it before you believe it: if your features are not altered, neither is their opinion of you, whatever may be pretended.[8]

> It might be wished that you would have suppressed your impatience, and have been content for the sake of religion, to enjoy it within yourselves, without the liberty of a public

exercise, till a Parliament had allowed it; but since that could not be, and that the artifices of some amongst you have made use of the well-meant zeal of the generality to draw them into this mistake; I am so far from blaming you with that sharpness which, perhaps, the matter in strictness would bear, that I am ready to err on the side of the more gentle construction. There is a great difference between enjoying quietly the advantages of an act irregularly done by others and the going about to support it against the laws in being: the law is so sacred that no trespass against it is to be defended: yet frailties may in some measure be excused when they cannot be justified. The desire of enjoying a liberty from which men have been so long restrained, may be a temptation that their reason is not at all times able to resist. If, in such a case, some objections are leapt over, indifferent men will be more inclined to lament the occasion than to fall too hard upon the fault ,whilst it is covered with the apology of a good intention; but where, to rescue yourselves from the severity of one law, you give a blow to all the laws by which your religion and liberty are to be protected; and instead of silently receiving the benefit of this Indulgence you set up for advocates to support it, you become voluntary aggressors, and look like counsel retained by the Prerogative against your old friend Magna Charta, who hath done nothing to deserve her falling thus under your displeasure.[9]

The first of these passages tends towards dependence on simple, discontinuous statements, and the second towards a relatively more complex, continuous form of utterance. But though to this extent the two passages resemble respectively those already quoted from Burnet, their differences from Burnet's prose are more fundamental and more striking than their similarities to it. To state these differences first briefly, whereas Burnet's longer sentences have a generally linear structure, with one statement leading on naturally to the next, Halifax's are more closely integrated, more deliberately conceived, it would seem, as complex structures: and whereas Burnet's short sentences tend to be no more than just that, Halifax's have an unmistakably aphoristic, epigrammatic quality. Burnet, to this extent then, is the more natural, Halifax the more stylized, artificial, 'eloquent' writer.

Looking in greater detail, first at Halifax's more extended style, the first sentence of the second of the two passages above from his *Letter to a Dissenter* is worthy of closer examination:

> It might be wished that you would have suppressed your impatience, and have been content for the sake of religion, to enjoy it within yourselves, without the liberty of a public exercise, till a Parliament had allowed it; but since that could not be, and that the artifices of some amongst you have made use of the well-meant zeal of the generality to draw them into this mistake; I am so far from blaming you with that sharpness which, perhaps, the matter in strictness would bear, that I am ready to err on the side of the more gentle construction.

Grammatically the structure of this sentence is that of two co-ordinate principal clauses linked by 'but', to which are added a pattern of subordinate clauses, some of which are themselves linked co-ordinately. Relative to modern practice it is both rather long and rather complex, but in its seventeenth-century context it is no more than typical – certainly by comparison with, say, Milton or Hooker, it is neither unduly long nor particularly complex. Semantically, however, it is more unusual in that, despite its basically co-ordinate grammatical structure, the pattern of meaning is closer to that of the 'suspended' structure of the so-called Ciceronian period – the main thought of the sentence seems to be contained, not in either of the principal clauses, but in the final subordinate clause 'I am ready to err on the side of the more gentle construction', this being held back to the end while the remainder of the sentence leads up to and prepares for it. In other words the semantic structure of the sentence is basically synthetic, the parts of it serving to bring together and hold the various elements of the idea until the final pattern emerges at its end.

In this type of sentence Halifax shows clearly the influence of the Latinate, oratorical style perfected in English by Hooker and carried to its extreme by Milton.[10] But as well as being far less complex than the typical period of the earlier Ciceronians, Halifax's sentence, by its failure to maintain a strict parallel between grammatical and semantic structures, suggests a greater freedom in adapting the period to the thought rather than the thought to the period – despite its preconceived 'artificial' structure, the total form of the sentence appears to some extent determined by the form of the thought. And

P

though this precise sentence structure may not be especially typical of Halifax, he does consistently achieve something of this impression of writing as he thinks, rather than primarily of moulding his thought to a particular sentence form.

If Halifax's long sentence indicates a more flexible development of thought within the structure of the complex period, Burnet, though his sentences can often be equally long, depends primarily, as we have seen, on a simpler sentence structure which allows the expression of each idea to arise from what has gone directly before it, and to lead on to what immediately follows. Semantically and grammatically the structure of his sentences is typically that of a straightforward, continuing train of thought rather than of a complex pattern of ideas. And this is true not only of his narrative passages – this passage for example, from the Preface to his *Life of Sir Matthew Hale* where his purpose is more expository than narrative:

> But the lives of heroes and princes are commonly filled with the account of the great things done by them; which do, rather, belong to a general, than a particular history; and do rather amuse the reader's fancy, with a splendid show of greatness, than offer him what is really so useful to himself. And, indeed, the lives of princes are either writ with so much flattery, by those who intended to merit by it, at their own hands, or others concerned in them; or with so much spite, by those, who, being ill used by them, have revenged themselves on their memory, . . . that there is not much to be built on them. And, though the ill-nature of many, makes what is satirically writ to be generally more read and believed, than when the flattery is visible and coarse, yet, certainly, resentment, as much as interest, may make the writer corrupt the truth of history. And, since all men have their blind sides, and commit errors, he that will industriously lay these together, leaving out, or but slightly touching, what should be set against them to balance them, may make a very good man appear in bad colours. So, upon the whole matter, there is not that reason to expect, either much truth, or great instruction, from what is written concerning heroes or princes; for few have been able to imitate the patterns Suetonius set the world, in writing the lives of the Roman Emperors, with the same freedom, that they had led them.[11]

But the rhetorical influence on Halifax's style which distinguishes him from Burnet goes further than simply helping determine his sentence structure. Although he is certainly not euphuistic, or anything even mildly approaching it, there is consistently a kind of neatness, a sententious smartness about his utterance that is altogether lacking in Burnet. Take for example the continuation of the passage quoted earlier from Halifax, beyond the sentence that was analysed. Here, relative to the previous sentence, the structure is less complex and the idea depends more on a feeling of balance for its effect:

> There is a great difference between enjoying quietly the advantages of an act irregularly done by others and the going about to support it against the laws in being: the law is so sacred that no trespass against it is to be defended: yet frailties may in some measure be excused when they cannot be justified.

Halifax is a more 'pointed' writer than Burnet, and this particular contrast between the two writers becomes more apparent from a comparison of their 'brief' styles. Burnet's style in his characters is simply a discontinuous form of his looser narrative style – virtually the same linear or trailing structure with most of the connectives left out. Despite Swift's 'pretty jumping sentences', Burnet's characters have little or nothing of the antithetic, aphoristic, pointed quality that was the main aim of brevity in much seventeenth-century writing – in Bacon's *Essays*, for example, or in the work of most of the character writers. In Halifax's prose this quality, while not particularly obtrusive, is none the less frequently unmistakable, and most in his briefer style. There is balance and epigrammatic neatness in the following passage, where brevity combines with a more extended type of structure, in which, however, there is little or no Ciceronian suspension. Notice, for example, the aphoristic quality, an echo perhaps of Bacon's 'Revenge is a kind of wild justice', in 'All force is a kind of foul play':

> Our Trimmer is of opinion that there must be so much dignity inseparably annexed to the royal function as may be sufficient to secure it from insolence and contempt; and there must be condescensions too from the Throne, like kind showers from Heaven, that the Prince may look so much the more like God Almighty's deputy upon earth. For power without love hath a terrifying aspect, and the worship which is paid to it is like that which the

Indians give out of fear to wild beasts and devils. He that feareth
God only because there is an Hell, must wish there were no God;
and he who feareth a King only because he can punish, must wish
there were no King. So that, without a principle of love, there
can be no true allegiance; and there must remain perpetual seeds
of resistance against a power that is built upon such an unnatural
foundation as that of fear and terror. All force is a kind of foul
play, and whosoever owneth it himself doth by implication allow
it to those he playeth with. So that there will be ever matter
prepared in the minds of the people when they are so provoked;
and the Prince, to secure himself, must live in the midst of his
own subjects as if he were in a conquered country, raise [armies]
as if he were immediately to make or resist an invasion, and all
this while sleep as unquietly from the fear of the remedies as he
did before from that of the disease – it being hard for him to
forget that more Princes have been destroyed by their guards
than by their people . . .[12]

This basic difference in style between the two writers is to be
seen clearly in their respective accounts of the character of
King Charles II. Here first is part of Burnet's account as it
appeared in his original memoirs – simple, straightforward,
distinguished only by a tendency towards discontinuity.

The king is certainly the best bred man in the world, for the
queen-mother observed often the great defects of the late king's
breeding and the stiff roughness that was in him, by which he
disobliged very many and did often prejudice his affairs very
much; so she gave strict orders that the young princes should be
bred to a wonderful civility. The king is civil rather to an excess
and has a softness and gentleness with him, both in his air and
expressions, that has a charm in it. The duke would also pass for
an extraordinary civil and sweet tempered man if the king were
not much above him in it, who is more naturally and universally
civil than the duke. The king has a vast deal of wit (indeed no
man has more), and a great deal of judgement when he thinks
fit to employ it; he has strange command of himself, he can pass
from business to pleasure and from pleasure to business in so
easy a manner that all things seem alike to him; he has the
greatest art of concealing himself of any man alive, so that those
about him cannot tell when he is ill or well pleased, and in
private discourse he will hear all sorts of things in such a manner
that a man cannot know whether he hears them or not, or whether
he is well or ill pleased at them. He is very affable not only in

public but in private, only he talks too much and runs out too long and too far. He has a very ill opinion both of men and women, and so is infinitely distrustful; he thinks the world is governed wholly by interest, and indeed he has known so much of the baseness of mankind that no wonder if he has hard thoughts of them; but when he is satisfied that his interests are likewise become the interests of his ministers then he delivers himself up to them in all their humours and revenges: for excusing this he has often said, that he must oblige his ministers and support their credit as necessary for his service; yet he has often kept up differences amongst his ministers and has balanced his favours pretty equally among them, which (considering his temper) must be uneasy to him, except it be that there is art necessary and he naturally inclines to refinings and loves an intrigue. His love of pleasure and his vast expense with his women together with the great influence they have had in all his affairs both at home and abroad, is the chief load that will lay on him; for not only the women themslves have great power, but his court is full of pimps and bawds, and all matters in which one desires to succeed must be put in their hands.[13]

And now Halifax's wittier, more stylized version:

He lived with his ministers as he did with his mistresses; he used them, but he was not in love with them. He showed his judgment in this, that he cannot properly be said ever to have had a *favourite*, though some might look so at a distance. The present use he might have of them made him throw favours upon them, which might lead the lookers on into that mistake; but he tied himself no more to them then they did to him, which implied a sufficient liberty on either side.

Perhaps he made *dear purchases*: if he seldom gave profusely but where he expected some unreasonable thing, great rewards were material evidences against those who received them.

He was *free of access* to them, which was a very gaining quality. He had at least as good a memory for the faults of his ministers as for their services; and whenever they fell, the whole inventory came out; there was not a slip omitted.

That some of his ministers seemed to have a *superiority* did not spring from his resignation to them, but to his ease. He chose rather to be *eclipsed* than to be *troubled*.

His brother was a minister, and he had his jealousies of him. At the same time that he raised him, he was not displeased to have him lessened. The cunning observers found this out, and at the same time that he reigned in the Cabinet he was very familiarly used at the private supper.

A minister turned off is like a lady's waiting-woman, that knoweth all her washes, and hath a shrewd guess at her strayings: so there is danger in turning them off, as well as in keeping them.[14]

There can be no doubt that something of the rhetoric of the earlier curt style, the striking turn of phrase, the love of balance and antithesis, entirely absent in Burnet, still lingers in Halifax – that Halifax sometimes achieves an *appearance* of weightiness of the kind that Francis Bacon objected to when he declared that:

Litle better is that kind of stile (yet neither is that altogether exempt from vanity) which neer about the same time succeeded this *Copy* and *superfluity of speech*. The labour here is altogether, *That words may be aculeate, sentences concise, and the whole contexture of the speech and discourse, rather rounding into it selfe, than spread and dilated*: So that it comes to passe by this Artifice, that every passage seemes more witty and waighty than indeed it is . . . And this kind of expression hath found such acceptance with meaner capacities, as to be a dignity and ornament to Learning; neverthelesse, by the more exact judgements, it hath bin deservedly dispised, and may be set down *as a distemper of Learning*, seeing it is nothing else but a hunting after words, and fine placing of them.[15]

There is something of this same rhetorical weightiness even in Halifax's *Advice to a Daughter*, generally natural but with every now and then a carefully contrived antithesis or the like:

If in the lottery of the world you should draw a covetous husband, I confess it will not make you proud of your good luck; yet even such a one may be endured, too, though there are few passions more untractable than that of avarice. You must first take care that your definition of avarice may not be a mistake; you are to examine every circumstance of your husband's fortune, and weigh the reason of everything you expect from him before you have right to pronounce that sentence. The complaint is now so general against all husbands that it giveth great suspicion of its being often ill-grounded; it is impossible they should all deserve that censure, and therefore it is certain that it is many times misapplied. He that spareth in everything is an inexcusable niggard; he that spareth in nothing is as inexcusable a madman.

The mean is, to spare in what is least necessary, to lay out more liberally in what is most required in our several circumstances; yet this will not always satisfy. There are wives who are impatient of the rules of economy, and are apt to call their husband's kindness in question if any more measure is put to their expense than that of their own fancy; be sure to avoid this dangerous error, such a partiality to yourself, which is so offensive to an understanding man that he will very ill bear a wife's giving herself such an injurious preference to all the family and whatever belongeth to it.[16]

Only to a very limited extent does this essay, or any other of Halifax's writing, depend on what Dryden decried as 'the jerk or sting of an epigram, . . . the seeming contradiction of a poor antithesis . . . the jingle of a more poor paronomasia' [I, 98]. But some taste of these things is there, and it would not be possible altogether to apply to Halifax Dr Johnson's description of Dryden's style in his Prefaces:

They have not the formality of a settled style, in which the first half of the sentence betrays the other. The clauses are never balanced, nor the periods modelled: every word seems to drop by chance, though it falls into its proper place. Nothing is cold or languid; the whole is airy, animated, and vigorous; what is little, is gay; what is great, is splendid. . . . Though all is easy, nothing is feeble; though all seems careless, there is nothing harsh; and though since his earlier works more than a century has passed, they have nothing yet uncouth or obsolete.[17]

Burnet's narrative style lacks the grandeur of Clarendon's but it is always adequate for his purpose, and at times can be superb – as it is in his account of happenings after the death of Charles II:

He continued in the agony till Friday at 11 o'clock, being the 6th of February 1684/5; and then died in the fifty-fourth year of his age, after he had reigned, if we reckon from his father's death, thirty-six years, and eight days, or if we reckon from his restoration, twenty-four years, eight months, and nine days. There were many very apparent suspicions of his being poisoned: for though the first access looked like an apoplexy, yet it was plain in the progress of it that it was no apoplexy. When his body was opened, the physicians who viewed it were, as it were, led by those who might suspect the truth to look upon the parts that were certainly sound. But both Lower and Needham, two famous physicians, told me they plainly discerned two or three blue spots on the outside of the stomach. Needham called twice to have it opened, but the surgeons seemed not to hear him; and when he moved it the second time, he, as he told me, heard Lower say to one that stood next him, Needham will undo us, calling thus to have the stomach opened, for he may see they will not do it. And they were diverted to look to somewhat else: and when they returned to look upon the stomach, it was carried away: so that it was never viewed. Le Fevre, a French physician, told me he saw a blackness in the shoulder: upon which he made an incision, and saw it was all mortified. Short, another physician, that was a papist, but after a form of his own, did very much suspect foul dealing: and he had talked more freely of it than any of the protestants durst do at that time. But he was not long after taken suddenly ill, upon a large draught of wine he had drunk in the house of a popish patient that lived near the Tower, who had sent for him, of which he died; and, as he said to Lower, Millington and some other physicians, he believed that he himself was poisoned for having spoke so freely of the king's death. The king's body was very indecently neglected. Some parts of his inwards, and some pieces of fat, were left in the water in which they were washed: all which were so carelessly looked after, that the water being poured out at a scullery hole that went to a drain in the mouth of which a grate lay, these were seen lying on the grate many days after. His funeral was very mean. He did not lie in state: no mournings were given: and the expence of it was not equal to what an ordinary nobleman's funeral will rise to.[18]

But the effectiveness of this passage is probably mainly accidental – the result of a striking contrast between Burnet's continued use of a normal, straightforward, unobtrusive style and the melodramatic quality of his material at this point. His style, here as elsewhere, does not rise or fall to meet the occasion. It is not, in fact, what could be described as a 'flexible' style – or such flexibility as it has comes not from its adaptability to varying demands but from the fact that, within a fairly wide range of relatively simple narrative and expository purposes, it serves more or less well, without the need for variation. If the emergence of modern prose is, as I suggested at the beginning of this essay, primarily the development of a prose style sufficiently unobtrusive and flexible to allow it to be adapted to a wide variety of uses, then Burnet's prose is not in this respect, I think, modern. The prose of Halifax, on the other hand, despite its greater dependence on rhetorical devices, has an unobtrusive variety that is closer to modern prose. *The Character of a Trimmer* is a political pamphlet; the *Advice to a Daughter* is a personal essay; in both of these, as in his other work as well, Halifax's basic style is essentially the same, but is adjusted to its subject with a subtlety that never draws attention to itself.

In the process of development of modern prose, therefore, Halifax is probably the more significant writer. Burnet, in seeking the plainness of utterance that the reaction against rhetorical eloquence had made fashionable in the seventeenth century, achieved a spontaneity, a lack of self-consciousness, that was one of the essentials of modern prose. But his very plainness is itself a limiting factor: he was not able – in fact does not attempt – to deal successfully with any sustained pattern of thought in which ideas do not follow each other in more or less linear succession. Halifax's prose is less plain – he was, as we have seen, closer to the rhetorical tradition that Burnet shunned, more inclined towards a carefully thought out structure in which ideas could fall into their place in a more complicated pattern. But Halifax is none the less more 'natural' than a Milton, a Browne, or a Hooker; and, too, his style is more viable over a wider range of material without the need for substantial adjustment. Where Burnet's naturalness consists of seeming to report the ideas in the order in which they come to him, Halifax achieves a more sophisticated naturalness in which thought still appears to impose its form on the words but in which the form of thought itself is enabled to be more varied and complex.

The highly rhetorical prose styles of the sixteenth- and earlier seventeenth-centuries were essential to the development of English prose, in that they provided the formal elements which earlier prose, except in its simplest forms, tended to lack. It was essential, too, that having achieved this sense of form prose should become more natural, less self-conscious. However, this does not mean that it was necessary for prose to abandon altogether the forms on which it had previously depended. An efficient multi-purpose prose must be unobtrusive, must have an appearance of naturalness; but in order to be able to give verbal form to a wide range of thought patterns of varying degrees of complexity and subtlety it needs also the assistance of the devices developed by the conscious stylists. Halifax's prose represents, at a more advanced level than Burnet's, the fusion of naturalness and stylistic sophistication which in the work of Dryden marks the emergence of modern English prose.

NOTES

1. Jonathan Swift, *Works*, ed. Sir Walter Scott. 19 vols. (London, 1883), XII, 177.

2. Swift, *Works*, XII, 193.

3. Burnet, *History of My Own Time*, ed. Osmund Airy. 2 vols. (Oxford, 1897), I, 543.

4. Burnet, *History*, I, 172-174.

5. Burnet, *History*, I, xxxi-xxxii.

6. From Harpsfield's *Life of More*, quoted by C. S. Lewis, *English Literature in the Sixteenth Century, excluding Drama* (London, 1953), pp. 272-273.

7. John Lyly, *Euphues, The Anatomy of Wit*; in *The Complete Works of John Lyly*, ed. R. W. Bond. 2 vols. (Oxford, 1902), II, 208-209.

8. Halifax, *Life and Letters*, ed. H. C. Foxcroft. 2 vols. (London, 1898), II, 367-8.

9. Halifax, II, 371.

10. See K. G. Hamilton, 'The Structure of Milton's Prose', in *Language and Style in Milton*, ed. R. D. Emma and J. T. Shawcross (New York, 1967).

11. Burnet, *Lives, Characters and an Address to Posterity*, ed. John Jebb (London, 1833), pp. 1-2.

12. Halifax, II, 291.

13. Burnet, *Supplement to Burnet's History of My Own Time*, ed. H. C. Foxcroft (Oxford, 1902), pp. 48-49.

14. Halifax, II, 351.

15. Francis Bacon, *De Augmentis Scientiarum*, trans. Gilbert Wats (Oxford, 1640), p. 29.

16. Halifax, II, 399.

17. Samuel Johnson, 'Dryden', in *Lives of the Poets*, ed. G. Birkbeck Hill (Oxford, 1905), I, 418.

18. Burnet, *History*, II, 461-462.

Dryden and Literary Good-breeding

JOHN FOWLER

I

Dryden in his discussion of satire in the *Discourse* on that genre prefaced to his translation of Juvenal and Persius assumes that the circumstances of satire's institution must afford clues – more than clues indeed – to its present nature. For poetry as Dryden conceives it, no less than government as Hobbes conceives it, is assumed to have been a thing rationally decided on, then deliberately performed with certain and delimited aims in view, and the whole account here given of the origins and progress of satire is governed by this assumption of deliberateness, this attribution of conscious intention to the remote ancestors of Horace. We find this notion operating as a premise, not to be questioned; we read that '. . . as all festivals have a double reason of their institution, the first of religion, the other of recreation, for the unbending of our minds; so both the Grecians and Romans agreed, after their sacrifices were performed, to spend the remainder of the day in sports and merriments . . .' [II, 98]. It was for such occasions that the first, lamentably coarse, satiric verses are said to have been devised; indeed, the fact that such rustics could not yet know the town gives the expected tone to the account of the nature of these merriments, 'amongst which, songs and dances, and that which they called wit (for want of knowing better) were the chiefest entertainments' [II, 98-99]. Yet, if this 'custom of reproaching each other with their faults, in a sort of extempore poetry, or rather of tunable hobbling verse' [II, 99] was rationally instituted for a properly conceived end, none the less its first stages were far from *comme il faut*, and the genre that was to reach its perfection in Horace was as yet but 'rude and barbarous and unpolished, as all other operations of the soul are in their beginnings, before they are cultivated with art and study' [II, 106].

As Dryden is writing here with Horace's Epistle II, i, in mind (*Our brawny clowns* giving us the origins of satire), and as we cannot expect to find him considering the possibility of complex, sophisticated verbal artistry existing anywhere but in a leisured, relatively idle class, aristocratic in ethos, inevitably his sketch of satire's improvement is simultaneously a sketch of its practitioners' social rise. 'When they began to be somewhat better bred, and were entering, as I may say, into the first rudiments of civil conversation, they left these hedgenotes for another sort of poem, somewhat polished, which was also full of pleasant raillery, but without any mixture of obscenity' [II, 107]. At a subsequent stage, successive men having cast deliberately about for further improvements, publicspirited Ennius, the first writer of 'satire abstracted from the stage, and new modelled into papers of verses on several subjects' turned from 'the coarseness of his old countrymen' to imitate 'the fine railleries of the Greeks' [II, 110].

But even while the developers of the genre, Livius Andronicus and Ennius, were consciously improving and refining it out of the clownish old way, so was the language too refining itself, though still in Lucilius' time 'not yet sufficiently purged from the dregs of barbarism' [II, 112] – just as Jonson's age was, as to correctness in language, 'content with acorns before they knew the use of bread' [I, 173]. And just as the rise of satire is written of as indistinguishable from the social improvement of its practitioners, so is linguistic change described as though it were a matter of advance towards a decent and courtly decorum. But a theoretical difficulty arises of this view if it is held – as it is by Dryden – of English and Latin alike. As it is visible that Latin continues to change long after it has reached politeness, how is the following of a literary and linguistic silver age upon a polite golden one to be expressed in the language of deportment? In the *Discourse* and in connection with Persius, the notion of language rotting away from purity and good-manners supplies the answer. Of this satirist we find that 'as his verse is scabrous, and hobbling, and his words not everywhere well chosen, the purity of Latin being more corrupted than in the time of Juvenal, and consequently of Horace,

who writ when the language was in the height of its perfection;
so his diction is hard, his figures are generally too bold and
daring, and his tropes, particularly his metaphors, insufferably
strained' [II, 118]. One is forced to assume that on judging
Persius guilty of breaches of literary manners similar in
tendency to those of our own Jacobeans (too strained, bold, and
daring), and yet finding him indisputably to have lived after
Latin's rustic coarseness was long outgrown, Dryden felt
himself constrained to place him well *after* the polite period, as
he could not go before it – and that this or something like it is
the reason for the curious error in chronology. What is important is the view that Persius, writing during the decline from
politeness, lapses not into coarseness again but rather into a
fantastic daring, a too-wilful boldness, consistent with good-
breeding though a perversion of it. That is, the view of languages
as organisms that necessarily grow ceaselessly forward through
inevitable stages has such priority in Dryden's concepts that
judgements as to stylistic quality must be tailored to it, facts or
mistakes about chronology take their meaning from it.

These are the ideas threading through Dryden's consideration of the relative politeness of Persius and Horace and which
help him counter Casaubon's view that Horace 'being the son
of a tax-gatherer, or a collector, as we call it, smells everywhere
of the meanness of his birth and education: his conceits are vulgar,
like the subjects of his satires; that he does *plebeium sapere*, and
writes not with that elevation which becomes a satirist: that
Persius, being nobly born, and of an opulent family, had likewise the advantage of a better master . . .' [II, 124]. The
counter to all of this is that, on the contrary, Horace's father
'bred him in the best school, and with the best company of
young noblemen' [II, 124] and that thereafter the conversation
of great men abroad 'form'd' him, and that moreover all this
occurred before 'his acquaintance with Maecenas, and his
introduction into the court of Augustus, and the familiarity of
that great emperor; which, had he not been well-bred before,
had been enough to civilise his conversation, and render him
accomplished and knowing in all the arts of complacency and
good behaviour . . . so that, upon the whole matter, Persius may
be acknowledged to be equal with him [*not*, as Casaubon claims,
superior] in those respects, tho' better born, and Juvenal

inferior to both' [II, 124-125]. But the passage pretends to be,
after all, about the relative excellence of the two men's satiric
styles; what it therefore demonstrates to *us* is that in Dryden's
opinion literary stylistic endowments, and those social-deport-
mental ones that give a young man the ability to carry it off
in an assembly, are inextricably entwined, are indeed perhaps
one and the same. Proof of competence in the one raises a
strong presumption of competence in the other. What made
Horace well-bred in manner would have given him elegance of
style. Dryden, that is, argues as though good-breeding must,
in literary judgement as in life, compel, as soon as mentioned,
all other arguments to yield. And the reason for the confidence
everywhere underlying this delightfully tentative veering and
lengthy three-cornered comparison is that Dryden, suspending
for a time what is of course to decide all things, for the moment
wanders as if with abandon from satirist to satirist applying
various provisional criteria not systematized one with another
and therefore yielding results which strike Dryden – and us – as
pleasingly free. If Horace wins while 'the delicacy of his turns' is
being considered, 'his choice of words, and perhaps the purity
of his Latin' [II, 125], and if Horace's poems are the most
useful in the sense that their lessons, being mundane, are more
frequently applicable to everyday urban life, yet on other and unrelated criteria Juvenal is found more fierily delightful, '. . . of a
more vigorous and masculine wit; he gives me as much pleasure
as I can bear; he fully satisfies my expectation; he treats his
subject home; his spleen is raised, and he raises mine . . .
Horace is always on the amble, Juvenal on the gallop' [II, 130].
Juvenal's political stance is equally a source of pleasure, for his
'indignation against vice is more vehement; his spirit has more
of the commonwealth genius; he treats tyranny, and all the
vices attending it, as they deserve, with the utmost rigour: and
consequently, a noble soul is better pleased with a zealous
vindicator of Roman liberty than with a temporizing poet, a
well-mannered Court slave, and a man who is often afraid of
laughing in the right place; who is ever decent, because he is
naturally servile. After all, Horace had the disadvantage of the
times in which he lived; they were better for the man, but
worse for the satirist' [II, 131-132]. Persius is, morever, in his
turn, the finest of them all when – for the moment – ideological

consistency, nobility of doctrine, and unity of design are the criteria being applied. How endearing, how directly the result of being hustled this way and that by the immediacy of literary experience relished, then re-expressed, must it be when after all this Horace is suddenly and finally elevated to the topmost place for the delicate decorum with which he accomplishes blaming and indecorous motions: 'How easy is it to call rogue and villain, and that wittily! But how hard to make a man appear a fool, a blockhead, or a knave, without using any of those opprobrious terms! To spare the grossness of the names, and to do the thing yet more severely, is to draw a full face, and to make the nose and cheeks stand out, and yet not to employ any depth of shadowing . . .' [II, 136-137]. The grossness of satire's origins has been purged but its railling function remains; and now its operation upon its victims is presented in the language of gentlemanly company-manners:

> The occasion of an offence may possibly be given, but he cannot take it. If it be granted that in effect this way does more mischief; that a man is secretly wounded, and though he be not sensible himself, yet the malicious world will find it for him: yet there is still a vast difference betwixt the slovenly butchering of a man, and the fineness of a stroke that separates the head from the body, and leaves it standing in its place. A man may be capable, as Jack Ketch's wife said of his servant, of a plain piece of work, a bare hanging; but to make a malefactor die sweetly was only belonging to her husband.
>
> [II, 137]

Broad sweeps of enthusiasm for Juvenal the court-scourger have, as we have seen, been indulged; Dryden has written his discussion of the three satirists for the most part as an extended judicial metaphor, casting himself as judge, depressing and elevating, umpire-like, one satirist after another as he reviews them under successive aspects; he has even at one point crowned the three together as victors and in the immediately succeeding triumphal procession has allowed Juvenal to ride a little ahead (*Primus equum phaleris insignem victor habeto*, quotes Dryden from *Aen.* V. 310); he has awarded the prize for some quality or other to each of the three at least once; he has combined the deferential tactics of a man out to offend the champions of none of the contenders[1], with that of a judge who must after all award the palm some way or other, perhaps by dividing it; the language of competition is never absent from the discussion, all three are rival contenders for *the prize of satire*. But when at last the whole charming and sceptical essay approaches its close, the judgement between the three ends with a sentence which gives last preference to Horace as the best model, after all, for the *manner*, at least, of satire. The satirist's gentlemanly manner is commended in a breath with that of the noble patron to whom all the *Discourse* is addressed. Horace and Dorset alike are paragons of elegant deportment:

> Of the best and finest manner of satire, I have said enough in the comparison betwixt Juvenal and Horace; 'tis that sharp, well-mannered way of laughing a folly out of countenance, of which your Lordship is the best master in this age.

[II, 147]

I think we are to infer from this that it is the courtly railler, the well-bred self-comporter, the client of Maecenas, who incarnates most perfectly that ethos which satire ought to be marked by. It is good-breeding which finally places us all, from pensioned poet to hangman.

II

But the passage just quoted introducing Jack Ketch as a type for the satirist, besides being one of Dryden's many agreeable metaphors for the delightfulness conferred by poetry upon equivocal subject-matter, is applied by him here directly to his own sketch of Buckingham as Zimri in *Absalom and Achitophel*. This reminds us of the curious fact that he, one of our major satirists, wrote no original work in the genre he principally means by satire. (What has *MacFlecknoe* to do with the *Discourse*?) His criticism might be expected to be as uncoordinated with his original poetry on this matter as in most – his critical theory is dominated by the heroic poem, but he never wrote one; he writes feelingly and with insight on character-creation by passionate empathy in his criticism of Ovid, Virgil, and Chaucer, but that gift is antithetical to his own; he writes perceptively on the importance and beauty of tight dramatic construction apropos of Jonson, but his original plots show very different qualities. Yet both *MacFlecknoe* and *Absalom and Achitophel* are indubitably satires and turn out eventually to be located in the sub-species Varronian or Menippean satire which is mentioned twice in the *Discourse*, most significantly near the end. Versification and choice of measure is there the immediate topic, and this time an appeal to Tassoni's mock-heroic *Secchia Rapita* and Boileau's *Lutrin* establishes the dogma – important for *MacFlecknoe* and *Absalom and Achitophel* – that it is the heroic verse form and style – not, that is, any Hudibrastic or burlesque form comic in itself – that has been found in modern languages the most appropriate for satire. Dryden quotes with approval Boileau's travesty of a famous Virgilian passage with the remark that, as Virgil in the fourth Georgic may be seen perpetually raising 'the lowness of his subject by the loftiness of his words, and ennobles it by comparisons drawn from empires, and from monarchs', so we see Boileau 'pursuing him in the same flights; and scarcely yielding to his master' [II, 149]. This, he considers 'to be the most beautiful and most noble kind of satire. Here is the majesty of the heroic, finely mixed with the venom of the other; and raising the delight which otherwise would be flat and vulgar, by the sublimity of the expression' [II, 149]. This remark, besides (perhaps inevitably) ranking most highly that species of satire most appropriately to be described as *noble*, locates and emphasizes the distinctive quality of Dryden's three great satiric poems (counting *The Medall* as one) better than any claims for continuing incongruity between style and content – locates it in the magniloquent splendour of diction that creates a consistent, homogeneous, loud-sounding sublimity by means of 'the beautiful turns of words and thoughts; which are as requisite in this, as in heroic poetry itself, of which the satire is undoubtedly a species' [II, 149]. The poem thus 'finely mixed' is made, by its diction, sublime; subject-matter thus reclothed actually loses its lowness.

But this impressive confidence in the real distinction – and unity – of tone achieved, this, along with Dryden's anxious rescuing of Horace from the charge of sounding ill-bred like any taxgatherer, shows that the speculations on epic intruding into the *Discourse* are less of a digression than a summary of that essay might suggest; they are rather an integral part of Dryden's attempt to clarify the nature of poetical good-breeding. Having found that satire is to avoid contamination from the lowness of its materials, Dryden now directly finds that its courtliness is to be learned specifically from heroic poetry. But why should it seem to him appropriate that the literary genre sired by Homer and portraying the deeds of men distant in time and greater than their descendants – why should such a genre lend its style to one that attacks, as its proper object, the corruptions of the eternal present? Horace – and the authority of his example – has been saved from the imputation of *plebeium sapere* himself, and from the shamefulness of encouraging uncouth manners – but it is surely to go wantonly further – too far – to make Horace's chattering genre a sub-species of what is essentially of the same kind as the *Aeneid* itself? Why does Dryden conclude in this way?

To reconstruct a possible Drydenian answer, the ends of poetry must be looked at, and attention paid to what seems to Dryden the most important of epic's claims to supremacy – namely that it is directed at an audience more august than that of any other genre: tragedy is 'only instructive', but the heroic poem or epopee 'forms a hero, and a prince' [II, 96]; it is about heroes and kings and princes, as everybody knows; but it is for their education as well. But satire's *raison d'être* is likewise that it instructs and *forms* through its 'amendment of Vices by Correction'. Epic is superior to tragedy through being both better-bred and *about* the better-bred, and directed *at* them as well. But satire too has been shown to be approaching the task here ascribed to epic throughout its self-conscious and deliberate history. It has left behind the days when it addressed and was forming rustics; but if it is to keep the status now won for it by Horace, it must necessarily speak the language of the court of Augustus. If, like the *Aeneid*, it is to edify future Augustuses, it is reasonable to rule that it must sound rather like the *Aeneid*, that eminently didactic poem according to Dryden's account of it. But if Dryden thus believes that the task of epic is as close as this to that of satire, then it is certainly not surprising that the composite ideal satire as it now ought to be written should be composed out of those qualities (detectable in satire-up-to-the-present) which are in closest conformity to the nature of heroic poetry. Nor is it surprising that Louis

XIV's Boileau should be accorded such rank as he is.[2] The best prince reigning over the best people at the best period of their language was by definition the best of all possible readers of the best satire.

So much for the theory, but how about the practice? The immediate intention of the *Discourse* was after all to introduce a translation by several hands of the Roman satirists. How does Dryden's notion of the requirements – the nature – of satire get reflected in his translations? How does he think of the act of translation? That his procedure in verse-translation must impose a theory of satire upon whatever he translates is clear from the primary fact that the sort of difference as to literary manners seen by him between Juvenal and Persius is not reflected in differences of metre or versification in the translations, nor of vocabulary where the subject-matter is comparable. It is clear, in fact, that he *intended* to impose a manner upon them different if necessary from that he found in them, as is plain from the way he boasts – after reproving the too boisterous imagery in Persius – that 'for once, I will venture to be so vain as to affirm that none of his hard metaphors, or forced expressions, are in my translation' [II, 121]. The latitude he and his co-translators have felt engaged – for poetry's sake – to claim is explained to us: 'The common way which we have taken is not a literal translation, but a kind of paraphrase; or somewhat, which is yet more loose, betwixt a paraphrase and imitation. It was not possible for us, or any men, to have made it pleasant any other way' [II, 152]. Their predecessors, Stapleton and Holyday, had in rough and obscure verses rendered the exact sense, but the latter 'wrote for fame, and wrote to scholars: we write only for the pleasure and entertainment of those gentlemen and ladies who, tho' they are not scholars, are not ignorant . . .' [II, 153]. 'We make our author at least appear in a poetic dress. We have actually made him more sounding, and more elegant, than he was before in English; and have endeavoured to make him speak that kind of English which he would have spoken had he lived in England, and had written to this age' [II, 154]. It is in any case clear enough from the conscious and principled modernization in verse technique and vocabulary found everywhere in them, that these translations were meant to *replace*[3] their predecessors, using those where necessary but making them always new, always as much like original seventeenth-century satire as should be consistent with faithfulness to at least the broad features of Roman institutions and civilization.

How do satires walk in modern dress?

> *Friend.* Once more, forbear.
> *Persius.* I cannot rule my Spleen.
> My scorn Rebels, and tickles me within.
>
> [Satire I, ll. 29-31]

As examples of scorn-deserving objects, Persius gives us what the Loeb translator renders thus: 'We shut ourselves up and write something grand – one in verse, one in prose – something that will take a vast amount of breath to pant out'[3] and Dryden thus:

> First, to begin at Home, our Authors write
> In lonely Rooms, secur'd from publick sight;
> Whether in Prose or Verse, 'tis all the same:
> The Prose is Fustian, and the Numbers lame.
> All noise, and empty Pomp, a storm of words,
> Lab'ring with sound, that little Sence affords.
>
> [Satire I, ll. 32-37]

One of the meanings of 'poetic dress' can from here be safely inferred; it means clarifying and ordering, and always does so. The first satire treats of writers, which is a topic *close to* Persius; the subsequent self-adornment is likewise done at home; but the public recitation is, when it comes, elsewhere; and to point the contrast more keenly than did Persius, additional phrases are needed to amplify *inclusi*. *Scribimus inclusi* therefore accepts clarifying assistance from 'First, to begin at Home', from 'our Authors', and from 'In lonely Rooms secur'd from publick sight'.

Another aspect of 'poetic dress' – an entirely predictable one – may be illustrated from the next two lines. Wherever a noticeable elegancy, an identifiable grace, a rhetorical trick, is accomplished by the original, something equally apparent must be worn by the English, apparent though not necessarily the same. Thus Persius' chiasmus *numeros ille, hic pede liber | grande aliquid* [ll. 13-14] is heavily marked by Dryden's doing a similar thing *twice over* and appending the comment that the literary product under description was equally bad in the two cases. Dryden, grinning in our faces, insists:

> Whether in Prose or Verse, 'tis all the same:
> The Prose is Fustian, and the Numbers lame.
>
> [ll. 34-35]

The lines at once following show still more of what is involved when heroic couplets of Dryden's sort have to cover satiric Latin hexameters: pairs of phrases (and therefore pairs of opposing or balancing thoughts), binary aspects, one-to-one relationships, have perpetually to be found implied in the Latin material in order that the expectations aroused by this quint-essentially well-bred form of English verse may be unfailingly and resoundingly satisfied. *Quod pulmo animae praelargus anhelet* [l. 14] must consequently yield some pairs, and does so: *words* against *Sense*, *Sound* against *Sense*; a group of nominative phrases in apposition forming one line and making a couplet with another line containing the verbs (a pair of verbs, more-over, *in* that line and placed like weights at opposite ends of it); a conceptual ironic coupling of the word *Lab'ring* with its barren result – that it *little . . . affords*, this conceptual pairing being marked by alliteration on *s* and *l*:

> All Noise, and empty Pomp, a storm of words,
> Lab'ring with sound, that little Sence affords.

Persius continues, according to the Loeb: 'This stuff you will some day read aloud to the public, having first lubricated your throat with an emollient wash; you will take your seat on a high chair, well combed, in a new white robe, and with a rakish leer in your eye, not forgetting a birthday sardonyx gem on your finger'.[4] Dryden no less than the Loeb translator upsetting the order of Persius' items, but with the purpose of separating them clearly from one another and putting them into the order in which they will happen and giving each a line to itself, writes three lines on the *toilette*. The first covers *pexusque* and intensifies the foppish care by a pair of verbs both focussed on one object:

> They Comb, and then they order ev'ry hair,

The next translates and glosses *togaque recenti . . . albus*, and, finding (quite justifiably) two connected possible meanings, gives both and produces a qualifying irony:

> A Gown, or White, or Scour'd to whiteness, wear:

Persius' *et natalicia tandem cum sardonyche* by a happy accident reflects a seventeenth-century practice:

> A Birthday-Jewel bobbing at their Ear.

The *toilette* completed, the poets are ready to be led by Dryden to the recitation, his *next* and *and thus prepar'd* organizing and separating things for clarity and introducing his splendid equivalent for Persius' sour disdain:

> Next, gargle well their Throats; and thus prepar'd
> They mount, a God's Name, to be seen and heard
> From their high Scaffold; with a Trumpet Cheek:
> And Ogling all their Audience e're they speak.
>
> [ll. 41-44]

Continuing, Dryden selects what he takes to be the next step in the poem's argument, namely that it is the highest-born in Rome who lend themselves degraded as audience at the present rehearsal, and puts it prominently at the head of his next paragraph, though Persius has allowed us to find it rather gradually:

> tunc neque more probo videas, nec voce serena
> *ingentis* trepidare *Titos*, cum carmina lumbum
> intrant et tremulo scalpuntur ubi intima versu.
>
> [ll. 19-21]

Dryden at the top of his form, selecting pairs of concepts, alliterating, and writing continuous logical sense that is fluently linear and yet so ordered that pairs of lines belong together as couplets, yet form unbroken larger units as well, assembles this:

> The Nauseous Nobles, ev'n the Chief of *Rome*,
> With gaping Mouths to these Rehearsals come,
> And pant with Pleasure when some lusty line
> The Marrow pierces, and invades the Chine.
> At open fulsom Bawdry they rejoice,
> And slimy Jests applaud with broken Voice.
>
> [ll. 45-50]

When Persius, continuing, introduces a scornful apostrophe whose scorn is perhaps clearer than its point:

> Tun, vetule, auriculis alienis colligis escas,
> auriculis, quibus et dicas cute perditus 'ohe'?
>
> [ll. 22-23]

["What, you old reprobate? Do you cater for other people's wanton ears? – ears to which, however hardened your hide, you might fain cry, "hold, enough!" ' [5]]
Dryden retains and intensifies the scorn and finds a turn of his own for *escas*, allowing a pair of scornful rhetorical questions to cover Persius' last clause:

> Base Prostitute, thus dost thou gain thy Bread?
> Thus dost thou feed their Ears, and thus art fed?
>
> [ll. 51-52]

then adds, to conclude the sketch by an *obvious* close (and thereby avoid one of Persius' un-Augustan abruptnesses), a couplet all his own, though inferable from what has preceded:

> At his own filthy stuff he grins, and brays:
> And gives the sign where he expects their praise.

Enough has now been quoted for Dryden's constant tendency towards the Ovidian *turn*, the near-paradoxical repetition of a word in opposing senses, or the coupling of a substantive with two opposing or alternative adjectives – his pursuit, in short, of small yet ostentatious grammatical neatnesses – to leap from the page to the contented eye. It should also be clear that such superbly adroit prinking is an integral part of the office of the well-bred translator. 'Had I time, I could enlarge on the beautiful turns of words and thoughts; which are as requisite in this [Varronian satire – but all satire, too, ideally, as we have already seen] as in heroic poetry itself . . .' [II, 149]. Such turns are indeed *most* of the poetic dress – certainly the most prominent part of it – that he is here putting the Roman satirists into. If they do not exhibit it very often themselves, yet their betters did: 'Virgil and Ovid are the two principal fountains of them in Latin Poetry'. And the politest modern nation, the French

> at this day are so fond of them, that they judge them to be the first beauties: *délicat et bien tourné* are the highest commendations which they bestow on somewhat which they think a masterpiece.
>
> An example of the turn on words, amongst a thousand others, is that in the last book of Ovid's *Metamorphoses*:
>
>> Heu! quantum scelus est, in viscera, viscera condi!
>> Congestoque avidum pinguescere corpore corpus;
>> Alteriusque animantem animantis vivere leto.
>>
>> [II, 151]

(subsequently translated by Dryden:

> O impious use! to Nature's Laws oppos'd,
> Where Bowels are in other Bowels clos'd:
> Where, fatten'd by their Fellows' Fat, they thrive;
> Maintained by Murther, and by Death they live.
>> [*Of the Pythagorean Philosophy*, ll. 125-128])

What stronger argument is conceivable than an appeal to the taste of the French?[6] What more obvious duty could lie upon a translator than to raise Persius and Juvenal to an Ovidian neatness, gracefulness, courtliness? How in any other form could they be fully pleasurable to and educative of a courtier – or a prince?

III

But the ideas thus imposed upon the Roman satirists more than double their interest when we find them so extended as to include in a single conceptual complex the English poets as well – Chaucer, whom Dryden translated, and the Elizabethans, who were the subject of his least durable, but not least fascinating, criticism – and it is in this act of extension that we become most acutely conscious of what has dated in Dryden. For a great deal of what is the most absurd and complacent in Dryden's critical thinking is organically related to – is indeed a part of – the ideas defined above, and is what gives meaning to, bodies out, this same correctness, this literary good-breeding, whenever he turns from the practice of Augustanism to any precise

theoretical consideration of its bases. Among and in spite of all
his generous enthusiasm for Shakespeare, his excitement at
Jonson's constructive powers, passages of foolish blight inter-
polate themselves, puffing, complacent references to 'the last
and greatest advantage of our writing, which proceeds from
conversation. In the age wherein those poets lived, there was
less of gallantry than in ours; neither did they keep the best
company of theirs. . . . Greatness was not then so easy of
access, nor conversation so free, as now it is' [I, 180-181].
And Dryden extends a grave, understanding pity to such as have
lived into his own generation with the uncourtliness of the last
still hanging upon them, 'old fellows who value themselves
on their acquaintance with the *Blackfriars*; who, because
they saw their [Jonson's, etc.] plays, would pretend a right to
judge ours. . . They were unlucky to have been bred in an unpolished age, and more unlucky to live to a refined one' [I, 181].

But it is easier to feel unthinking scorn for such passages as
this than to do what is only appropriate, which is to discover, if
possible, some meaning in them; and this in this instance seems
to be, not that Dryden claims everyone in England now to be
reformed from the boorish state they were formerly in (indeed
his own audiences are blamed enough for containing bullies and
roarers indifferent to sense, and clamorous for the farce, the
dance, and the black joke, nor does he doubt, besides, but that
there *were* gentlemen to be found among our earlier ancestors);
it is merely that these materials, these genres, and these elements
in the audiences were not properly paired-off against one
another; of Jonson he complains that 'to entertain an audience
perpetually with humour [that is, with exaggerated obsessive
types, the scenes being not lightened with admixtures of airy
gentlemanly wit] is to carry them from the conversation of
gentlemen, and treat them with the follies and extravagances
of Bedlam' [I, 150]. The remedy that was necessary follows
plainly from what has been said; Dryden would separate,
choose, distinguish: 'I would have the characters well chosen,
and kept distant from interfering with each other [humour-
types from witty gentlemen]; which is more than Fletcher and
Shakespeare did: but I would have more of the *urbana, venusta,
salsa, faceta*, and the rest which Quintilian reckons up as the
ornaments of wit. . . . As for repartee in particular; as it is the

very soul of conversation, so it is the greatest grace of comedy, where it is proper to the characters' [I, 149]. That is, comedy needs to be about and to contain smart talkers of the best new sort. That is, a proper *social* stratification must be induced into literature, a stratification that was not there to be found – or too rarely and not clearly enough – in the dramatists of the last age. But if comedy, in order to attain its proper and pre-determined form, is busy doing what satire did, which is purging itself of all its original lowness, what further can be found in Dryden concerning the stylistic courtliness the attain-ment of which is a sign of maturity in comedy as it was formerly in satire?

Unhappily Dryden endeavours to discover and then to show what he means by improvement in language, by refinement, indeed by progress itself in any developing genre. His essay on the *Dramatic Poetry of the Last Age* faces, very squarely, the prob-lem, assuring us first, tautologically enough, that refinement is *'an improvement of our wit, language, and conversation; or, an alteration in them for the better'* [I, 170]. The problem is only to show that – in the matter of language, for instance – the changes visible since Jonson *are* improvements, 'For many are of a contrary opinion, that the English tongue was then in the height of its perfection; that from Jonson's time to ours it has been in a continual declination, like that of the Romans from the age of Virgil to Statius, and so downward to Claudian; of which not only Petronius, but Quintilian himself, so much complains, under the person of Secundus, in his famous dialogue *De causis corruptae eloquentiae*' [I, 171]. Dryden does not and cannot be expected to guard himself against the very assumption that a language in changing must be getting better or worse; his business, as he conceives it, is to determine *which* of these processes is happening; and in deciding he is aware that his taste is sensitive to faults in what he called the *manners*, faults that must, that is, be distinguished from other more purely linguistic ones. He accordingly takes care to make it clear that he finds in both manners *and* language, separately, baseness in his predecessors, baseness not only in breaches of decorum in anachronisms like 'Demetrius afterwards appearing with a pistol in his hand, in the next age to Alexander the Great' and a Shepherd falling 'twice into the former indecency of wounding women' – former, because already before (shockingly against the known manner of princes) Philaster was shown 'wounding his mistress' [I, 172] – not only in offences like these against the stability of Renaissance, socio-literary sterotypes, but in the incidence of double-negatives, 'antiquated words', freedoms of word-order, here Dryden assumes he can demonstrate indubitable improvement since Ben Jonson's time. Discarding now the question of manners improving, in what, according to Dryden, if we pursue him, *does* the refinement of language consist? '*Either in rejecting such old words or phrases which are ill sounding, or improper, or in admitting new, which are more proper, more sounding, and more significant*' [I, 171]. It is useful to note the vacuity of reason that here coexists with such confidence of utterance and directness of demonstration, for it shows that Dryden's intense animus against his predecessors' language is fetched from something in him other than thought about language. The faults in Jonson are of this order:

> And be free
> Not Heaven itself from thy impiety.

A *synchysis*, or ill placing of words, of which Tully so much complains in *Oratory*.

> The waves and dens of beasts could not receive
> The bodies that those souls were frighted from.

The preposition in the end of the sentence; a common fault with him, and which I have but lately observed in my own writings . . .

> So Asia, thou art cruelly even
> With us, for all the blows thee given;
> When we, whose virtue conquered thee,
> Thus by thy vices ruin'd be.

Be there is false English for *are*; though the rhyme hides it. . . . I think few of our present writers would have left behind them such a line as this:

> Contain your spirit in more stricter bounds.

But that gross way of two comparatives was then ordinary; and therefore, more pardonable in Jonson.

[I, 174–176]

This is perhaps as naked a passage on language as is to be found in Dryden. It shows his familiarity – such as it is – with Jacobean usage prompting him to exculpate Jonson personally but not prompting him to ask whether that usage which *was* ordinary *is* now to be rated gross, *an sich*. One can but note that an intense feeling against the language as it was then conceals from Dryden himself whatever motives may be driving his mind. Soon, when language has so petulantly been asserted to have improved relative to some standard of refinement never defined but appearing to be, *tout court*, the usage of Dryden's own generation, a like improvement in wit is proved, not by adducing examples of better repartee than was formerly to be heard, but by appealing to a cause that must inevitably have produced in us a wit superior to theirs:

> Now, if any ask me whence it is that our conversation is so much refined, I must freely, and without flattery, ascribe it to the Court; and, in it, particularly to the King, whose example gives a law to it. . . . At his return, he found a nation lost as much in barbarism as in rebellion. And as the excellency of his nature forgave the one, so the excellency of his manners reformed the other. The desire of imitating so great a pattern first wakened the dull and heavy spirits of the English from their natural reservedness, loosened them from their stiff forms of conversation, and made them easy and pliant to each other in discourse.
> [I, 181-182]

What, implies the passage, could be more obvious than that, having an Augustus, we are the Augustans, and therefore – as the appeal to Latin's history is sufficient to demonstrate – *not* the succeeding Silver Age? It may be that the coupling of rebellion with barbarism in an essay about progressing literary refinement tells us quite a lot. If we take up the hint and follow his judgements on the last age's wit into the Epistle Dedicatory to *The Spanish Friar*, we find the same plain marks of a mind not able to analyze the springs of the disgust he feels at the whole manner of his forebears but able to express it with colourful and imaginative vehemence: 'I have sometimes wondered, in the reading, what was become of those glaring colours which amazed me in *Bussy D'Ambois* upon the theatre; but when I had taken up what I supposed a fallen star, I found

I had been cozened with a jelly; nothing but a cold, dull mass, which glittered no longer than it was shooting; a dwarfish thought, dressed up in gigantic words . . .' [I, 275-276].

And that the wild disorder he finds in the last age's metaphoric style inspires him with a horror that is quasi-political by nature is hinted by his saying of Statius and Virgil that '*Quae superimposito moles geminata Colosso* carries a more thundering kind of sound than *Tityre tu patulae recubans sub tegmine fagi:* yet Virgil had all the majesty of a lawful prince, and Statius only the blustering of a tyrant' [I, 277]. Dryden had, as we may remember, not only liked the style of Chapman but had written verses on the death of the Lord Protector as well; but then before a nation, and before a man, reaches a decent discretion it is indeed dangerous bluster that each delights in.

> I remember, when I was a boy, I thought inimitable Spenser a mean poet in comparison of Sylvester's *Dubartas*; and was rapt into an ecstacy when I read these lines:
>
>> Now, when the Winter's keener breath began
>> To crystallize the Baltic Ocean;
>> To glaze the lakes, to bridle up the floods,
>> And periwig with snow the bald-pate woods.
>
> I am much deceived if this be not abominable fustian, that is, thoughts and words ill sorted, and without the least relation to each other; yet I dare not answer for an audience, that they would not clap it on the stage: so little value there is to be given to the common cry that nothing but madness can please madmen, and a poet must be of a piece with the spectators to gain a reputation with them.
>
> [I, 277-278]

Besides, then, demonstrating the nervy passion with which he speaks of the monstrous breed that lived and roared before and through the Commonwealth, and the fervour with which he craves standards of secure good-breeding and gentle deportment *now*, in letters no less than politics, besides showing that these needs are expressed from a different part of his mind, as it were, from that which gave such cool and sceptical expression to the quasi-technical problems of the unities, of *liaison des scènes* and of rhyme as against blank verse, his criticism on Comedy shows us in constant operation the *idée fixe* that a civilization's excellence in language and politeness in wit is bound always to grow slowly through roughness towards the culminating grace, politeness, finish, with the language and style of each several kind distinct from that of the others, but also, and equally, bound thereafter silverly to decline. We have seen him wonder about the present condition of English as though this process were certainly happening – the visible phenomenon of linguistic change is the guarantee of that – and as though the only problem were to establish in which phase of this process is our language now? The problem as he conceives it is *how* exactly to synchronize the Elizabethans and his own time with the rise from Lucilius to Horace and Virgil, then the decline to Claudian and the rest; the unquestioned assumption is that, of course, it all *can* be synchronized, and indeed *has been*, by the nature of things which ensures that, like literary genres and national literatures, so languages as well grow to maturity, then decay; nor is anything more self-evident than that a courtliness of the present sort and of that of Maecenas' circle is unquestionably the golden maturity.

It is at this point that we can see the real significance of Dryden's urge to modernize earlier English poets. Why did he recommend the world to rescue Dr Donne's satires from the obscuring dress they were clogged with? Why assume it necessary to try to save Chaucer for his own contemporaries and for all tasteful posterity? 'We can only say that he lived in the infancy of our poetry, and that nothing is brought to perfection at the first. We must be children before we grow men. There was an Ennius, and in process of time a Lucilius, and a Lucretius, before Virgil and Horace; even after Chaucer there was a Spenser, a Harington, a Fairfax, before Waller and Denham were in being; and our numbers were in their nonage till these last appeared' [II, 281]. Despite *infancy* and *nonage*, these two sentences are clearly not meant ungenerously; Dryden's encomium of Chaucer emphasizes not the obstacles to enjoyment that infancy throws down, but rather the extraordinary delights that genius provides. However, these sentiments unquestionably imply that the necessary prerequisite for the enjoying of Chaucer is the willing suspension of some of the most important lessons of good-breeding. Dryden knows, that is, what it is hopeless to expect from Chaucer, for, having built his whole criticism upon the Humanists' Horace-based, Quintilian-based, single, and immutable paradigm for a language's growth, ripening, then decay – which is simultaneously the paradigm for the growth and fall of literatures, of civil societies in the sense that makes the Court civil, the arena not – Dryden knows where in that paradigm Chaucer belongs, and expects from him, and is delighted to get, as much pleasure, as much nature, as could be expected from *there*. It is because he enjoys, as Gibbon did, the inestimable good-fortune of being himself on the best part of the paradigm that Dryden in translating not only Chaucer but Boccaccio as well is concerned before all to breed up their language and manner to where their natural genius *ought* to have *chronologically* placed them. Dryden's sympathy with Chaucer no less than with Shakespeare and Jonson is explicitly restricted to such of their qualities as suit them for the best part of the paradigm; they understand and they portray human nature, the passions and the manners; they understand the immutable types – such as the lover, the hypocrite, the angry man, the heroine. Only the dress was wanting, and Dryden out of disinterested veneration for that founder of English poetry who 'in the beginning of our language' laboured so well to write good things – Dryden, the restorer, is charitably willing to cover the nakedness of this Father.

NOTES

1. For example: 'This manner of Horace is indeed the best; but Horace has not executed it altogether so happily, at least not often. The manner of Juvenal is confessed to be inferior to the former; but Juvenal has excell'd him in his performance' [II, 138].

2. '. . . if I would only cross the seas, I might find in France a living Horace and a Juvenal, in the person of the admirable Boileau; whose numbers are excellent, whose expressions are noble, whose thoughts are just, whose language is pure, whose satire is pointed, and whose sense is close; what he borrows from the Ancients, he repays with usury of his own, in coin as good, and almost as universally valuable; for, setting prejudice and partiality apart, though he is our

R

enemy, the stamp of a Louis, the patron of all arts, is not much inferior to the medal of an Augustus Ceasar' [II, 81].

3. To *replace* them – as is so aptly suggested of Dryden's greatest translation by L. Proudfoot in *Dryden's Aeneid and its Seventeenth Century Predecessors* (Manchester, 1960), p. 267.

4. *Juvenal and Persius*, with an English translation by G. G. Ramsay, rev. ed. (Loeb Classical Library, 1957), p. 319.

5. *Juvenal and Persius*, p. 24.

6. *Juvenal and Persius*, p. 27.

John Dryden, Gavin Douglas
and Virgil

MARK O'CONNOR

I

Twentieth-century criticism, since Eliot and Mark van Doren, has succeeded in rescuing Dryden's satirical and argumentative works from the charges of being 'unpoetical' and 'prosaic'. However, it is still largely content to leave the reputation of his most ambitious work, the translation of Virgil's *Aeneid*, roughly where it stood in the Victorian age. In many studies it is passed over as if, being a mere translation, of very inferior importance; and, while nobody denies that it has many fine passages, few critics would claim that the whole work can be read with pleasure. Thus, for instance, Mr L. Proudfoot, whose study of the translation is the fullest to date, concedes that 'It has become customary to regard Dryden's *Aeneid* as a distinguished failure, and with this judgement I am not disposed seriously to quarrel'.[1]

All this, of course, is strikingly different from the view of Dryden and his contemporaries. Dryden's own sense of the magnitude of the undertaking is sufficiently indicated by the opening sentence of his *Dedication of the Aeneis*: 'A Heroick Poem, truly such, is undoubtedly the greatest Work which the Soul of Man is capable to perform' [Kinsley, III, 1003]. The time and energy which Dryden had devoted to pondering the nature of the *Aeneid* and the manner in which it could best be Englished are sufficiently indicated by the length and critical complexity of his dedicatory essay. He declares that: 'Long before I undertook this Work, I was no stranger to the Original. I had also studied *Virgil's* Design, his disposition of it, his Manners,

his judicious management of the Figures, the sober retrench-
ments of his Sense, which always leaves somewhat to gratifie
our imagination, on which it may enlarge at pleasure; but
above all, the Elegance of his Expressions, and the harmony of
his Numbers' [p. 1051].

Although he emphasized the impossibility of doing justice
to Virgil's eloquence – 'If I cannot Copy his Harmonious
Numbers, how shall I imitate his noble Flights; where his
Thoughts and Words are equally sublime?' [pp. 1058-59] –
and chose as the motto for his title-page 'Sequiturque patrem
non passibus aequis', he was still confident enough to remark in
his *Postscript to the Reader* that 'what I have done, Imperfect
as it is, for want of Health and leisure to Correct it, will be
judg'd in after Ages, and possibly in the present, to be no dis-
honour to my Native Country; whose Language and Poetry
wou'd be more esteem'd abroad, if they were better understood'
[p. 1424]. Similarly, he was at pains in his *Dedication* to assert
the clear superiority of his version to the best-known French
and Italian ones [pp. 1049-51].

To his contemporaries, in fact, the work seemed an outstanding success. More than eighty years later we find Johnson
in his *Life of Dryden* praising it, not, as one might expect, for
its 'correctness', accuracy, or clarity, but for its allurement
and sustained imaginative power. He concedes that the translation is, like all others, 'sometimes erroneous, and sometimes
licentious', but argues that 'It is not by comparing line with line
that the merit of great works is to be estimated, but by their
general effects and ultimate result. . . . Works of imagination
excel by their allurement and delight; by their power of attract-
ing and detaining the attention'.[2]

Clearly we are faced here with some radical change in
sensibility or reading habits, for I suspect that most contemporary readers would actually reverse Johnson's verdict and
find Dryden's *Aeneid* a large and imposing edifice but insufficiently animated with spirit or imaginative power.[3] It may
therefore be worth while to consider more closely the possible
merits of Dryden's version.

Dryden's most obvious advantage lies in an essential similarity between his Augustan style and Virgil's. Both writers
had polished, 'perfected', and (inevitably) conventionalized

their respective languages in order to express a new kind of national confidence and cultural sophistication; and this had in both cases involved choosing to concentrate on the verse-form which seemed to best express the kind of polished elegance and confident refinement of expression which they desired to reconcile with the pre-existing genius and practice of the language. This verse-form, in turn, had in both cases forced them to prefer certain words and turns of phrase which came to be characteristic of their verse. Dryden, before he came to translate the *Aeneid*, had spent years in perfecting the pos-sibilities of the English heroic couplet, just as Virgil had spent years in perfecting the Latin hexameter. Admittedly neither Dryden nor Virgil was the first initiator of such a movement, but both might have claimed to represent its culmination. In both cases it was a matter of partly re-designing the idiom of the language, of learning to select and rely upon those words, groups of words, devices of style, and turns of syntax which had been found to adapt themselves most readily to the demands of the verse-form in question. Both the heroic couplet and the hexameter were, in fact, quite rigorous forms. Features of the fully-developed heroic couplet with which the poet was generally required to comply included the end-stop, the antithetical 'turn', the presence of polysyllables within the line and of strong-sounding and often monosyllabic rhyme-words at the end, and the use of trochaic adjectives in certain positions. In the case of the Latin hexameter the necessary adjustments were at least as great. There were some very common word-forms – for instance, *milites*, 'soldiers', *arbores*, 'trees', and *consules*, 'consuls' – which, because of their scansion, could never be used. Moreover, as the rules became more stringent particular word-forms tended to appear at particular places in the line. Thus a dactylic form like the adjective *saucia* would tend to appear in either the first or the fifth foot of the hexa-meter; while an iambic form like *gravi* could not, unless augmented by an enclitic particle, be used anywhere except after a weak caesura in the first, second, or third foot. It was necessary, moreover, to control the innate tendency of Latin towards long and often heavily spondaic polysyllables.[4] Hence one can readily recognize in English lines like 'One Cave a grateful Shelter shall afford / To the fair Princess, and the *Trojan*

Lord' [IV, 174-175] and Latin ones like 'At regina gravi iamdudum saucia cura / Volnus alit venis et caeco carpitur igni' [IV, 1-2] that, while the diction employed is not alien to that of the same language a century earlier, it still represents a very deliberate and fairly drastic selection and arrangement of those elements which most suit the metre.

Because of these similarities in style and outlook, Dryden readily recognized in Virgil the existence of a poetic rhetoric, of a workable brand of studied eloquence, commonly running to magniloquence. He attempted therefore to develop and use an English poetic style or rhetoric that should correspond to the Latin one and give the same effect of ease and epic dignity.

Overall Dryden's epic style serves him well enough. Except when he strains to heighten it, it is generally brief, lucid, and forceful, often capable of carrying conviction by its sheer clarity and syntactical neatness. For pages and pages, even when, as often in the later books, Dryden is not very interesting, one is still forced to admire the firm, clear re-sorting of Virgil's fluid material into the standard units of couplets, lines, and half-lines, and then the neat, perspicuous, and reasonably sonorous arrangement of this material into effective verse paragraphs.

Moreover, Dryden succeeds in his translation not only with those passages which one would certainly expect him to relish – the erotic, political, and argumentative ones, for instance – but with a wide variety of others. Here, for instance, in an example taken almost at random, he adjusts his style finely to a quiet moment in the Fourth Book, shortly before the suicide of Dido:

> 'Twas dead of Night, when weary Bodies close
> Their Eyes in balmy Sleep, and soft Repose:
> The Winds no longer whisper through the Woods,
> Nor murm'ring Tides disturb the gentle Floods.
> The Stars in silent order mov'd around,
> And Peace, with downy wings, was brooding on the ground.
> [IV, 757-762, cf. Virgil, IV, 522-525]

The well-chosen long vowel and lingering *z* sound of 'close', the first line-break which is placed so as to slow the voice even in the middle of the sentence, the placing of *w*s, *m*s, and *s*s, and the variation provided by the final lingering alexandrine are all effects of conscious art; they are typical of Dryden at his most studied, and at the same time very like Virgil, with his meticulous care to place the right sounds in the right places and his love of carefully-controlled cumulative effects.[5]

One can imagine, then, what a contemporary reader might have found to admire in Dryden's translation: such smoothness and harmony in the verse, and such precision and lucidity in the individual statements, combined with such length and complexity of narrative interest, and yet again with such authoritative and sustained magniloquence.

There are, however, some very solid reasons for finding Dryden's version unsatisfactory. Mr Proudfoot has effectively documented what he calls the 'coarsening of tone', and concludes that ' . . . he [Dryden] damaged Virgil in his most precious qualities, his tenderness, his epic grandeur and his refinement and delicacy in describing love. Relative to Virgil, Dryden was a little obtuse, perplexed by hostility to women and a false idea of courtliness, and lacking in a really noble sense of the purpose of human effort, or the scale of human destiny'.[6]

With Mr Proudfoot's analysis there is, unfortunately, little opportunity to disagree. One of the worst examples is Dryden's treatment of Dido which, throughout Book Four, is insensitive and half-hostile; in the *Dedication* he almost exults, with a kind of rakish masculine egotism, in her having been worsted by Aeneas in the battle of the sexes.

Moreover, in handling the sufferings or deaths of such characters as Priam, Andromache, Nisus, Euryalus, Palinurus, Pallas, and Turnus, he greatly underplays Virgil's pathos. This is a fault which has become more noticeable since his day, and come to seem a greater departure from Virgilian sensibility. The nineteenth-century English poets and critics became much more aware of this element in Virgil, which they understood not as being something like the mediaeval sense for 'pity' but as the expression of a more general sorrow, or even indignation with the human condition – 'the sense of tears in mortal things' – a feeling that was perhaps not fully compatible with the confident celebration of Rome's imperial destiny in other passages. They laid stress on emotions of reverence and spiritual yearning which Dryden did not especially recognize, stressing Virgil's empathic melancholy and associating it often with the melancholy produced by their own religious and philosophical uncertainty. Hence Tennyson's Virgil:

> Thou that seëst Universal
> nature moved by Universal Mind;
> Thou majestic in thy sadness
> at the doubtful doom of human kind.[7]

This Victorian appreciation of Virgil, though since heavily modified, has rarely been completely rejected[8]; in fact, it has sometimes been reinforced by the work of critics like Robert Cruttwell and W. F. Jackson Knight[9] who are concerned to demonstrate Virgil's use of ancient mythical or even archetypal patterns and beliefs. More recently, it is true, critics like Michael Putnam and Kenneth Quinn[10] have suggested that Virgil's human sympathy is less universal or, rather, more discriminating than used to be thought, that there are ironic points and implied judgements in even the most pathetic passages, and that passages like the account of the death of Turnus in Book Twelve are not meant merely to evoke a vaguely melancholy view of the indignities to which the human condition condemns men's spirits, but are part of a systematic investigation of the nature and consequences of military violence ('Furor impius') and of the irrational emotions that go with it. Such criticisms go some way towards absolving Dryden from the objections of his Victorian critics. R. D. Williams has pointed out that the *Aeneid* contains a variety of expressive modes 'direct and oblique, intimate and distanced, sensitive and detached, luxuriant and severe, hyperbolical and real, emotional and intellectual': the sympathetic 'private' voice, 'derived from the Alexandrians and Catullus, preoccupied with the individual and his feelings', is certainly prominent in the *Aeneid* but it is held in tension against the 'public voice' which is derived from the older, harsher, more distanced tradition of Ennius: 'We are not asked to weep for Dares or Cacus'.[11]

Of course, these modern interpretations are still rather different from Dryden's. Though the element of deliberate imperial propaganda is more fully recognized today than fifty years ago, few modern critics would consent to see this as the prime meaning of the *Aeneid*. Where Dryden attempts to defend Virgil by demonstrating that Aeneas is an ideal hero

and a 'perfect Prince' [Kinsley, III, 1020-25], critics like
Kenneth Quinn and Michael Putnam see Aeneas as a struggling,
imperfect, and often backsliding hero who even at the very end
of the epic betrays his civilized ideals by killing Turnus in a
moment of wild fury ('furiis accensus', XII, 946) and unreasonable anger. Consequently too their view of the way in
which Virgil intended his portrayal of Aeneas to reflect upon
the behaviour of the Emperor Augustus (Aeneas' descendant)
is more complex than Dryden's. Nevertheless, such interpretations, if accepted, must inevitably lead to a more favourable
appreciation of the translation, for there is no doubt that its
unreasonably low reputation over the last hundred years is
primarily due to Dryden's failure to emphasize those aspects of
Virgil's sensibility upon which Victorian criticism seized.

However the translation has, whether rightly or wrongly,
been considered open to another major objection, most
memorably stated in Wordsworth's famous letter to Scott:
'That his [Dryden's] cannot be the language of the imagination must have necessarily followed from this, that there is not a
single image from Nature in the whole body of his works; and
in his translation from Virgil, wherever Virgil can be fairly said
to have his eye upon his object, Dryden always spoils the
passage'.[12] Whatever one may think of Wordsworth's terms it
is clear that he has indicated an important quality of Dryden's
version. Dryden, as his *Dedication* makes quite clear, thinks of
an epic poem primarily as a verbal construction, not as a series of
vivid descriptions of visible realities. The task of translating
Virgil, as he conceived it, was essentially a matter of creating
an English literary artifact that should correspond to a Latin
one, not of imagining or experiencing the sights, scenes, and
emotions that Virgil describes and then rendering them back
into English words. Thus we find him informing his patron in
the *Dedication*:

> I am also bound to tell your Lordship, in my own defence:
> That from the beginning of the first *Georgick* to the end of the
> last *Aeneid*; I found the difficulty of Translation growing on me
> in every succeeding Book. For *Virgil*, above all poets, had a stock,
> which I may call almost inexhaustible, of figurative, Elegant, and
> sounding Words. I who inherit but a small portion of his Genius,
> and write in a Language so much inferiour to the Latin, have

found it very painful to vary Phrases, when the same sense returns upon me. Even he himself, whether out of necessity or choice, has often express'd the same thing in the same words; and often repeated two or three whole Verses, which he had us'd before. Words are not so easily Coyn'd as Money: And yet we see that the Credit not only of Banks, but of Exchequers cracks, when little comes in, and much goes out. *Virgil* call'd upon me in every line for some new word: And I paid so long, that I was almost Banckrupt. So that the latter end must needs be more burdensom than the beginning or the middle. And consequently the Twelfth *Aeneid* cost me double the time of the first and second. What had become of me, if *Virgil* had tax'd me with another Book?

[pp. 1057-58][13]

The *Aeneid* is a long epic poem, most of it concerned with the narration of plausible enough human actions and experiences (the presence of the supernatural does not, after all, exclude the natural) and with the reasonably vivid description of various scenes and settings. Yet Dryden speaks as if his endeavour in translating it were not to make his readers feel these experiences or 'see' these scenes as vividly as the Latin and his own earlier theory, as expressed in the preface to *Annus Mirabilis* [I, 98], require, but only to match elegant and impressive phrases with Virgil. It seems probable that Dryden did not consider the details of Virgil's narrative and description scenes especially subtle or complex and was aware of no particular challenge in translating them. He thought of the *Aeneid's* narrative primarily as a mere design to be dressed up as fittingly as possible by the application of a kind of external eloquence. Mark van Doren remarks, in discussing the translation, that 'Dryden generalized. His feeling for details was not keen, and his interest in them was nil', and relates this to the rather shallow neoclassical theory that Dryden advances in his *Parallel of Poetry and Painting* and elsewhere: 'He conceived color in painting as a kind of splendid wash applied after the drawing is done. It is decoration. So with elocution in poetry; it is, "in plain English," says Dryden, "the bawd of her sister the design . . . ; she clothes, she dresses her up, she paints her, she makes her appear more lovely than naturally she is; she procures the design, and makes lovers for her''. That is, diction in poetry is a splendid wash that is spread over the framework of the plot'.[14]

The question raised by Wordsworth must therefore be given consideration: whether Dryden's too-literary, too-purely-stylistic concept of epic writing did not prevent him from adequately rendering many vivid scenes, descriptions, and touches of detail that are in fact present in the *Aeneid*. This suspicion has been strengthened by the increasing popularity this century of a rival translator, Gavin Douglas, Bishop of Dunkeld, whose translation into early sixteenth-century Scots has precisely that quality of vividness that Dryden seems to lack, and is therefore considered by some critics the better version.

Douglas, like Dryden, recognized in Virgil a studied elevation of style. However, unlike Dryden, who was prepared to alter Virgil's 'figurative' expressions where they would not 'retain their Elegance in our Tongue' [p. 1055], Douglas, finding, as he claims, that he could not adequately render both Virgil's *sentens* and also his *eloquens*, preferred to concentrate on vividly and precisely rendering the *sentens*. As he explains with conventional modesty, 'My studyus brayn to comprehend his sentens / Leit me nevir taist hys flude of eloquens'.[15]

In the contrast between Douglas's decision to let the *Aeneid* stand or fall largely by the value of the story and the 'sentens' it contains, and Dryden's belief that the basic 'design' was of value only if it could be set off by elevated style and rhetorical graces, we may trace the difference between a common mediaeval view of literature and most later attitudes. As C. S. Lewis has remarked, the art of even the best mediaeval narrative poets 'is the art of people who, no less than the bad mediaeval authors, have a complete confidence in the intrinsic value of their matter. The telling is for the sake of the tale; in Chapman or Keats we feel that the tale is valued only as an opportunity for the lavish and highly individual treatment'.[16] Lewis connects this mediaeval confidence in the intrinsic value and interest of the accepted stories and myths with two other common traits: firstly with the air of ease and unstrained conviction that characterizes many mediaeval narratives, and secondly with the fashion for providing vivid close-up details, such as the description in Henryson's fables of the ineffective

mouse running up and down the river-bank with many a
'piteous peep'. He might well have used Douglas's *Eneados* as
an example of both these qualities. It is, despite some elevated
and ornate passages, essentially a rather homely and even
racy version, written in loose but fluent Chaucerian pentameter
couplets, verbose but clearly determined to bring out the full
sense of the original, sensitive, and full of vivid touches which
often make the characters and situations seem more real and less
purely literary than in Dryden's version.

Douglas's work has worn surprisingly well. An actor who
desires to revive the humours of an old play is well advised to
lean towards over-acting; and something similar applies to a
translator who wishes his version to retain its freshness.
Douglas is always prepared to emphasize or even over-
emphasize the emotional suggestions of the original. Thus, in
the scene in Book IV [ll. 305-392] where Aeneas admits to
Dido his intention of deserting her, when Virgil calls Dido
'aegra', Douglas renders it 'ful dolorus in hir thocht'; when
Virgil speaks of Dido's maids supporting her 'conlapsa membra'
(and Dryden writes 'Her fearful Maids their fainting Mistress
led'), Douglas says that Dido was 'in dedly swoun plat for
dispar'. In Book II [ll. 622-623], where Virgil writes 'Apparent
dirae facies inimicaque Troiae / Numina magna deum', Douglas
has 'Than terribil figuris apperis to my sycht / Of gret goddis,
semand with Troy aggrevit'. This is not necessarily better than
Dryden's 'And the dire Forms of hostile Gods appear' (which,
with its conventional but elevated vocabulary, is rather similar
in style to the Latin) but it certainly survives all changes in
poetic fashion and retains its freshness today in a way in which
Dryden's more artificial version does not.

It is, in fact, possible to argue that Douglas's version is
better than Dryden's precisely because he breaks the spell of
spurious Augustan classicality and recognizes that Virgil is
talking about real things. This judgement has been adopted
with characteristic verve by C. S. Lewis in his *English Literature
in the Sixteenth Century*:

> Douglas shocks us by being closer to Virgil than we. Once a
> man's eyes have been opened to this, he will find examples
> everywhere. *Rosea cervice refulsit*: 'her nek schane like unto the
> rois in May'. Do you prefer Dryden's 'she turned and made

appear / Her neck refulgent'? But *refulsit* cannot possibly have
had for a Roman ear the 'classical' quality which 'refulgent' has
for an English. It must have felt much more like 'schane'. And
rosea has disappeared altogether in Dryden's version – and with
it half the sensuous vitality of the image. . . .

It is not the real Virgil; it is that fatal 'classical' misconcep-
tion of all ancient poets which the humanists have fastened
upon our education – the spectral solemnity, the gradus epithets,
the dictionary language, the diction which avoids every contact
with the senses and the soil. (Dryden tells us that though he
knew *mollis amaracus* was sweet marjoram, he did not dare so
translate it, for fear 'those village words' should give the reader
'a mean idea of the thing'.) Time after time Douglas is nearer to
the original than any version could be which kept within the
limits of later classicism. And that is almost another way of
saying that the real Virgil is very much less 'classical' than we
had supposed.[17]

Lewis's claim is so important that it seems to me worth while
to test it in the present essay, by considering a larger and more
representative set of parallel passages from the two translators
than his brief review could find space for. In doing so I shall
be concerned more with the relationship of Dryden's sensibility
to Douglas's and Virgil's, than with the merits of his translation
considered as a seventeenth-century poem in its own right.
Nevertheless, if Lewis is right – or even half-right – it may
be possible to demonstrate that Dryden's translation failed
to 'allure' post-Augustan readers essentially because he had,
perhaps along with most of his contemporaries, mistaken the
nature of the work he was translating.

II

It will be useful to begin by stating the case against Lewis. It is
clear straightaway that he is loading the dice a little. 'Her neck
refulgent' is for Dryden an unusually artificial turn of phrase;
he more often runs to the other extreme of being too colloquial
and irreverent for the Latin. It is, in any case, no more artificial
than Virgil's frequent Hellenisms and Latin archaisms. Similarly,
Dryden's argument, that if Virgil used the name *mollis amaracus*
in an epic context this was because the resonant Latin name
did not sound so 'low' as 'sweet marjoram' in English, is not

necessarily nonsense. Virgil may well have subscribed to principles similar to those of his friend Horace, from whose *Ars
Poetica* the (English) Augustans' theory of decorum was largely
drawn.

It is, in fact, possible to adduce many quite typical passages,
especially those containing the 'images from Nature' which
interested Wordsworth, where Dryden's translation, though
perhaps less attractive to modern taste, is closer to what Virgil
offers than Douglas. Consider, for instance, the following
passage from the description of Dido's hunt in Book Four.
After a rich and glowing account of dawn, of the spirited horses
and hounds awaiting the Queen's pleasure outside the palace,
of Dido's appearance, and of Aeneas' Apollo-like, manly
beauty, Virgil abruptly continues:

> Postquam altos ventum in montis atque invia lustra,
> Ecce ferae saxi deiectae vertice caprae
> Decurrere iugis; alia de parte patentis
> Transmittunt cursu campos atque agmina cervi
> Pulverulenta fuga glomerant montisque relinquunt.
> At puer Ascanius mediis in vallibus acri
> Gaudet equo, iamque hos cursu, iam praeterit illos,
> Spumantemque dari pecora inter inertia votis
> Optat aprum aut fulvum descendere monte leonem.
> Interea magno misceri murmure caelum
> Incipit. . . .
>
> [IV, ll. 151-161]

which the Loeb translator renders:

> When they came to the mountain heights and pathless lairs,
> lo! wild goats dislodged from the rocky peaks ran down the
> ridges; in another part stags scurry across the open moors and
> amid clouds of dust mass their bands in flight, as they leave the
> hills behind. But in the midst of the valleys the young Ascanius
> glories in his fiery steed, galloping past now these, now those,
> and prays that amid the timorous herds a foaming boar may be
> granted to his vows or a tawny lion come down from the
> mountain. Meanwhile in the sky begins the turmoil of a wild
> uproar. . . .

What strikes one most immediately about this passage is its
brevity, the characteristic Virgilian brevity which is less a

matter of concision within a given sentence than of passing very rapidly over any material that is not quite essential. Virgil seems here to have no space for visual effects. There is not even any vivid detail of the garb of Ascanius or the trappings of his horse, and the adjectives *spumantem* and *fulvum* are entirely conventional. The whole hunt scene to which Virgil has been building up for some time is disposed of in nine lines. The 'Interea magno . . .' comes as suddenly and unexpectedly as the thunder that it announces.

But if Virgil is not interested in vivid scene painting, we should be able to say what he *is* doing in these lines. Essentially he appears to be building up, in preparation for the contrast that will follow, a confused but excited sense of a successful hunt in full swing. Lo! there are the wild goats the beaters were hoping to flush, fleeing down the ridges; at the same time, in another place, the stags are heading out across the plain. The scene is not to be too precisely visualized but the general geography is clear. The hunters wait down in the valleys on horseback; the beaters drive the game down from the hills; the goats run down along the ridges, offering one kind of chase for the huntsmen; the stags flee out across the open plain, offering a different one. In the middle of the excitement is young Ascanius, the great hope of future Rome, excited, full of precocious courage, naïvely confident of his ability to deal with a boar or a lion. All attention is on the thickets and the game, not on what Juno (as the reader knows) is brewing.

Moreover, if visual suggestiveness is weak audial suggestiveness is tremendously strong. The four spondees and four elisions in the first line suggest the sound of hunting-horns; the three dactyls of 'Pulverulenta fuga glomerant' are clearly onomatopoeic; and the build-up of *m*s and spondees in 'Interea magno misceri murmure caelum / Incipit . . .' is unashamedly ominous.

The significance, therefore, of the scene that Virgil describes has little to do with those elements in it which lend themselves to precise visual imagery. Douglas translates the greater part of it as follows:

> And eftyr thai ar cummyn to the chace,
> Amang the montanys in the wild forest,
> The rynnyng hundis of cuppillys sone thai kest,

And our the clewys and the holtis, belyve,
The wild beistis doun to the dail thai dryve.
Lo! thar the rays, rynnyng swyft as fyre,
Drevyn from the hyghtis, brekkis out at the swyre;
Ane othir part, syne yondyr mycht thou see
The herd of hartis with thar hedis hie,
Ourspynnerand with swyft courss the plane vaill,
The hepe of duste upstowryng at thar taill,
Fleand the hundis, levand the hie montanys.

[IV, iv, 44-55]

This is superbly vivid and fully visualized but five lines of
Virgil have become twelve English (or Scots) pentameters.[18]
Douglas clearly has to set out to imagine the scene as fully as
possible, no doubt remembering his experience of Scottish
deer-hunts, and has then put it back into his own words with
the addition of several plausible touches. He is translating a
scene rather than a text. This is in one way a sensitive mode of
translation and would doubtless meet with Wordsworth's
approval; but stylistically it is quite unfaithful: its excellencies
are not germane to those of its original. Nevertheless, the last
four lines are enough to show that such poetry may be of a high
order, even if it has to be thought of ultimately rather as an
indigenous Scottish than a classical masterpiece.

Dryden's translation is much more neat and succinct. It can
be seen that it works in a more purely 'literary' way, relying
on a steady flow of well-regulated words rather than on
sharply-focused images:

Now had they reach'd the Hills, and storm'd the Seat
Of salvage Beasts, in Dens, their last Retreat;
The Cry pursues the Mountain-Goats; they bound
From Rock to Rock, and keep the craggy Ground:
Quite otherwise the Stags, a trembling Train,
In Herds unsingl'd, scour the dusty Plain;
And a long Chace, in open view, maintain.

[IV, 216-222]

Admittedly, if Douglas has overtranslated the visual quality of
the passage Dryden has slightly undertranslated it. 'A trembling
Train' certainly sounds well and provides a convenient strong
rhyme with 'Plain' but the generic use of the adjective 'trembling'

is, as it were, visually incompatible with 'scour the dusty Plain'.
(Or can Stags tremble on the run?) Nevertheless, although no
single line is especially striking Dryden *has* very briefly and
lucidly conveyed into English most of what Virgil has to offer.
Like Douglas he effectively conveys the general sense of
excited movement, but where Douglas has concentrated on the
visual effects Dryden may almost be said to have concentrated
on the logical rationale of the description. We do not *see* the
mountain-goats or the stags but the distinction between the
behaviour of the two species is made very clear. The emphasis
given to the connective phrase 'Quite otherwise' is characteristic. There is no diffuseness about the passage. Everything is
lucid, everything fits and connects; the translator's style is
sufficiently evocative of that of the original. If Dryden began
with the view that, as Johnson later expressed it, 'the business
of the poet is to examine, not the individual, but the species:
to remark general properties and large appearances', then he
can have found little in this passage to make him suspect that
Virgil thought differently. Douglas's preference for adding
particulars and close-up detail may, as Lewis himself suggests,
be considered a mediaeval peculiarity.

Dryden's handling of this passage can be seen then to proceed
from the assumption (or perhaps the perception) that Virgil,
like himself, was practising a sophisticated form of poetic
rhetoric in which verbal and audial effects take precedence over
visual, and generalities over specific details. In general I think
it can be said that, as this example indicates, the greater visual
vividness of Douglas's version does not necessarily make it any
better and often, in fact, makes it less faithful to the spirit of
the original. Dryden's lack of particularizing visual imagination was not, at least when it came to translating the *Aeneid*, a
major handicap.

But Wordsworth's and Lewis's criticisms still hold. In fact, it
is not especially in those passages where it is primarily a matter
of visualizing or not visualizing that Douglas's method appears
at its best by comparison with Dryden's. It is rather where
Virgil is demonstrating a large amount of human sympathy or
where he is assuming a fairly coherent social or cultural background that Douglas's technique of imagining and re-creating
the scene as fully as he can in terms of his own experience

s

before translating it, may preserve more of what Virgil has to offer. Consider, for instance, this passage in Book Four where, after Dido has discovered his intention of deserting her and bitterly taxed him with it, Aeneas attempts, awkwardly enough, to pacify her:

> Dixerat. Ille Iovis monitis immota tenebat
> Lumina et obnixus curam sub corde premebat.
> Tandem pauca refert: 'Ego te, quae plurima fando
> Enumerare vales, numquam, regina, negabo
> Promeritam, nec me meminisse pigebit Elissae,
> Dum memor ipse mei, dum spiritus hos regit artus.
> Pro re pauca loquar. Neque ego hanc abscondere furto
> Speravi (ne finge) fugam, nec coniugis umquam
> Praetendi taedas aut haec in foedera veni.'
>
> [IV, 331-339]

[She ceased: he by Jove's command held his eyes steadfast and with a struggle smothered the pain deep within his heart. At last he briefly replies: 'I will never deny, O queen, that thou hast deserved of me the utmost thou canst set forth in speech, nor shall my memory of Elissa be bitter, while I have memory of myself, and while breath still sways these limbs. For my course few words will I say. I did not hope – think not that – to veil my flight in stealth. I never held out the bridegroom's torch nor entered such a compact'.]

Here is a passage to test any translator. Its tone depends on so precise and crucial a balance of attitudes that he can hardly dare change it, much less add additional details of his own, without running the risk of destroying the whole concept of Aeneas' *virtus* as Virgil has developed it. It is important that before making this reply Aeneas pauses for some time with his eyes fixed, steadfast, struggling to force down the love-pain in his breast. His reply, when it does come, is brief and disjointed, marked by a kind of troubled and faltering courtliness. The translator should observe the disjointed syntax of 'Ego te, quae plurima fando / Enumerare vales, numquam, regina, negabo . . .'; the contrast between the stiff formality of the opening 'regina' and Aeneas' later, faintly maudlin, attempt to use Dido's more intimate personal name, Elissa; and also the sudden transition from the heroics of 'Pro re pauca loquar' and then to the inglorious equivocation of 'neque ego hanc abscondere furto / Speravi (ne finge) fugam'.

Douglas offers us:

> Thus said the queyn Dido, in febil estate.
> Bot, apon Iovis message fermly he
> Stude musyng so, he movit nocht ane e,
> Refrenyt his will, hydand in hart his thocht,
> And, at the last, thir few wordis hess furth brocht:
> 'O gentil queyn, that sall I nevir deny,
> Thy gude deid and desart is mair worthy
> Than thou with wordis or tong may expreme;
> Nor it sal nevir me irk, na yyt mysseym,
> The worthy Dido to hald in fresch memory,
> So lang as that my self remembir may I,
> Or quhil the spreit of lyfe this body steris.
> As the mater requiris, a litil heris:
> I purposyt nocht forto hyde thyftuusly
> My vayage, nor, as ye weyn, secretly
> Away to steil; quhat nedis you sa tofeyn?
> For I pretendit nevir, be na meyn,
> With you to mak the band of mariage,
> Nor in that yok, ne frendschip in Cartage,
> Yyt come I nevir:'   [IV, vi, 100-119]

Once again we notice that Douglas expands on Virgil's text but the expansions are not insensitive or haphazard. They often result from the determination to bring out, perhaps a little too explicitly, the full meaning of Virgil's hints. Thus in the lines 'I purposyt nocht *forto hyde thyftuusly* / *My vayage*, nor, as ye weyn, *secretly* / *Away to steil*; quhat nedis you sa tofeyn?' the two italicized phrases may represent different 'unpackings' of Virgil's somewhat vague 'hanc . . . furto . . . fugam' rather than mere doublets; while the 'as ye weyn' and 'quhat nedis you sa tofeyn?' undoubtedly represent different possible applications of Aeneas' parenthetical 'ne finge'. Thus this may be prolix but is certainly not insensitive translation.

Moreover, though this may not be great epic writing, it is a very effective and plausible piece of rhetoric. It succeeds and becomes credible because of the (almost unconscious) anachronism by which Douglas has unobtrusively placed Aeneas and Dido within the world of mediaeval chivalry. Beyond this speech, slight enough in itself, there seems to be a fully imagined world with known objects, laws, and, above all, manners. Of course it is not quite the world that Virgil envisaged; it is a mediaeval equivalent; but it is an acceptable equivalent, one that does not lead the translator to grossly distort the tone or meaning of his original. In fact, Virgil's basic meaning and his variations of tone are reproduced with great accuracy, but a few slight touches – 'O gentil queyn' for 'regina' and 'to hald in fresch memory' for 'meminisse' – assimilate him to a mediaeval setting. In this context both the personalities and the plight of Aeneas and Dido seem far more solid, less overtly fictional, than in Dryden's version:

> Here paus'd the Queen; unmov'd he holds his Eyes,
> By *Jove*'s Command; nor suffer'd Love to rise,
> Tho' heaving in his Heart; and thus at length, replies.
> Fair Queen, you never can enough repeat
> Your boundless Favours, or I own my Debt;
> Nor can my Mind forget *Eliza*'s Name,
> While vital Breath inspires this Mortal Frame.
> This, only let me speak in my Defence,
> I never hop'd a secret Flight from hence:
> Much less pretended to the Lawful Claim
> Of Sacred Nuptials, or, a Husband's Name.
>
> [IV, 480-490]

Dryden is certainly more concise and his syntax is far sharper; and yet the spirit of the original is almost lost. His tone is quite false to the courteous and courtly effect which the Latin demands; it seems to have been borrowed from his own satires. Even the suggestion of Aeneas' being ill-at-ease and the deliberately tentative syntax of the original have disappeared. The couplets enact harsh, neat, confident judgements rather than regretful decision.

The question must, in fact, be raised whether it is the heroic couplet that is really to blame for Dryden's weakness in this and similar passages. In many cases Dryden's apparent inferiority to Douglas may be due not so much to his having missed Virgil's subtleties or failed to feel his emotions as to the sheer difficulty of rendering into the heroic couplet the kind of feeling that the original conveys. The couplet, as Dryden has mastered it, was designed to give primarily an effect of definiteness, force, and clarity. Hence in the last example the temptation to give Aeneas' speech a quality of lucid, emphatic decision, which unfortunately tends to mask its more important qualities.

A similar phenomenon may be observed in the opening lines of Book Four. Virgil has:

> At regina gravi iamdudum saucia cura
> Volnus alit venis et caeco carpitur igni.
> Multa viri virtus animo multusque recursat
> Gentis honos; haerent infixi pectore voltus
> Verbaque, nec placidam membris dat cura quietem.
>
> [IV, 1-5]

[But the queen, long since smitten with a grievous love-pang, feeds the wound with her life-blood, and is wasted with fire unseen. Oft to her heart rushes back the chief's valour, oft his glorious stock; his looks and words cling fast within her bosom, and the pang withholds calm rest from her limbs.]

This is very studied writing. One is conscious of the Latin language being regulated by the hexameter form as carefully as ever English was by the heroic couplet. The vocabulary and choice of metaphors to describe the progress of love are both conventional. The subdued alliteration and even the placing of long vowels and particular consonants can be seen as highly self-conscious. Immediately after the impressive close of Aeneas' narration in Book Three the initial adversative conjunction *At* (which means something like 'but moreover'), recalling us to the effect on Dido which, although as yet ignored, is already half-expected, and itself followed by the sonorous key-word 'regina', sets a fine note of regret and tragic foreboding which the passage well maintains. Here, one would think, is a passage that Dryden could handle well. He has:

> But anxious Cares already seiz'd the Queen:
> She fed within her Veins a Flame unseen:
> The Heroe's Valour, Acts, and Birth inspire
> Her Soul with Love, and fann the secret Fire.
> His Words, his Looks imprinted in her Heart,
> Improve the Passion, and increase the Smart.
>
> [IV, 1-6]

Virgil's regretful tones have been replaced by a kind of swift erotic relish. No doubt this is partly an example of the hostility to women which, as Proudfoot has demonstrated, caused Dryden to ignore the pathos of Dido's position; but I think that the nature of the heroic couplet is also a factor. What, if anything, does the movement of the couplets 'enact' here? I should say two things. Firstly the couplets enact their own lucidity, or perhaps, rather, the lucidity and intellectual comprehensibility of the process they describe. Secondly they enact the swiftness, the innate force, and perhaps ultimately the inevitability of the process. This combination effect of kinaesthetic perspicuity is characteristic of Dryden, though perhaps found at its best in his more satirical work (cf. the opening of *Absalom and Achitophel*). On the one hand his verse communicates a kind of excited sympathy, which can almost be felt in the muscles, with the force or the vitality of some physical action; on the other hand a kind of clear-headed, logical awareness of what the situation amounts to. The former component, the kinaesthetic, tends to compensate for any lack of precisely *visual* vividness and is almost always a source of strength. However, the latter, the quality of self-conscious clarity and decisiveness, is much less appropriate to the task of translating Virgil's epic style. It is, of course, a very common effect, even in the more pathetic or affecting passages of the translation. After all, the effect of the predominantly end-stopped couplet, as Dryden was perfecting it, was almost inevitably one of crisp precision.

It would be too mechanical, however, to think of Dryden as being imprisoned by a limiting form to which he was committed by fashion. If he (and his age) preferred a form which would tend to emphasize the comprehensibility rather than the pathos of Dido's plight it was partly because that was, in fact, the way he felt. That he was conscious of a 'scientific' interest in the general nature and course of love, rather than of any feeling of pity for poor Dido caught between the aspirations of love and the decrees of Fate, is sufficiently indicated by his account of the Fourth Book in the *Dedication*:

> Love was the Theme of his Fourth Book; and though it is the shortest of the whole *Aeneis*, yet there he has given its beginning, its progress, its traverses, and its conclusion. And had exhausted so entirely this Subject, that he cou'd but resume it but very slightly in the Eight ensuing Books.

> She was warm'd with the graceful appearance of the Heroe,
> she smother'd those Sparkles out of decency, but Conversation
> blew them up into a Flame. Then she was forc'd to make a
> Confident. . . . See here the whole process of that passion, to
> which nothing can be added.   [III, 1028]

I have loosely described this interest as 'scientific'. However, the approach is in no sense empirical or inductive. What Dryden reveals is rather a concern with the nature of love as expressed in its most generalized form. He is interested in codifying universally-known truths in the most memorable and appropriate way. It would be unwise, however, to assume that such passages as the above need represent insensitivity on Dryden's part. After all, to relish the lucidity, comprehensibility, and typicality of a process is not necessarily to be insensitive to its human consequences. The problem for the modern reader is that of these two aspects it is commonly rather the 'scientific' rationale than the human emotion that Dryden's verse chooses to enact. 'Improve the Passion, and increase the Smart'. *It is presumed that the reader is intelligent enough to be sensitive to the human significance.* This, in fact, is the way in which the heroic couplet is designed to work, and it was not until people ceased to admire Ovid that the couplet became unsuited to English sensibility.

Perhaps this is ultimately the answer to the question which I originally proposed: why does a poem which seemed to Dr Johnson full of allurement and imaginative power, and to Pope 'the most noble and spirited translation that I know in any language' fail to move us today? The answer may be that Dryden's epic verse belongs to a different and more Ovidian school of poetry than we are familiar with. It is not impossible for us partly to recapture the taste that admired his version so highly. Compare, for instance, Dryden's vigorous opening of Book Four, quoted earlier, with James Rhoades's careful late-Victorian version:

> But stricken long since with anguish deep, the queen
> Feeds at her veins the wounds, whose hidden fire
> Consumes her. To her heart comes surging back
> Full oft the manhood of the man, full oft
> The lustre of his line: his looks, his words,
> Cling rooted fast within her bosom's core,
> And anguish to her frame calm sleep denies.[19]

Surely the basic difference between Rhoades's and Dryden's version (which is very nearly the same as that between Virgil's and Dryden's) is as simple as the formula suggested above. Dryden's verse enacts primarily the rationale and cause of Dido's falling in love, relishing the comprehensibility of the process, without necessarily being insensitive to Dido's plight. In Rhoades, conversely, the movement and disposition of the words is designated to enact the pathos of the process (without necessarily being indifferent to the rationale). No neat antithesis for him, though he permits the mournful repetition 'Full oft . . . full oft . . .' which the Latin invites.

Such seems to be the basic difference between the two, and surely one could argue that Dryden's version is much the better. It has stronger and more striking technical effects, there is a virile, bracing tone about the whole movement of the passage, it suggests by implication everything that Rhoades is mournfully at pains to bring out about Dido's plight, and it does so from a more complex (or at least duplex) point of view. Rhoades's approach when used by a great poet will in the long run take him further, but there is nothing weak or despicable, or necessarily callous, about Dryden's version.

The apparent insensitivity of Dryden's version when contrasted with Douglas's may therefore be partly illusory; and to this extent what had previously appeared as a kind of 'classical' obnubilation foisted upon the text by Dryden may be defended from C. S. Lewis's strictures and seen as a more positive quality. However, the complaint that Dryden has, whether consciously or not, altered the tone of the original, made Virgil sound more like Ovid, would remain. In fact, when all has been said in favour of a fairer understanding of Dryden's mode I think it must still be admitted that he has commonly failed to perceive Virgil's melancholy, pathetic, and suggestive qualities and has supplied in their place, and often rather tastelessly, a greater emphasis on merely technical and rhetorical effects. Thus:

> . . . ingeminant curae, rursusque resurgens
> Saevit amor, magnoque irarum fluctuat aestu.
> [IV, 531-532]

may be in Virgil a neat exercise in elegant variation as well as an affecting statement of Dido's condition but it does not deserve to be turned into:

> Despair, and Rage, and Love divide her heart;
> Despair and Rage had some, but Love the greater part.
>
> [IV, 771-772]

Nor is it necessary for:

> Quis tibi tum, Dido, cernenti talia sensus,
> Quosve dabas gemitus, cum litora fervere late
> Prospiceres arce ex summa . . .
>
> [IV, 408-410]

which Douglas correctly renders:

> Quhat thocht thou now, Dydo, seand thir thingis?
> Quhou mony sobbys gave thou and womentyngis? *etc.*
>
> [IV, viii, 1-2]

to be turned, no doubt in the interests of maintaining an epic height of diction, into the remote third person:

> What Pangs the tender Breast of *Dido* tore,
> When, from the Tow'r, she saw the cover'd Shore . . .
>
> [IV, 591-592]

Examples might be multiplied. The great problem, it becomes clear, is the basic difference between the sensibilities of Dryden and Virgil; a difference that is in part caused by and in part merely reflected in their different verse-forms. It was suggested earlier that the heroic couplet and the Golden-Age Latin hexameter were alike in that they were both fairly rigorous forms which had been laboriously perfected and shaped to express a newly-found kind of national confidence and civilized articulateness, which we characterize as 'Augustan', both Virgil and Dryden having played major parts in the shaping of the respective forms. However, in some more essential respects they are opposite. The effect of the hexameter is certainly one of cultivated articulacy but it is not normally one of definiteness. Ruth Wallerstein has spoken of 'the syntactical distinctness . . ., the terse completed thought that marks the fully developed couplet',[20] but the Virgilian hexameter (unlike the elegiac couplet which Ovid preferred) is rarely end-stopped. The recurrent pattern of the last two feet of the hexameter line, though strong, is not nearly so forceful as the rhyme of the heroic couplet and does not encourage the same terse sententiousness. The unit of verse, therefore, is not the single line or couplet but, as in Milton's epic style, the flowing verse paragraph. To a limited extent Dryden can and does create flowing verse paragraphs and where he succeeds, as in the opening lines 'Arms, and the Man I sing' *etc.*, or in the passage quoted earlier beginning "Twas dead of Night, when weary Bodies close . . . ', the result is almost always admirable. But the disruptive effect of the couplet form is strong and the paragraph must have a strong internal unity if it is not to split up into a series of discrete units of information. The difficulty Dryden felt in achieving simultaneously a fair imitation both of Virgil's thought and of his music is suggested by his remarks in the *Dedication* about the sad lot of the translator – '. . . For being ty'd to the Thoughts, he must make what Musick he can in the Expression' [III, 1058] – and the inconvenience of rhyme – 'What it adds to sweetness, it takes away from sense; and he who loses the least by it, may be call'd a gainer' [III, 1050].

Moreover, not only Virgil's metre but also the very nature of the Latin language (leaving aside the question of Virgil's own poetic personality) makes his style less definite than Dryden's. Because literary Latin has comparatively few words, individual words tend in literature to have fewer precise connotations and larger and vaguer areas of meaning than English words. They may be thought of as having large empty spaces within them which become filled with meaning only through the proximity of the right companion-words.[21] Thus, the suggestions of many of Virgil's lines – for instance, Aeneas' famous comment when he finds the episodes of Troy depicted upon a temple in faraway Carthage: 'Sunt hic etiam sua praemia laudi / Sunt lacrimae rerum et mentem mortalia tangunt' [I, 461-462] – are so much a matter of the interacting of words vague in themselves, like *rerum, mentem, mortalia*, that it would require exceptional skill for a translator to find an equivalent in the more definite idiom of English. (That the heroic couplet added to this difficulty is suggested by Dryden's complaint that, though Virgil has sometimes two figurative expressions in a line, 'the scantiness of our Heroick Verse, is not capable of receiving more than one' [III, 1055]). Certainly one does not need to be addicted to finding in Virgil the expression of a Victorian melancholy to feel that Dryden's version of the lines quoted above – 'Ev'n the Mute Walls relate the Warrior's Fame / And *Trojan* Griefs the *Tyrians* Pity claim' [III, 648-649] – misrepresents the feeling of the original. 'Ev'n the Mute Walls relate the Warrior's Fame' is a fair attempt to express the major meaning of 'Sunt hic etiam sua praemia laudi' (or at least one of the major meanings) but Virgil's words have no such naked specificity. His poetry, like music, is nothing without the overtones. The second half of Dryden's couplet is even cruder.

It seems that Dryden had quite largely mistaken the nature of Virgil's style. His over-concern with elevation of style and with 'harmony' corresponded to a certain unawareness of the way in which Virgil's language works. His translation is full of admirably clear and forceful statements but it fatally lacks the quality which E. M. W. Tillyard calls 'obliquity'.[22] Sometimes a couplet or a brief passage like 'The Hearer on the Speaker's Mouth depends; / And thus the Tragick Story never ends' [IV, 113-114, for Virgil's 'pendetque iterum narrantis ab ore', IV, 79] will prove an exception and imitate Virgil's power of suggesting several applications at once; but it is more common to find such crudely explicit lines as 'Strange Voices issu'd from her Husband's Tomb: / She thought she heard him summon her away; / Invite her to his Grave; and chide her stay' [IV, 668-670, for 'Hinc exaudiri voces et verba vocantis / Visa viri', IV, 460-461] or 'Amaz'd he stood, revolving in his Mind / What Speech to frame, and what Excuse to find' [IV, 564-565], where Virgil has 'Linquens multa metu cunctantem et multa parantem / Dicere' [IV, 390-391] and Douglas 'On seir materis leifand hym pensyve wight' [IV, vii, 56].

Overall, we may say that Dryden was misled by certain Augustan similarities between his mode and Virgil's into imagining that he knew Virgil's mind better than he did. He had studied Virgil's rhetoric and the 'judicious management of his figures' and was often able to achieve a similar polished magniloquence; but he too often failed to render Virgil's melancholy and human tenderness (especially in the Dido episode – in the Sixth Book, where he met similar feelings expressed in more generalized form he sometimes rendered them admirably). He was also insufficiently aware of the *Aeneid* as a historical romance, a re-creation of fabled events. Those emotions which he did recognize, his couplets often failed to enact. He was generally unable to achieve that effect of smooth-flowing opulence that is characteristic of Virgil's epic style, as of Homer's and Milton's. Indeed, to judge from his *Dedication*, he was unaware of this essential difference between Virgil's style and his own. It might also be argued, though this is not the place, that Dryden had little grasp of the historical, as opposed to the political, element in the *Aeneid*, the sense of a specifically Roman past enriching a specifically Roman present which anthropology is helping us to rediscover. In these senses Lewis is right: the Augustan understanding of the classics, at least as exemplified by Dryden's handling of the *Aeneid*, was often a narrow and mistaken one. Dryden's concept of heroic sublimity had an inhibiting effect upon his poetic range and his modes of achieving it led to a certain monotony.

Nevertheless, Dryden's achievement remains impressive. The essential weakness of his translation – the concept of epic 'elevation' as magniloquence not necessarily backed by any very profound view of life, and the unsuitability of the heroic couplet for rendering Virgilian style and sensibility – were imposed upon him by the culture of his age; and in his understanding of Virgil, as of Shakespeare, he often showed the ability to rise above the limitations of Augustan theory by a rare combination of generosity and intelligence. If he failed to write a successful epic on these principles, no one else succeeded. The English Augustans, following the ideas of the French Augustans, could finely re-create the spirit of Horatian discourse – Pope's imitation of the *Epistle to Augustus* is flawless Horace – but they never fully understood the nature of classical epic: at least they never produced a fully successful imitation. The form which they placed on the pinnacle of their literary pyramid was half-chimera.

NOTES

1. *Dryden's Aeneid and Its Seventeenth Century Predecessors* (Manchester, 1960), p. 183.

2. *Lives of the Poets*, ed. G. B. Hill, 3 vols. (Oxford, 1905), I, 454.

3. See, for instance, Mark van Doren, in *John Dryden: A Study of His Poetry* (Indiana, 1963), p. 63.

4. On this point, see Kenneth Quinn, *Virgil's Aeneid* (London, 1968), p. 352.

5. On these characteristics, see L. P. Wilkinson, *Golden Latin Artistry* (Cambridge, 1963), pp. 74–83 and 198–200. Also W. F. Jackson Knight, *Roman Vergil* (London, 1966), pp. 296–308.

6. Proudfoot, p. 219.

7. 'To Virgil', ll. 11–12; *The Poems of Tennyson*, ed. Christopher Ricks (London: Longmans, 1969), p. 1313. For an account of the development of this view, which arose partly in opposition to the disparaging attitude fostered by the Romantic movement – Byron called Virgil 'that harmonious plagiary and miserable flatterer' – see R. D. Williams, 'Changing Attitudes to Virgil: A Study in the History of Taste from Dryden to Tennyson', in *Virgil*, ed. D. R. Dudley (London, 1969).

8. There has, of course, been an interesting attempt by Robert Graves, most notably in his 1961 Oxford lecture 'The Anti-Poet', printed in *Oxford Addresses on Poetry* (London, 1961), to present Virgil as an artificial Alexandrian rhetorician who wrote, not under the inspiration of the Muse, but by the barren rules of Apollo, God of Reason. (Cf. Byron's view.) This is an interesting line. The obvious and immense calculatedness of so many of Virgil's effects might well seem at variance with the 'received' view. Unfortunately Mr Graves's method of argument is not convincing. The Oxford lecture, for instance, is primarily an *ad hominem* argument which depends on conjectures and interpretations stated as though they were accepted fact. Thus, for instance: 'Virgil's chief delight [!] was to mourn beautiful boys cut off in the flower of their youth – ah, what a waste!' [p. 43] and 'Virgil never mentions Cicero . . . but caricatures him as the abominable 'Drances' in the Eleventh Book' [p. 48]. His few examinations of particular passages are in several places marred by similar eccentricity. Thus his comments on the opening lines of Book Two are all dependent on the odd assumption that the 'all' of

'Conticuere omnes intentique ora tenebant' is undefined. It would be interesting, however, to see what sort of case a more careful critic could build up by a more disciplined examination of passages like those to which Mr Graves objects.

9. Robert Cruttwell, *Virgil's Mind at Work* (Oxford, 1946). W. F. Jackson Knight, *Vergil: Epic and Anthropology* (London, 1967).

10. Michael Putnam, *The Poetry of the Aeneid* (Harvard, 1965), especially Chapter 4, 'Tragic Victory'. Kenneth Quinn, *Virgil's Aeneid*.

11. In D. R. Dudley, ed., *Virgil*, p. 136. See also William's pamphlet *Virgil, Greece and Rome*, offprint, New Surveys in the Classics, No. 1 (1967).

12. *Early Letters of William and Dorothy Wordsworth*, ed. Ernest de Selincourt (Oxford, 1935), p. 541.

13. It is interesting to note that Dryden appears not to consider the possibility that Virgil's repetitions may have thematic significance, that they may be designed, for instance, to suggest relationships between various episodes. The tracing of such patterns of verbal similarity in the *Aeneid* is popular today and is one of the major concerns of Michael Putnam's book.

14. Van Doren, p. 53.

15. *Virgil's Aeneid Translated Into Scottish Verse*, ed. Coldwell, S. T. S., 4 vols. (London, 1957), Volume II, Prologue to the First Book, ll. 309-310. All references are to this edition. As Douglas divided each of the Books of the *Aeneid* into a series of small chapters, references are given to Book, chapter, and line.

16. *The Discarded Image* (Cambridge, 1964), p. 205.

17. *English Literature in the Sixteenth Century* (Oxford, 1954), pp. 83-84.

18. Douglas's translation cannot entirely be excused from charges of metrical uncertainty. Nevertheless, for the time that it was written, the iambic beat is surprisingly distinct, and there is little reason to doubt that the departure from regular pattern in lines like 'Drevyn from the hyghtis, brekkis out at the swyre' is intentional. It should be remembered that the *-is* or *-ys* termination of plural nouns and singular verbs may be counted as a syllable where convenient.

19. *The Poems of Virgil: Translated into English Verse* (London, 1893).

20. Ruth Wallerstein, 'The Development of the Rhetoric and Metre of the Heroic Couplet', *PMLA*, L (1935), 168.

21. For a fuller discussion of this point, see *Roman Vergil*, W. F. Jackson Knight, pp. 239-243, and Chapter 6, 'Style', in Kenneth Quinn's *Virgil's Aeneid*.

22. See E. M. W. Tillyard, *Poetry Direct and Oblique* (London, 1945), especially Chapter 3.

John Dryden's Jacobitism

WILLIAM J. CAMERON

Both John Dryden and Alexander Pope owed deeply-felt allegiance to the *de jure* 'King over the water' while holding strong opinions about the necessity for a stable society that forced them into equally strong allegiance to the *de facto* monarch of England. Little or no investigation has been done into the effects of this ideological conflict on the literary work of the two men. It is my intention here to probe into some of the literary manifestations of Dryden's adherence to the lost cause of Jacobitism in order to open up the subject for more detailed study.

As early as 1660, Dryden's lifelong literary, political and ethical beliefs were knotted together in this characteristic piece of mythical history:

> Of Morall Knowledge Poesie was Queen,
> And still she might, had wanton wits not been;
> Who like ill Guardians liv'd themselves at large,
> And not content with that, debauch'd their charge:
> Like some brave Captain, your successfull Pen
> Restores the Exil'd to her Crown again;
> And gives us hope, that having seen the days
> When nothing flourish'd but Fanatique Bays,
> All will at length in this opinion rest,
> 'A sober Prince's Government is best.'
> ['To my Honored Friend, Sir Robert Howard']

There was no conflict of allegiance here, for the sober Prince was England's legitimate King, and under his ensuing stable government Poetry would surely flourish again. Until Charles II's death in 1685 Dryden could therefore

T   277

wholeheartedly support England's monarchical state against all rebellious factions. But James II, who succeeded his brother in 1685, was not the 'sober Prince' (despite his impeccable legitimacy) that Charles had been, and signs of conflict and strain began to show in Dryden's poetry.

Louis Bredvold, in his important book *The Intellectual Milieu of John Dryden* (1934)[1] succeeded in portraying for us the uneasy conflicts within a loyal but moderate Catholic subject of James. In charting Dryden's course through the polemical shoals of seventeenth-century religious controversy, Bredvold brought him safely into the haven of Catholicism and succeeded in destroying forever the false grounds for the charges of 'turncoat' and 'time-server' that must have disturbed Dryden in his own day and that have certainly bedevilled his reputation ever since. But although Bredvold helped to gain sympathetic modern readers for Dryden's *Hind and Panther*, and although he focused attention on Dryden's political predicament before 1688, he did not consider it his business to treat Dryden's second intellectual voyage into a changed milieu – that of William III's reign.

Despite his age (he was 57 when the Revolution took place in November 1688) Dryden remained extraordinarily sensitive to the intellectual currents of his time. The fact is that Catholicism was not entirely a sheltered haven for him, but he rode the heaving, troubled waters of political and religious allegiance with great skill and seeming serenity. It might well be said of him that, over a hundred years before the term came into vogue, Dryden had already developed the concept of 'His Majesty's Loyal Opposition'. It was his conscious solution to the ideological conflict of divided allegiance. He was helped towards the solution by his firm belief in the doctrine of passive obedience and non-resistance. This age-old Tory doctrine helped him remain firm in his allegiance to James II, while resolutely doing nothing to shake the stability of William's *de facto* régime.

The theme of lines 41-50 of Dryden's 'To my Dear Friend Mr. Congreve on his Comedy, call'd the Double Dealer', where the poet apparently adopts a very personal stance, is firmly based upon just such an attitude towards the Revolution Settlement. Dryden has in the first forty lines of his poem established the general thesis that a new age of wit has begun with Congreve, and has subtly outlined a history of [dramatic?] poetry which explains mythopoeically how Congreve has brought this about. In the next ten lines Dryden takes up the theme of succession in the empire of wit (a theme satirically exploited eighteen years before in *MacFlecknoe*) and, by subtle allusion to state affairs, is able to distinguish a true succession of wit from a false:

> Oh that your Brows my Lawrel had sustain'd,
> Well had I been Depos'd, if You had reign'd!
> The Father had descended for the Son;
> For only You are lineal to the Throne.
> Thus when the State one *Edward* did depose;
> A Greater *Edward* in his room arose.
> But now, not I, but Poetry is curs'd;
> For *Tom* the Second reigns like *Tom* the first.
>
> [ll. 41-48]

James II and Dryden were deposed in 1688; the one lost his crown, the other the laurel. Dryden implies that the lineal successor of James II should have been James III and wishes openly that Congreve had been his. The first implication is thinly disguised by a careful allusion to the deposition of Edward II and praise for his youthful successor, Edward III. This preserved Dryden from being accused by his contemporaries of blatant Jacobitism; however, we need not be so careful as he was. We may make explicit what Dryden delicately hints at. Dryden tells us both indirectly and directly that in 1693 it is not James II and Dryden who are cursed; it is England and Poetry. For William III and Tom Shadwell succeeded to the crown and the laurel respectively in 1688. What is worse, Tom Rymer succeeded 'Tom the First' to part of the laurel in 1692. Dryden chooses to name Rymer, the new Historiographer Royal, rather than Nahum Tate, the new Poet Laureate, because 'poetry' as a topic in this poem is confined by principles of decorum to dramatic poetry, the field in which Congreve had established the new age of wit, and the field in which Rymer was critically most active. Dryden himself refuses to curse or to protest against the badness of the age; however, his love for Congreve and for poetry demands that he at least pay tribute to goodness in the age. He makes it quite clear that his forbearance in the realm of poetry (and, by implication, in the realm of state affairs) must not be misunderstood:

> But let 'em not mistake my Patron's part;
> Nor call his Charity their own desert.
>
> [ll. 49-50]

Bad poets and disgraceful critics, like ungrateful rebels against true monarchic succession are still bad people even though the poet withholds his censure. Thus, instead of censuring, the deposed laureate uses the remaining twenty-seven lines of the poem to prophesy the return of the true monarchs in both realms.

The prophetic vision, in which Congreve is restored to the throne of wit (and, by implication, James II to his rightful throne), includes an ironic allusion to William III's motto (now part of England's royal arms), 'Je Maintiendray', for Dryden begins his last paragraph with the words:

> Maintain Your Post: That's all the Fame You need;
> For 'tis impossible you shou'd proceed.
>
> [ll. 64-65]

Those loyal to true monarchy and loyal to the Queen of Morall Knowledge will prevail by simply enduring 'the short parenthesis' that must occur between legitimate rulers in both the state and Poesy. Passive obedience and non-resistance acquire a new dignity when applied with so much clarity and sense to both realms. And the doctrines take on a new mythic significance for lesser thinkers than Dryden when the great poet thus embodies them in a revitalizing poem of this kind. Dryden was helping to maintain the right in both realms; and he was justified after all, for Alexander Pope was to put himself into the true succession thirty-four years later by building Dryden's myth into his *Dunciad*:

> Say great Patricians! (since yourselves inspire
> These wond'rous works; so Jove and Fate require)
> Say from what cause, in vain decry'd and curst,
> Still Dunce the second reigns like Dunce the first?[2]

It is not my intention here to deal with Pope's solution to his own conflicts of allegiance, but it must be noted that Pope was undoubtedly aided and inspired by Dryden's example. That example was embodied most clearly in Dryden's most ambitious work under William III's 'sober government' – his translation of Virgil. However, this embodiment is no longer as clear to us as it was to Pope, for we do not read Dryden's *Aeneid* in quite the way his contemporaries did. As will be demonstrated later, Dryden was undoubtedly conscious of the tendency for Englishmen to read the *Aeneid* as Virgil's *Mirror for Magistrates* – an heroic ideal held up by a court poet to his magistrate Augustus as a tactful guide for his conduct and as subtle flattery of his success in filling the heroic mould. The notion that Virgil was writing deliberately as a court poet tends to call Dryden's motives into question, for his Jacobite friends could easily be persuaded that here, too, in the translation, was a court poet flattering an illegitimate monarch. Dryden was certainly holding up a mirror for his new magistrate but careful study reveals that his political acumen had not deserted him. Both in the poem and its long dedicatory preface the deposed laureate steers a skilful course.

However, even a superficial reading of the dedication to Dryden's *Aeneid* will demonstrate that it was a hasty, ill-thought-out piece of writing, at least in comparison with the dedication to the *Juvenal and Persius* of four years before. Dryden frequently calls attention to the 'loose epistolary way' in which he is proceeding, and almost as frequently denies that he is writing a formal treatise on heroic poesy. Even if we refuse to accept these statements at their face value, there can be no doubt that Dryden was uneasy about the rambling nature and the general implications of the essay. L. Proudfoot, irked by Dryden's failure to appreciate Virgil's pathos either in his critical comments or in his actual renderings, was exasperated enough to generalize: 'In short, it is fair to say that to many of the qualities of the poem Dryden was blind. His whole account can be reduced to the following: structure; political purpose; character of the hero; function of similes; literary ornaments; I cannot after repeated reading of it find that Dryden had any more to say of it than comes under these heads. What he says is good: usually sound and sometimes helpful. It is what he does not say that is so surprizing.'[3] This is quite unfair, and even somewhat obtuse. For Dryden was not attempting a formal critical analysis of Virgil. What he does attempt (ostensibly, at any rate) is a traditional 'defence' of the poet. This defence is divided rather arbitrarily under about seven heads, some of which are determined by Dryden's real or imagined adversaries among French and English critics, and some by specialized interests of Dryden himself. The defence is preceded by a perfunctory but fairly serious comparison between the functions and value of epic and tragedy – another traditional form of critical utterance. And the defence is followed by a section on the more technical aspects of Dryden's own translation methods, a section restricted in topic because of Dryden's awareness of having dealt at length with the more important issues elsewhere.

Two facts, however, make it impossible to accept even this formal structure as an expression of Dryden's real aims in the dedication. One is that Dryden chose John Sheffield, Earl of Mulgrave and Marquis of Normanby, as the dedicatee; the other is that Dryden is predominantly concerned with the political and constitutional implications of the poem. Only when we take for granted that Dryden and his contemporaries were especially sensitive to these implications does Dryden's dedication take on its true significance. Dryden's friends of Jacobite sympathies (among whom Mulgrave was prominent) would certainly question his motives in making Virgil's *Aeneid* English. If Virgil were flattering Augustus, must not Dryden be flattering William III? Lurking beneath the easy urbanity of Dryden's stated intention to defend Virgil from detractors are the answers to that embarrassing question. In defending Virgil, Dryden is also defending himself and the Earl of Mulgrave.

Dryden's decision to dedicate his poem to the Earl of Mulgrave (now the Marquis of Normanby) was subtly tactful both in the literary and the political sense. Dryden's latest biographer, Charles E. Ward, stresses the literary tact by linking the dedication to an episode in Dryden's life, to which he devotes a chapter entitled 'The Epic Dream 1673-1676'.[4] On very little evidence Ward reiterates the theme that Dryden was from 1673 to 1676 deeply engaged in study for a projected epic. Ward, who is somewhat insensitive to political innuendo throughout Dryden's writings, is also slow to detect the snobbish delight with which Dryden reveals his social intimacy during this three-year period with the circle known now as the Court Wits, those aristocratic aesthetes who imagined themselves, in the 1670s, to be the literary arbiters of the time. The charm and the harmony of the circle was soon to be broken for Dryden by Rochester's *Allusion to Horace*. Dryden had been carrying on a running critical battle with Thomas Shadwell since 1668, centred upon their conflicting views of Ben Jonson and upon their different views of the nature of 'wit'. Both men were accepted into the Court Wit circle in the years 1673-1676, and their differences were somewhat forgotten, or at least submerged, in the Wits' boisterous and enthusiastic war against would-be wits such as Settle and Sir Carr Scrope. But in the latter part of 1675 Rochester wrote *An Allusion to Horace* to teach the professional poet Dryden to know his proper place, which was a position inferior to that of the courtly writer of sense and wit. Many of the censures of Dryden's writings expressed in that poem are remarkably similar to, and merely develop, Shadwell's earlier criticisms. And undoubtedly the most telling blow Rochester delivered was his numbering of Shadwell among the true Wits.

Dryden's overt reaction to this attack on him is carefully displayed in his preface to *All for Love*, written (or at least prepared for the press) a little over two years later. But his covert reaction was to plan and within a few months to execute the literary satire we know as *MacFlecknoe*. It may be possible that Dryden wrote it with the connivance of one of his Court Wit patrons (perhaps the Earl of Mulgrave) in reprisal for Rochester's attacks on his fellow-Wits, as well as for having elevated Shadwell to the proud position of a true Wit. His use of the Wits' names, or his 'in-group' allusions to them, support the conjecture. But in the narrowest context the poem must be read as Dryden's superb attempt to put Shadwell back where he belongs – among the would-be wits. The publication of Shadwell's *The Virtuoso* in the summer of 1676, with its incorrigible reiteration of literary theories that Dryden had already blasted (and its satire on Royal Society wits) sealed Shadwell's doom. Dryden used the potent theme of monarchical succession and the mock-grandeur of heroic poetry to defend wit against the encroachment of dullness and to demonstrate his own claims to being in all senses a true Wit. Dryden's sureness of touch, and his easy mastery of a variety of poetic styles and genres, demonstrates that he could easily outwit a Wit, and this makes Ward's 'epic dream' seem an over-solemn attempt to account for Dryden's activities in the period. He was in fact enjoying the common pursuits of his aristocratic patrons on an almost equal footing.

When he dedicated *The Assignation* to Sir Charles Sedley in 1673, Dryden revealed publicly for the first time that he had been accepted into the exclusive circle of the Court Wits, among whom Mulgrave was a leader. At some time Mulgrave gave Dryden the opportunity to talk to Charles II and James, Duke of York, about an English epic. Dryden reminded Mulgrave in 1676 (in the dedication to *Aureng-Zebe*) that the Royal brothers 'were then pleased both to commend the design, and encourage it by their commands. But the unsettledness of my condition has hitherto put a stop to my thoughts concerning it' [I, 191]. His revival of the proposal in 1676 and his flattering of Mulgrave to assume patronage of the intended epic were no doubt prompted partly by discussion among the Wits of the recent spate of French criticism on the epic. Le Bossu's *Le poème épique* (1675) was probably for Dryden the climax of this upsurge of critical interest. Nevertheless, Dryden asked Mulgrave to bring up the subject once more with Charles and James, not for critical encouragement but for financial assistance. The economic necessity that prompted Dryden to ask for Mulgrave's intercession in such a public document as a dedication was undoubtedly the result of the decay of economic support in the theatre. In the event, Dryden turned to a new vein of writing – and found every rift loaded with ore. This was translation of heroic poetry. For it is of great significance that Dryden and Mulgrave, during the period of Dryden's intimacy with the Court Wits, collaborated in translating one of Ovid's heroic epistles – *Helen to Paris*.

When Jacob Tonson published his *Ovid's Epistles* in 1680, the volume included translations in the heroic style by many of the leading writers of the fashionable heroic play. The publication in fact marked a very important rechannelling of creative literary effort in the field of heroic poetry. Even as early as 1671, the two playhouses had reached a point of financial difficulty that made union seem inevitable, and union,

or even the threat of union, brought with it a consequent restriction in financial support for writers who had perfected their
heroic verse style in the theatre. Tonson's interest in translation was thus opportune and helped to bring about a major
shift in literary taste. He was to follow up his initial success
(*Ovid's Epistles* ran to many reprints, and was parodied and
imitated again and again) by publishing his very influential
series of poetical miscellanies, literary publications which
helped to provide financial support for some poets of the day
(chief among them being Dryden) and a literary outlet for
gentlemen poets such as the Court Wits. Dryden's collabora-
tion with both Mulgrave and Tonson in establishing the taste
for polite translation of the classics led ultimately to the growth
of that literary public for which his Virgil was designed. It is
therefore to be concluded that Dryden's choice of Mulgrave
on literary grounds has much greater significance than the
theory of an 'epic dream' implies.

Another literary reason for the choice of Mulgrave is hinted
at in the dedication itself. In 1682 Mulgrave published anonymously a verse treatise on poetry in imitation of Boileau (and,
ultimately, of Horace). Dryden's chagrin at having had com-
mendation of his patron unwillingly extorted from him when he
publicly praised the anonymous work is delightfully told and
adroitly placed in the dedication.[5] After having debated the
pre-eminence of epic over tragedy (a debate deriving its
tradition from Aristotle himself), Dryden calls upon Mulgrave
to support him in his claim that his present opinion is the same
as that he held when he was himself writing heroic drama. He is
able to drop this topic soon after because Mulgrave had so
authoritatively dealt with it in 1682:

> By painfull steps we are at last got up
> *Pernassus* hill, upon whose Airy top
> The *Epick* Poets so divinely show,
> And with just pride behold the rest below.
> Heroick Poems have a just pretence
> To be the chief effort of humane sence,
> A work of such inestimable worth,
> There are but two the world has yet brought forth,
> *Homer* and *Virgil*. . . .[6]

Dryden, after his flattering digression on Mulgrave's *Essay*, develops briefly his support for Mulgrave's opinion on the superiority of Homer and Virgil, before beginning his main design – the defence of Virgil against the confederacy of Virgil's enemies. All this prefatory material is in fact a sop to Cerberus, a rhetorically dictated form of personal flattery of Mulgrave's literary opinions.

Despite the appropriateness of choosing Mulgrave on account of his literary opinions, it seems likely that Mulgrave's political opinions were more influential in prompting Dryden to choose him for the honour of having the *Virgil* dedicated to him. A contemporary satire analyzes Mulgrave's attitudes:

> Mulgrave flatters in public and libels in private,
> Talks for the Court and, against it does write;
> This way and that way, a place he does drive at,
> But nothing for Mulgrave, alas, will hit right.
> Petre today and Burnet tomorrow,
> Knaves of all sides and religions he'll woo:
> At Syon in triumph, at Whitehall in sorrow,
> Yet neither White Staff nor Marquis will do.[7]

In other words, Mulgrave had the reputation of being a Jacobite who nevertheless wanted a place in William III's court. He was in fact a considerable leader in the House of Lords of the constitutional 'loyal opposition' that was gradually forming in English parliamentary practice.

The only detailed anecdote of Mulgrave's political behaviour under William III is to be found in *A Short Character*, appended to the 1729 edition of Mulgrave's *Works*. For want of more reliable and more detailed evidence it is quoted here in full:

During the time that one of the fore-mention'd bills (I forgot which) was in a likely way to pass the houses, King William sent one day for the Earl of Mulgrave; and after some little discourse, offer'd to give him an additional title, with an annual pension of 3000 pounds, and to make him of the cabinet-council. The Earl gave him many thanks for his intended favours, and ask'd, with humblest submission, what his Majesty expected from him in return; adding, that he could not deny but that he was engag'd in assisting those bills which his Majesty did not at present approve of; he was sorry his Majesty did not, but whether he had the honour or not of serving him, he could not give them up, but must assist their success to his utmost ability. The King

seem'd a little surpriz'd; but as that Prince was a very good
Politician, he chang'd the discourse, and settled his countenance
into a seeming good humour: He then told him, that upon
hearing he was not much satisfy'd, for some time before King
James left *England*, with the measures then taken, a person whom
he had employ'd to consult and treat with those Lords who
invited him to come over, propos'd at one of their meetings to
bring over Lord Mulgrave, and to communicate their design
to him; upon which the Earl of Shrewsbury said, *If you do, you'll
spoil all, he'll never join with us*. The King telling him this Story,
ask'd with a smile, Pray, my Lord, what would you have done,
if my agent had acquainted you with the whole business? *Sir*,
said the Lord Mulgrave, *I should have discover'd it to the Master I
serv'd*. The king reply'd, *I cannot blame you*; and 'tis probable,
lik'd him the better for it. For tho' he did not then confer upon
him the favours he mention'd, sometime in his reign he had them
all, and was generally pretty well in his favour and confidence,
tho' the bills he did not like, had success, and pass'd both in the
houses of Parliament.   [pp. 12-13]

Despite the *naïveté* and partiality, this anecdote probably
reflects accurately Mulgrave's own interpretation of the incident,
and Mulgrave's autobiographical fragments lend credence to
its authenticity simply because they reveal something of the
same self-aggrandizement. What seems especially significant
when one reads Mulgrave's prose pieces (even though they have
probably been heavily revised by Alexander Pope) is the way
in which he seems to coarsen and make more violent and stark
those attitudes to William that are delicately hinted at in
Dryden. In *A Feast of the Gods*, a piece suppressed from the
1723 edition of the *Works* by an anti-Jacobite government,
Mulgrave speaks of William's title to the throne in these words:

All the Gods admir'd that odd Mixture, of which his Successor
was compos'd; so very lazy, heavy, and easily impos'd on by
Favourites; and yet so very ambitious, and enterprising: which
they attributed to the different Characters of his Ancestors; who
on his Mother's Side were *only* Sovereigns (*Henry* the Fourth
of *France* excepted); but, on his Father's, such as *deserved* to
be so.

Yet *Jupiter* himself shew'd great Esteem of him; but was
suspected a little of some Partiality, on Account of his own
Proceedings with old Father *Saturn*.   [pp. 165-166]

The Jacobite opinion that William overthrew his father-in-law by violence and gained the throne by conquest is here disguised as an understated, wry joke loaded with malice. Dryden manages the opinion with much more subtlety. For instance, in *Don Sebastian*, his first play presented after the Revolution, the concept of 'conquest' runs through the play like a leitmotiv and is accompanied by barely-suppressed Jacobite innuendo. Again, in the dedication to the *Aeneid*, Dryden loads his seemingly innocent attempt to determine the 'moral' of Homer and Virgil with even more delicately managed innuendo. First of all, he expresses the opinion that Homer 'liv'd when the *Median* Monarchy was grown formidable to the *Grecians*: and that the joint Endeavours of his Countrymen, were little enough to preserve their common Freedom, from an encroaching Enemy. Such was his Moral . . .' He goes on to say: 'Had *Virgil* flourish'd in the Age of *Ennius*, and address'd to *Scipio*, he had probably taken the same Moral, or some other not unlike it. For then the *Romans* were in as much danger from the *Carthaginian* Commonwealth, as the *Grecians* were from the *Assyrian*, or *Median* Monarchy. But we are to consider him as writing his Poem in a time when the Old Form of Government was subverted, and a new one just Established by *Octavius Caesar*: In effect by force of Arms, but seemingly by the Consent of the *Roman* People' [III, 1012]. That last sentence is disingenuous. Substitute Dryden for Virgil, and William III for Octavius Caesar, and we have the situation (as interpreted by moderate Jacobites like Mulgrave and Dryden) in England in the mid-1690s. The four paragraphs which follow the quotation in the dedication, though ostensibly dealing with the political and religious history of Rome, could be (and certainly were) read as Dryden's comment on the recent history of England. The parallel is not exact, but it lurks in every line. Dryden's characteristic political attitudes are quite clearly formulated: '. . . the Cause of Religion is but a Modern Motive to Rebellion, invented by the Christian Priesthood, refining on the Heathen . . .' [III, 1012]. Factional rivalry between Nobles and Commons, he asserts, leads to destruction of political institutions and substitution of Tyranny: 'This comes of altering Fundamental Laws and Constitutions' [III, 1013]. His characteristic condemnation of the mob and its leaders, of

'Reformation' or the pretence of it, and his dubiety about the
stability of an 'elective' king are also expressed. Nevertheless,
his present principles are summed up in Montaigne's principle:
'. . . . that an Honest Man ought to be contented with that
Form of Government, and with those Fundamental Constitutions
of it, which he receiv'd from his Ancestors, and under which
himself was Born . . .' [III, 1014]. He is sure that Virgil was
at heart a republican, and that Cato's presence as a lawgiver in
Elizium was a gentle hint to Augustus, the arbitrary monarch,
of the origins of Roman monarchy – elective kings governing
with a senate. Dryden, despite his disapproval of William as an
elective and not an hereditary monarch, was still being a consistent and firm adherent to the principles of passive obedience
and non-resistance. Moreover, it would seem that he, the
moderate supporter of kingly prerogative against parliamentary
power in the 1680s, was a firm enough believer in the English
constitution to support parliamentary limitations upon the prerogative of an elective king. His pragmatism and common-sense
attitude to stability thus allowed him to respect the *de facto*
King William in theory, but to refuse the oaths of allegiance to
him in practice.

Given these complex political principles, it would be wrong to
read into his *Virgil* a covert criticism of William III. It is certain
that Dryden insists upon the elective nature of the *de facto* King
of England, but he will not countenance rebellion against him.
The hero of his poem is a mirror held up to a genuine king whose
title was regrettably gained by conquest and seeming consent
of the people but who is nevertheless a 'sober prince'. Dryden,
like Virgil (who could not approve the unlawful basis of
Augustus' title), concluded 'that this Conquerour, though of a
bad kind, was the very best of it: that the Arts of Peace
flourish'd under him: that all Men might be happy if they would
be quiet . . .' [III, 1014] and more to the same tune. And both
Dryden and Virgil 'concluded it to be the Interest of his Country
to be so Govern'd: To infuse an awful Respect into the People,
towards such a Prince: By that respect to confirm their Obedience
to him; and by that Obedience to make them Happy. This was
the Moral of his Divine Poem . . .' [III, 1015]. There can be
no doubt that this was also the moral of Dryden's poem. The
famous passages inserted by Dryden with little or no hint from

Virgil consistently point up this honest aim. Take the heroic similitude in Book I which describes the regal authority of Neptune when he commands the waves to subside:

> As when in Tumults rise th'ignoble Crowd,
> Mad are their Motions, and their Tongues are loud;
> And Stones and Brands in ratling Vollies fly,
> And all the Rustick Arms that Fury can supply;
> If then some grave and Pious Man appear,
> They hush their Noise, and lend a list'ning Ear;
> He sooths with sober Words their angry Mood,
> And quenches their innate Desire of Blood:
>
> [ll. 213-220]

The second line and the last lines have little justification in the Latin. The whole passage infuses an awful respect for a monarch, but the two additional lines increase it by stressing the awful *need* for such monarchical authority. Dryden is not merely taking an opportunity of expressing his prejudice against the mob; he is using his fear of anarchy to enhance monarchic authority. Many extreme captains of the mobile (Lord Delamer or Lord Lovelace are examples) thought of themselves as William's best friends and supporters; Dryden indirectly attempts to expose what was for him their inherent enmity to monarchy, their innate bloodthirstiness.

Or take the passage in Book VI which is usually quoted to show Dryden's enmity to the House of Orange; among the list of miscreants to be tormented in Tartarus are the following:

> Then they, who Brothers better Claim disown,
> Expel their Parents, and usurp the Throne;
> Defraud their Clients, and to Lucre sold,
> Sit brooding on unprofitable Gold:
> Who dare not give, and ev'n refuse to lend
> To their poor Kindred, or a wanting Friend:
> Vast is the Throng of these; nor less the Train
> Of lustful Youths, for foul Adultry slain.
> Hosts of Deserters, who their Honour sold,
> And basely broke their Faith for Bribes of Gold:
> All these within the Dungeon's depth remain:
> Despairing Pardon, and expecting Pain.
>
> [ll. 824-835]

There can be little doubt that Dryden was thinking of William when he misconstrued Virgil in the first two lines; it is no less doubtful that he was thinking of the Earl of Marlborough as the chief of the host of deserters; it is even possible that he had particular examples in mind when he listed the cozening lawyer, the miser (who refuses either to lend or give to friend or kindred), and the adulterer. But antipathetic critics who assume that Dryden merely seized an opportunity to castigate William III, Marlborough, or others of his contemporaries and thus allowed political prejudice to undermine his artistic conscience are misconstruing Dryden. For his intention was much more subtle. Throughout the poem he is attempting to bolster up constituted authority; he is not betraying this purpose in this particular context. Dryden's conscience will not allow him to countenance rebellion in the state against William, or in the army against Marlborough. Punishment, he affirms, will be meted out to such men after their death (when they will be 'Despairing Pardon, and expecting Pain'). Dryden is anticipating God's punishment but using that anticipation to support his general thesis – that constituted authority, despite its illegal or doubtful origins, must be respected. As a Christian and a Catholic, Dryden is thus taking the opportunity to assert that sinful behaviour by holders of authority will receive its just rewards in the proper place.

Another passage in Book VI has been misconstrued as an attempt to slight King William; Dryden, in his list of the sinful denizens of Tartarus, describes Theseus and Phlegias, and then continues:

> To Tyrants others have their Country sold,
> Imposing Foreign Lords, for Foreign Gold:
> Some have old Laws repeal'd, new Statutes made;
> Not as the People pleas'd, but as they paid.
> With Incest some their Daughters Bed prophan'd,
> All dar'd the worst of Ills, and what they dar'd, attain'd.
> [ll. 845-850]

Dryden's xenophobia chimes fairly well with Virgil's words to produce the first couplet, so one need not infer a specific thrust at William III. In any case, there is no hint anywhere in Dryden's writings that he considered William to be a tyrant, even though he might be a usurper. There is plenty of evidence that, if William's right to the throne were legitimate, Dryden would be only too happy to commend him. The wording of the preface of *King Arthur* (in the rare first issue) is sufficient to establish Dryden's attitude: 'But not to offend the present Times, nor a Government which has hitherto protected me (and by a particular Favour would have continued me what I was, if I could have comply'd with the Termes which were offered me), I have been oblig'd so much to alter the first Design . . . '.[8] The fact that he suppressed the phrase in parentheses from the second issue is adequate proof that Dryden was not actively opposed to a benevolent but unlawfully-originated government.

The second couplet of the passage from Book VI also has sufficient basis in the Latin to be free from suspicion of topical allusion. If one were intended, the second line must be read as favouring parliamentary honesty against factional bribery which tended to pervert the Commons. Only determination to find lurking prejudice could read it otherwise. It is perhaps significant that the third couplet has not tempted a critic to find a topical allusion.

Part of this determination to find personal malice towards William and his régime is based on a false simplification of Dryden's attitude to James II. Dryden was disturbed by James II's more immoderate and arbitrary acts, but some commentators seem to imply that because Dryden was a Catholic he was incapable of holding an independent opinion. But, as Dryden asserted: 'I shall continue still to speak my Thoughts like a free-born Subject as I am; though such things, perhaps, as no *Dutch* Commentator cou'd, and I am sure no *French*-man durst' [III, 1016]. Despite his reverence for James II, as a king by inheritance, Dryden was fully aware that he had acted arbitrarily. When he refers to Mezentius as Virgil's example of a tyrant, he pithily says: 'He Govern'd Arbitrarily, he was expell'd: And came to the deserv'd End of all Tyrants' [III, 1017]. On the other hand, in outlining the character of Latinus, commending him as both a king by inheritance and one born to be the father of his country, Dryden describes Latinus' attitude to his Senate. It is precisely that of William III and the complete antithesis of James II. Dryden was intelligent enough and sufficiently informed to know that neither James II nor William III was in all respects the perfect monarch. Dryden, like Virgil, was determined, however, to repay his *de facto* monarch's eschewal of arbitrary government '. . . with good Counsel, how to behave himself in his new Monarchy, so as to gain the Affections of his Subjects, and deserve to be call'd the Father of his Country' [III, 1016].

Perhaps this is pressing the parallel too far, but Dryden was willing to press home even more complicated parallels. Anchises was only the second branch of the Royal family, just as William's father was. (Compare Mulgrave's comments in *A Feast of the Gods* quoted above.) Aeneas, like William, married the heiress of the crown, but Helenus (the Old Pretender) could lawfully claim before her. Virgil rightly gave Aeneas the title of an elective king. Augustus, though he or his uncle Julius claimed the throne by descent from Aeneas, could not therefore lawfully be called an hereditary king.

All this smacks of special justification. Dryden must have felt the need to excuse himself to both friends and enemies. In suggesting moral justification for seeming to support the usurper's reign by endorsing the political and constitutional implications of Virgil's epic (and especially of its hero), Dryden also helps to justify the political activity of the Earl of Mulgrave. If this is one of Dryden's main preoccupations, we may readily see why it was irrelevant for Proudfoot to assume that Dryden was blind to qualities other than the political in Virgil's poem. He would not presume to tell Mulgrave what he already knows about the literary values of the poem. Nevertheless, it must be admitted that Dryden's critical comments on the poem and upon the 'manners' of its hero frequently do not entirely account for the characteristics of his rendering of both poem and hero. This is partly due to the slovenly way in which he relies on Segrais for comments on the topics that are not of central interest to him, partly to inadequate analysis of the assumptions he made during the process of translating, but mainly to the distorting effect of his political preconceptions.

Indeed it is worth studying Dryden's presentation of Aeneas in order to reveal how his critical comments in the dedication fall short of his actual achievement. Even more important, it will reveal how Dryden in fact gave William III good counsel

U

without flattering him. Aeneas' characteristics are not only
heroic in the martial sense, but princely in the truest sense of
Dryden's concept of a 'sober prince'. The pattern for William
III's behaviour is Virgilian, but only as interpreted by Dryden.

Dryden's hero in the epic is 'the Father of his people', a man
whose relationship with those younger, less wise, less sober
than he, is the true key to his character. Something of Dryden's
feeling for the centrality of Aeneas' 'virtues' in the making of a
monarch can be detected in his early work, but it might be best
to select 'To the Memory of Mr. Oldham' to demonstrate
the depth of his perception. Despite T. S. Eliot's frigid com-
mendation of the poem as an elegy in which lack of suggestiveness is compensated by the satisfying completeness of the
statement,[9] the poem is a noble fragment of a deliberately
implied and intentionally unwritten 'heroic poem'. The poem
suggests its own discursive context by both conscious and
unconscious allusion to Virgil's *Aeneid*. Dryden (with Virgilian
example constantly before his mind's eye) sees the hero-poet
as an active, courageous, resolute, and determined fighter
against the enemies of 'Virtue', in all the special meanings that
the word had been given by humanist writers. But at this
moment in the unwritten heroic poem celebrating this poet's
Odyssey, the hero, touched by self-reproach, utters a noble and
graceful tribute to yet another hero – his friend. It is a measure
of Dryden's skill as a poet that in his poem on Oldham he is
able to suggest such an heroic context very succinctly by the
language, tone, rhythm, and rhetoric of the first eight lines.
The full heroic context is provided by what seems on the surface
to be a simple classical parallel or 'similitude' as Dryden would
call it:

> Thus *Nisus* fell upon the slippery place,
> While his young Friend perform'd and won the Race.

The couplet is not merely an *explanation* by classical allusion;
it is an extension of context. The reader of Virgil will immediately recall his account of the footrace in which Nisus,
having slipped, ensured his friend Euryalis' victory by tripping
a competitor. But he will also recall the heroic death of Euryalis,
and how it inspired his surviving friend, Nisus, to kill his
slayer in a last burst of courage. This suggests a great deal

that is not stated, for it delicately implies that the death of the brilliant young satirist, John Oldham, will serve to spur John Dryden on to greater poetic (i.e. moral) endeavour. The theme of the dignity of the poet and his princedom in the realm of moral knowledge is of a piece with the self-portrait in *To my Dear Friend Mr. Congreve* a decade later. The theme of friendship for the young and the promising is very much in keeping with the portrait of Aeneas (or William III) conceived of as a prince in the larger world of statecraft. Before demonstrating that Dryden was capable of portraying the ideal prince without actually flattering William III, we may point out the subtleties with which Dryden could treat the subject of heroic friendship even in a short poem like the Oldham farewell.

It is significant that, just after writing the Oldham poem, Dryden was engaged in translating the classics, as he tells us in the preface to *Sylvae*, a poetical miscellany published in 1685. After translating two or three pastorals of Theocritus and two or three odes of Horace, he encouraged himself to renew his old acquaintance with Lucretius and Virgil, and immediately fixed upon some parts of them that most affected him in the reading. It is no surprise to learn that the two episodes he chose to translate from Virgil were the stories of Nisus and Euryalis from Books V and IX, and of Mezentius and Lausus from Book X. The first of these was to Dryden the finest example of heroic friendship, and the second the finest pattern of filial piety and virtue (always excepting Aeneas himself). Dryden's allusion to Nisus in the Oldham poem can thus be seen to be of great importance to Dryden, for it embodies a great deal of his highest values. The last four lines of the poem (another 'similitude') also suggest a great deal that is not stated. They read:

> Once more, hail and farewel; farewel thou young,
> But ah too short, *Marcellus* of our Tongue;
> Thy Brows with Ivy, and with Laurels bound;
> But Fate and gloomy Night encompass thee around.

The reference to Marcellus is more complex than that to Nisus. It refers (as 'statement') to the nephew of Augustus, who was married to Augustus' daughter Julia, and died young. But the last two lines of the poem are a direct translation of two lines from near the end of Virgil's *Aeneid*, Book VI, the book which suggests most clearly that Dryden read the poem as Virgil's mirror for a magistrate. Indeed, we have Dryden's own word for it that Book VI was the work of a court poet attempting to influence the Emperor.[10] He believed the story that Virgil read the book to Octavia, the sister of Augustus and mother of Marcellus, and that Octavia was so affected by the reading that she fainted.

The implication – that in one sense the whole book is aimed at providing the finest possible narrative context for his panegyric of Marcellus at the end – is a sound one. It comes at the climax to Aeneas' heroic visit to the Underworld. After several encounters with various spirits which lend so much significance and depth to the rest of the *Aeneid*, Aeneas achieves the aim of his pious mission – he meets the spirit of his father Anchises. When Aeneas expresses curiosity at seeing ghosts drinking from the river Lethe, Anchises explains in great detail the doctrine of the transmigration of the soul [ll. 978-1020]. For Dryden's purposes, this is highly relevant, because (as he delicately hints) John Oldham has assumed the soul of Marcellus. For Virgil's purposes (as interpreted by Dryden) this gives point to Anchises' explanation of the future of some of the souls drinking forgetfulness at the stream. These heroic souls will one day animate the bodies of great Romans. Anchises, as he touches on one hero after the other in high epic discourse, prophesies the greatness of Rome and the heroism of the old Romans who will ensure its greatness. Among the panegyrics is one on Augustus, but the finest and last is reserved for an unnamed youth (it is, of course, Octavia's son Marcellus) who keeps equal pace with one of Rome's greatest heroes – the Marcellus who was the third and last Roman to gain the coveted 'spolia opima'. But let Dryden speak for himself, even though his verse here is below his usual level. Aeneas asks who the godlike youth might be:

> Observe the Crowds that compass him around;
> All gaze, and all admire, and raise a shouting sound:
> But hov'ring Mists around his Brows are spread,
> And Night, with sable Shades, involves his Head.
> Seek not to know (the Ghost reply'd with Tears)

The Sorrows of thy Sons, in future Years.
This Youth (the blissful Vision of a day)
Shall just be shown on Earth, and snatch'd away.
[ll. 1196-1203]

Then follows the panegyric.

The last four lines of the poem on Oldham thus refer us to what Dryden probably felt was the finest discursive context ever provided for an elegiac panegyric. At the same time the four lines broaden the meaning of his poem to such an extent that we find Dryden elevating Oldham yet higher than Virgil's 'godlike youth.' Even more subtly, Dryden has suggested that he himself may be cast in the heroic mould of the dedicated poet, the legislator, moralist, and philosopher so eloquently defended by Sir Philip Sidney. In casting himself in this role, Dryden is objectifying himself and not, as an unsympathetic or prejudiced critic might claim, glorifying himself. Paradoxically, Dryden is humbling himself in the very act of heroicizing his craft. The poetical richness achieved in the poem by using Virgil in such fashion should warn us to expect similar allusiveness and richness in the great translation itself. If Dryden's mythopoeic placing of himself and Oldham into the heroic tradition can be done with such sureness of touch, we must at least be aware of the possibility that William III could be shown how he too could be placed in the heroic tradition. More to the point, Dryden's skill in heroicizing himself in 1684 without bringing unwarranted charges of self-glorification down upon his head makes it at least probable that he could heroicize William's kingly office without bringing unwarranted charges of flattery down upon his own or William's head. In other words, William need only model himself on Dryden's hero, and he would automatically become a true monarch 'so as to gain the Affections of his Subjects, and deserve to be call'd the Father of his Country' [III, 1016].

There is ample evidence in Dryden's correspondence that he was an affectionate and kindly father to his sons, and (in his old age) a gentle, kindly, and warm friend to younger poets such as Congreve. It is interesting, therefore, that he should project his paterfamilias image upon Aeneas and blow it up to heroic proportions. For there can be no doubt that Aeneas is not the overboiling hero of the Herculean or Homeric kind that

Eugene Waith has so perceptively analyzed[11]; he is a hero in whom 'piety' or human respect and affection is the leading trait. The trait of kindliness and protective affection seems to have been so important to Dryden that he specially emphasizes it in his dedication: 'Piety, as your Lordship sees, takes place of all, as the chief part of his Character: And the word in Latin is more full than it can possibly be exprest in any Modern Language; for there it comprehends not only Devotion to the Gods, but Filial Love and tender Affection to Relations of all sorts' [III, 1018]. On the one hand, one might recall the last lines in Dryden's controversial *Heroick Stanzas* (which already in 1659 reveal that Dryden was intent on detecting Virgilian traits in a 'sober prince' who was not a legitimate monarch), for his English diction is full of the Latin implications:

> His Name a great example stands to show
> How strangely high endeavours may be blest,
> Where *Piety* and *valour* joyntly goe.
>
> [ll. 146-148]

And on the other hand, one should realize that much of the diction of the great translation of the 1690s must be read with sympathetic attention to the Virgilian overtones if we are to respond fully to Dryden's blueprint for a monarch.

The heroic similitudes in the Oldham poem have already been analyzed to show how Dryden's use of Virgil has enriched his noble tribute; but the similitudes themselves help us to determine the way that Dryden read Virgil. They were used quite consciously, but other Virgilian qualities in the poem may not have been quite so conscious. The diction of the poem owes a great deal to Virgil, but a major critical problem is posed by it. Dryden's conscious Latinisms in other poems have been traced to Virgil, simply because the English word is so similar in form to the original. It is, however, very difficult to decide, when there is no obvious morphological similarity, which English words that Dryden habitually used carried overtones that he consciously derived from Virgil. But one way of detecting a possible Virgilian echo in an English line of Dryden's is to detect an echo between that line and one translating Virgil. Thus two lines in 'To the Memory of Mr. Oldham' take on some significance when they are found to be later echoed in *Virgil's Aeneis*:

> To the same Goal did both our Studies drive,
> The last set out the soonest did arrive.
> ['To the Memory of Mr. Oldham', ll. 7-8]

> Beyond the Goal of Nature I have gon;
> My *Pallas* late set out, but reach'd too soon.
> [*Virgil's Aeneis*, XI, 244-245]

The Latin reads:

> contra ego vivendo vici mea fata, superstes
> restarem ut genitor.
> [*Aeneid*, XI, 160-161]

Dryden thus used his lines for the Oldham poem to render part of Evander's lament over the corpse of his son Pallas. Does this mean that, when he was lamenting Oldham's death, Dryden had in mind the lament over Pallas? The opening line of the poem and the first line of the Marcellus similitude certainly seem to support the probability, for they both seem to echo Aeneas' famous valediction over Pallas:

> salve aeternum mihi, maxime Palla,
> aeternumque vale.
> [*Aeneid*, XI, 97-98]

Indeed, one might even hypothesize a tendency for the race of Nisus and Euryalis to be conjured up in Dryden's mind whenever the death of a young hero was presented to him.

Only three other instances may be found in Dryden's poems of the idea of a race or 'course' used metaphorically. One is in *The Secular Masque* (1700), where it is used for the sidereal year. The other two instances are much more significant, for they are laments over a dead hero. The first expresses Dryden's sympathy with the Duke of Ormonde over the death of his son, Thomas, Earl of Ossery:

> His Eldest Hope, with every Grace adorn'd,
> By me (so Heav'n will have it) always Mourned,
> And always honour'd, snatcht in Manhoods prime
> By unequal Fates, and Providences crime:

Yet not before the Goal of Honour won,
All parts fulfill'd of Subject and of Son;
Swift was the Race, but short the Time to run.
            [*Absalom and Achitophel*, ll. 831-837]

Dryden's obvious debts to Virgil, *Aeneid*, V, 49-50, II, 257, and
X, 380, in this passage have been pointed out, but the use of the
image of a footrace coupled with heroic endeavour has not been
hitherto connected with Virgil. The second example is Sigis-
monda's words over the heart of her murdered lover Guiscardo:

The Course is finish'd, which thy Fates decreed,
And thou, from thy Corporeal Prison freed:
Soon has thou reach'd the Goal with mended Pace,
A World of Woes dispatch'd in little space.
            [*Sigismonda and Guiscardo*, ll. 655-658]

Boccaccio's words are:

O molto amato cuore, ogni mio uficio verso te è fornito;
né piu altro mi resta a fare, se non di venire con la mia
anima a fare alla tua compagnia.[12]

Dryden has thus wrought up the passage by using Virgilian
heroic techniques, one of which may have been derived from
Dryden's customary linking of the race metaphor with a lament
over a dead hero.

The link in Dryden's mind between a lament for a dead
hero – of whom Pallas is the classic type – and the Nisus and
Euryalis episodes in the *Aeneid* can be accounted for by only
one common theme: friendship, especially of an older hero for a
younger one. It might well be concluded that Dryden read the
Nisus and Euryalis episodes as a microcosm of the Aeneas and
Pallas macrocosmic friendship.

This may perhaps be best illustrated by attention to the ending of *Virgil's Aeneis*. There, the wounded and defeated Turnus
appeals to Aeneas for mercy, and Virgil's hero (in Dryden's
words)

ev'ry Moment felt
His manly Soul with more Compassion melt.
            [XII, 1362-63]

Part of the reason for the compassion is that Turnus' appeal is
based upon Aeneas' love for his father and for his son. However,
when Aeneas sees that Turnus is wearing the golden belt of
Pallas, he immediately reacts to another claim on his affections.
Roused anew to wrath, Aeneas cries:

> Traytor, dost thou, dost thou to Grace pretend,
> Clad, as thou art, in Trophees of my Friend?
> To his sad Soul a grateful Off'ring go;
> 'Tis *Pallas, Pallas* gives this deadly Blow.
>
>   [XII, 1370-73]

Aeneas' delivery of the death-blow ends the epic. Dryden's
(and Virgil's) emphasis upon the importance of heroic friendship at the climax of the poem proves that it was a very important trait of the Virgilian hero as it was understood by
Dryden. Its particular importance can be stressed by tracing
the origin of this friendship in the poem.

Aeneas, advised by Tiber in a dream to seek an alliance with
Evander, the leader of the Greek colony precariously settled
at Palanteum, sets off up the river. The Greeks, fearful at the
sight of the approaching fleet, break off their sacred rites to
Hercules, but are reassured by the dauntless Pallas. Aeneas then
first sees Pallas, armed with a javelin upon a rising ground, in the
pose of a fearless challenger of a possible enemy. With olive
branch in hand, Aeneas begs 'the King's Relief' [VIII, 159].
Pallas' heroic reaction to the fame of Aeneas' name is to welcome
him as a guest and a friend. The first major act towards that
union which is part of Aeneas' destiny then ensues. Greek and
Trojan join in friendship against an enemy that will one day also
be reconciled – the Ausonians. Aeneas' statesmanship is rewarded
with success not solely because of the ties of kinship, but also
because of the kind of heroic friendship that can be formed only
through admiration for heroic qualities in a stranger. Evander
had once longed to join 'in Friendship's holy Bands' with
Anchises, whose visit fired his youthful breast with wonder.
Anchises had encouraged the youth by giving him appropriate
martial presents. The application of such principles of statesmanship to the political events of Dryden's own day need not be
elaborated here, but they should at least be noted.

Warm friendship is often celebrated in Virgil; if anything,

Dryden places even more emphasis upon it in his translation. The major theme of union in the last six books is again and again re-emphasized by episodes stressing admiration for friendship. That in Dryden's mind it was at least as important as filial piety and paternal care is attested by the Virgilian episodes he chose to translate for *Sylvae*. It is fairly obvious, too, as one reads *Virgil's Aeneis,* that Dryden assumed that Virgil's heroic figures were built upon the very human affections that a man feels for his family and friends. In the wider world of political and martial endeavour, the family virtues and the virtues of friendship become important elements in the hero who is to be both 'Father of his People' and a true friend to them.

Dryden himself clearly expressed his own belief in the origins of the Princely virtues:

> When Empire first from families did spring,
> Then every Father govern'd as a King;
> But you that are a Soveraign Prince, allay
> Imperial pow'r with your paternal sway.

These four lines occur in Dryden's poem called *To His Sacred Majesty* written to celebrate Charles II's coronation on St George's Day, 1661. An extension of the idea might very well be that heroic friendship originated in the social tie that bound family to family and protective age to unprotected youth. 'Imperial pow'r' wielded by a sovereign must be allayed with both paternal and friendly sway.

The commonplace view of Aeneas may perhaps be best expressed in the words of Alexander Ross in his *Mystagogus Poeticus, or the Muses Interpreter*: '*Aeneas* is the *Idea* of a perfect Prince and Governour, in whom we see piety towards his gods . . . ; piety also towards his old father . . . ; his love was great to his wife *Creusa* . . . ; his love was great to his sonne *Ascanius*, in the good breeding and counselling of him; to *Palinurus*, *Mysenus*, and others; his vigilancy in guiding the helme at midnight, when his people were asleep; his liberality to his souldiers; his magnanimity; constancy, wisdome, fortitude, justice, temperance, are fit by all Princes to be imitated and the *Aeneads* to be diligently read'.[13] If this garrulous moralizer, intent on proving the moral usefulness to Christian readers of reading the classics, can so sum up the virtues of Aeneas, it is with some disappointment that we find Dryden summing up the 'manners' of his hero in the following words: 'Piety to the Gods, and a dutiful Affection to his Father; Love to his Relations; Care of his People; Courage and Conduct in the Wars; Gratitude to those who had oblig'd him; and Justice in general to Mankind' [III, 1018]. The inadequacies of Dryden's dedication of *Virgil's Aeneis* have already been accounted for, but it seems worth while reiterating that the hero who actually emerges from the pages of Dryden's poem has a great number of traits not properly enumerated in the dedication. The particular combination of these traits in his hero makes Dryden's bald list seem even more inadequate. Dryden does indeed discuss the relative importance of piety and courage (drawing heavily upon Segrais for the discussion), but there, too, he does less than justice to his own and Virgil's work. And to mitigate the seeming inadequacies of his critical comments, it is only fair to point out that Dryden puts a wide range of meanings into some of his favourite words signifying emotional qualities in his hero. For instance, 'care' bears a far greater load of meanings than modern readers are apt to derive from it.

Nevertheless, we must depend upon a close reading of the poem rather than an exposition of his critical writings to discover what Dryden understood to be the outstanding traits of the Virgilian hero. We might take as a first example Aeneas' 'Justice in general to Mankind'.

Obviously, the earliest full-length attempt to illustrate Aeneas' sense of justice is the account of his actions at the Funeral Games in Book V. At the heart of it is the passage describing his judgements when awarding prizes after the footrace in which Nisus tripped Salius in order to ensure Euryalis' victory. But justice, it will be seen, is tempered by a number of qualities not mentioned by Dryden in his list of the hero's 'manners':

> Then thus the Prince; let no Disputes arise:
> Where Fortune plac'd it, I award the Prize.
> But Fortune's Errors give me leave to mend,
> At least to pity my deserving Friend.
> He said, and from among the Spoils, he draws,
> (Pond'rous with shaggy Main, and Golden Paws)
> A Lyon's Hide; to *Salius* this he gives:

Nisus, with Envy sees the Gift, and grieves.
If such Rewards to vanquish'd Men are due,
He said, and Falling is to rise by you,
What Prize may *Nisus* from your Bounty claim,
Who merited the first Rewards and Fame?
In falling, both an equal Fortune try'd;
Wou'd Fortune for my Fall so well provide!
With this he pointed to his Face, and show'd
His Hands, and all his Habit smear'd with Blood.
Th' indulgent Father of the People smil'd;
And caus'd to be produc'd an ample Shield;
Of wond'rous Art by *Didymaon* wrought,
Long since from *Neptune's* Bars in Triumph brought.
This giv'n to *Nisus*; he divides the rest;
And equal Justice, in his Gifts, express'd.

[ll. 454–475]

Aeneas is a shield between Fortune and his people, but it is pity
for a friend that prompts his consolation prize to Salius. (This
gains point because it was friendship which assisted Fortune to
reward Euryalis.) Justice, one of the necessary functions of
'Imperial pow'r', is thus 'allayed' with friendship.

Again, when Nisus attempts to equate his bad luck with
the bad luck of Salius, it is not the cold 'justice' of the equation
that sways Aeneas. Dryden makes him smile with indulgence in
awarding a consolation prize to Nisus. Presumably he awards
consolation prizes, not on the basis of impartial justice alone,
but as a result of his fatherly and friendly feelings for his
people – those attitudes which are included in Dryden's word
'Care'. The result, however, as Dryden explicitly states, is
'equal justice'.

This carefully-wrought excerpt is typical of the general
excellence of the whole of Dryden's Book V. The book is as
architectonically sound as any in the epic, and its style is
uniformly appropriate throughout. Yet the disparity between
Dryden's achievement and his analysis of it is nowhere more
surprising. Of the Funeral Games he remarks in the dedication:
'*Virgil* imitated the Invention of *Homer*, but chang'd the Sports.
But both the *Greek* and *Latin* Poet, took their occasions from
the Subject; though to confess the Truth, they were both
Ornamental, or at best, convenient parts of it, rather than of

necessity arising from it' [III, 1003]. And later he stresses Virgil's flattery of certain Roman families in the awarding of prizes and his poetical revenge on those who had disoblig'd the poet, his patron, or his Emperor: 'When a Poet is throughly provok'd, he will do himself Justice, however dear it cost him, *Animamque, in Vulnere ponit.* I think these are not bare Imaginations of my own, though I find no trace of them in the Commentatours: But one Poet may judge of another by himself' [III, 1016]. Despite these offhand comments, Dryden does not attempt himself to add overtones of lampoon to his treatment of the contestants at the games, nor does he treat the games themselves as either ornamental or convenient.

The structure of the Book reveals the truth of this. The Book begins with a proper emphasis upon Palinurus, the loyal pilot who is the chief instrument in ensuring that Aeneas escapes from the toils of Dido; and it ends with his symbolic or ritual murder at the hands of the God of Sleep. That Palinurus alone becomes the victim of the gods is a direct result of the piety of Aeneas in initiating the annual games in honour of his dead father.

The description of the games might perhaps seem a convenience for stressing the theme of justice, especially as one suspects that Dryden developed the theme with proper decorum and understanding simply because he was conscious of the traditional charges of injustice levelled against Aeneas in his relations with Dido in Book IV. Nevertheless, Aeneas' piety leads him to institute warlike play (the truly civilized form of war) as one of the Arts of Peace, an action that foreshadows his great and divine purpose – the permanent establishment at Rome of the civilization under which such Arts will flourish. Dryden is at his best when portraying such an adumbration of this desired civilization, and although the sojourn in Sicily is merely a pale shadow of what is to come Dryden describes it with proper appreciation. Far from being ornamental, the Funeral Games become a powerfully functional episode of the epic. Dryden is careful not to destroy the structural links provided by Virgil, and by appropriate emphasis (both rhetorical and stylistic) is able to bring out the thematic value of the episodes.

For instance, the danger of Aeneas' sacred mission represented by Dido's actions in Book IV is palely reasserted in the actions of the Trojan women in their attempt to burn the ships. Their actions prove to be unsuccessful and are turned to good, simply because Aeneas has acted in the recent past with exemplary piety, justice, and leadership, and acts in the emergency with proper protectiveness, piety, and princely order. His first action in Sicily after accepting the warm welcome from the Acestes is to honour his father by instituting the games. While he is fulfilling his religious duties before his father's tomb, a serpent appears as an omen to confirm him in his intentions. As a result of his conduct of the games, Acestes' flaming arrow warns him of coming treachery. Aeneas, careful of his people, hides his private fears behind a public smiling face, and dispenses what might seem strange justice. But by awarding the prize to Acestes, Aeneas is acting from protective instincts towards his people, and from proper respect for the gods who have shown themselves in the otherwise purely human endeavour of the shooting-match.

But the games themselves are not arbitrarily chosen. The naval games come first – an appropriate tribute to Neptune. The footrace (as Dryden was well aware) celebrates friendship as well as justice, and introduces the two young men whose heroic death in Book IV plays for Dryden such a significant part in the thematic structure of the epic. The boxing-match with its implications of present violence matched against past violence is thematically important too, for with the intercession of the Prince the civilizing role of Aeneas in controlling violence is linked with an implied condemnation of the brutality of the past – and a promise of peace in the settled commonwealth to come. The archery contest (already touched on above) is then followed by the *Lusus Troiae*. This warlike play of the youths is a fitting end to the games and a deliberate emphasizing of the import of the whole – the foreshadowing of the much-to-be-desired civilization towards which both Aeneas and Virgil are struggling. The games begin with a tribute to Anchises and end with one to Ascanius – stressing the succession theme, and opening up the vista of grandeur that will be developed further at the end of Book VI.

In the emergency created by Juno, attention is firmly switched from the pleasures of a peaceful civilization to that civilization's leader. Warned by the flaming arrow, Aeneas takes appropriate action. While Ascanius vainly attempts to put out the flames, Aeneas is piously but heroically calling on his gods. The gods immediately answer his prayer. But what is more important for Dryden and his contemporaries are the constitutional actions which follow. Aeneas is depicted as uncertain of his next decision. He takes counsel of Nautes, like a good constitutional monarch, but remains disturbed. His pious and correct behaviour while in Sicily is then rewarded in the evening by the appearance of his father's ghost, who confirms the good counsel of Nautes, but enjoins him to visit the under-world before proceeding to face the Italians.

Once his duty is clear, Aeneas acts with exemplary resolution and proper princely order. His religious duties come first, and his duties to his host next. Dryden then describes (in thirteen masterly lines) the founding of the city of Acesta and its govern-ment. Though peopled by the women and the weaklings among the Trojans, the city marks the first positive fulfilment of Aeneas' divine purpose. At the beginning of Book V the Trojans were a company of voyagers fleeing from a civilization that was not their own. At the end, they are a resolute company of heroes who have already founded a token city and are intent on founding a greater one. After the death of Palinurus, Aeneas himself takes the helm. The Trojans are thus completely prepared for their destiny.

We need go no further in the analysis of Dryden's transla-tion, for enough has already been said to show the nobility of Dryden's conception of a sober prince's motives and actions to ensure that we consider with some sympathy the probable application of this conception to political thinking in Dryden's own day. The postscript to *Virgil's Aeneis* is a document that eloquently pays tribute to the magnanimity of Williamites whose sense of the importance of the 'Arts of Peace' allowed them to overlook Dryden's Jacobite opinions and Catholic 'Perswasion' in order to be bountiful to the Poet [III, 1425]. This is not conventional flattery of patrons, but a genuine com-mendation of those who understood the nature of his dilemma, and who appreciated his solution of it. Even if William himself could not appreciate fully the poet's contribution to making the Revolution Settlement passively acceptable to Jacobites, it is to be hoped that some of his courtiers (Derby, Peterborough, Trumball, and others) actually did. One has only to recall the savage irony of Alexander Pope in his *Epistle to Augustus* to realize that Dryden's hope was, with the Hanoverians, to turn to contemptuous despair. Pope had to cope with a much more complex problem than did Dryden. But that is another story.

NOTES

1. Louis Bredvold, *The Intellectual Milieu of John Dryden: Studies in Some Aspects of Seventeenth-Century Thought* (*repr.* Ann Arbor, 1956).

2. Alexander Pope, *The Dunciad*, ed. James Sutherland, 2nd ed. (London and New Haven, 1953), ll. 1-4.

3. L. Proudfoot, *Dryden's Aeneid and Its Seventeenth Century Predecessors* (Manchester, 1960), p. 261.

4. Charles E. Ward, *The Life of John Dryden* (Chapel Hill, 1961), pp. 93-115.

5. Kinsley, III, 1008-09.

6. *Critical Essays of the Seventeenth Century*, ed. J. E. Spingarn (Oxford, 1908), II, 295.

7. William J. Cameron, ed., *Poems on Affairs of State* (Yale edn., New Haven, 1971), V, 5-6.

8. Hugh Macdonald, *John Dryden: A Bibliography* (Oxford, 1939), p. 132.

9. T. S. Eliot, 'Homage to John Dryden', in *The Hogarth Essays* (New York, 1928), p. 211.

10. Kinsley, III, 1028.

11. Eugene Waith, *The Herculean Hero in Marlowe, Chapman, Shakespeare, and Dryden* (New York, 1962), pp. 152-201.

12. Giovanni Boccaccio, *Il Decamerone*, ed. Giulo Einaudi, 7th ed. (Torino, 1963), p. 268.

13. Alexander Ross, *Mystagogus Poeticum*, 3rd ed. (London, 1653), p. 7.

Appendix

[see p. 150]

The last Night's Ramble.   1687
[Bodl. MS. Firth. c. 15. pp. 268-274]

Warm'd with the pleasures, which Debauches yeild
Brain, stufft with fumes, Excesse of Wine had fill'd,
I took last Night a Ramble being drunk
To visit old Accquaintance Bawd and Punk.
'Twas madam *Southcot* near old Dunkirk square,⎫
That House of ease for many a Rampant peer   ⎬
For only the lewd Quality f—k there. –   ⎭
The first divertisement I found was this,
I heard the Treble note of yeilding Misse.
Whisp'ring, Lord, S^r what pleasant Tales you Tell!
You'l find th'Enjoyment worth your mony well.
Then in Base viol voice I heard him swear
Dam me a Guiney Madam's very fair.
The utmost Fee I ever gave to swive,   ⎫
She answer'd, How d'ye think that we can live? ⎬
I'le Swear Sr *William R—ch* s^r gave me five. ⎭
While thus I listned I observ'd at last,
Tho' she ask't more, she held the Guinea fast.
When Grand procuresse to each standing *P—k* ⎫
Came in half fluster'd from her Stallion *Dick* ⎭
With Varnish'd Face of paint three Inches Thick,   p. 269
Daub'd on by Art and wise Industry laid
To hide the wrinkles Envious tyme had made.
This necessary freind I wou'd have staid;
When came an Implement she call'd her Maid,
Bred in the Art and skillfull in the Trade,
And whisper'd her away. I guess'd the matter,

And at a little distance Saunter'd a'ter:
Anon I heard one knocking at the door
Who entring, cry'd give me a ready Whore;
Let her be clean and sound, and bring her strait,
You know me (Bawd) I am not us'd to wait.
At *Grayden's* such a dam'd defeat I've had
With *Lady Mary Ratcl*— I am mad,
And must the fflame that's kindled by her Eyes,
Quench 'twixt some coṁon vulgar Beauties Thighs.
And to advance my Gust of Lechery ⎫
Just in the Act, dear *Ratcl*— I will cry ⎬
ffancying at least I swive with Quality. ⎭
By that same Cock't up nose (thought I) and Mein
That haughty spark shou'd be Lord Chamberl—
To be convinc'd I follow'd but mistook,
The Room, and did into another look.
Where who the divel doe you think I found?   p. 270
But one (Oh Frailty) of the Reverend Gown.
Stinking mouth'd *Chest*— to my best discerning
Who gravely was a fine young Whore Confirming.
Nay If't be soe cry'd I, we need not doubt, ⎫
Since our good Clergy=men are soe devout ⎬
But we shall keep all fears of Pop'ry out. ⎭

Then down I went and thro' a Wainscot flaw ⎫
Wallowing upon a Tir'd out Whore I saw,   ⎬
Fumbling in vain, old Griping *Renel—h*,   ⎭
With whores and pox, These forty years worn out
He sweats and stinks for one poor single 'Bout.
'Till Wench half stifl'd cry'd, my Lord, I'le Fr-g
You[r] P—k's too short, your Belly is too big.

I left them at it, when I heard a Noise ⎫
Of Gentle Rage, in an affected voice.   ⎬
What have we here (thought I) for a Sʳ Nice? ⎭
Twas *Cand—sh* who the faithlesse Baud was schooling
ffor giving him a Heat instead of Cooling:
G-d damme Madam were not you a Bitch
Last sunday with a Clap, to cure mine Itch,
Just when I shou'd have had an Assignation
With the most Courted Beauty of the Nation?
Baud –   How Clapt! Gad this my Reputation touches   p. 271
*a whore   Twas my best ware my Lᵈ Zounds twas my *Dutchesse
soe call'd   Who never yet was by foul Gamester leap't,

And soe uncõmon, by the Lord shee's kept.

L^d. And is she sound, may I depend upon her?

Baud. Your Fears are vain, for she's a whore of Honor;
Altho' your Lordship Bilk'd her, as they say⎫
You doe the Hacks, and Boxes at the Play; ⎬
Which tho' soe often us'd you never pay. ⎭
Soe out he went, quite eas'd of his despair
By Knowing he might venture with *Kild—re*.

Then in comes *N—burgh Gr-y & Manch—ster*.
Oh Cry'd the matron, have I got you S^r?
And wou'd you think it? Damme my L^d *Gr-y*
This *Manch—ter* stole my best whore away:
I Gad hence forth I'le watch your L^dships waters
And bring you City wives, but noe more daughters.
But you my little *Ruthen* kind and true, ⎫
I have most delicate fine things for you, ⎬
My *Lady Litchfeilds'* woman, brisk and New.⎭
Quoth *N—burgh* have you noe fine things for me?⎫
ffor I am tir'd with F—king Quality ⎬

Baud. Yes ith' next Room I've such a Rarity! ⎭
The Lady *Within's* 'tis, whose Husbands old,
She comes to S—ve for pleasure not for Gold:
While Quondam Judge is taking fees at home,
She for That same sometymes abroad does roam:
Such a Belle talle, such a Bon' Mein and Air
Soe witty soe well shap'd, and such a Hair!
A snowy skin! such sparkling eyes! and then
Rough as you'd wish, strait as a Girl of Ten.

This dear description did my nerves assail
And over all my facultyes prevail;
And while they barter'd, I stole in before
Where longing Beauty was and bar'd the door.

There on a Couch, all carelessely extended,
I saw what Bawd before soe much cõmended
Just as she said fair as the morning skies:
Lust heav'd her Breasts, and Lechr'y drest her Eyes.
I saw to Court her was but tyme Ill spent
She by my looks gues't at my kind Intent:
Yet that fair play might on both sides be shown,
As Soldiers parly e're beseige a Town;
I her unguarded virtue soe assail'd,
That shewing *Pego*, she her C—t unveil'd.   p. 273

I cou'd noe longer hold but rushing on
The short but pleasing sally we begun:
Soe eager and soe Vigorously free,
We gave not o're 'till wee repeated Three.
Our Raptures hardly finish'd were before
The peer and Bawd were knocking at the door.

Baud.   Open Fair *Venus*, to a fair *Adonis*.
The Youth must wait (said I) she not alone is,
Mars now possesses all with pleasures fervent,
Lord.   Is't soe? Then Dam me Sʳ Your humble servant.
Then cursing wond'ring Bawd, he went away
While I alone was master of the day.
I need not tell you when with Toying tir'd,
We sought with Clarret to be new Inspir'd;
Or how we kiss'd, and laught & Towz'd again,
And try'd soe often that we try'd in vaine.
This only therefore I'le recount you more,
my Body weak, my prick severely sore,
My Linnen foul, my hair with feathers stuck,
And half Ten Guineas spent in wine & F—k
I like a Ruffl'd Bully Rock came trudging   p. 274
And just at five this morning found my Lodging.

Index